P9-DUH-629

JERRY GRAHAM'S BAY AREA BACKROADS
REVISED AND UPDATED

OTHER BOOKS BY JERRY AND CATHERINE GRAHAM

Jerry Graham's More Bay Area Backroads
Jerry Graham's Bay Area Backroads Food and Lodging Guide

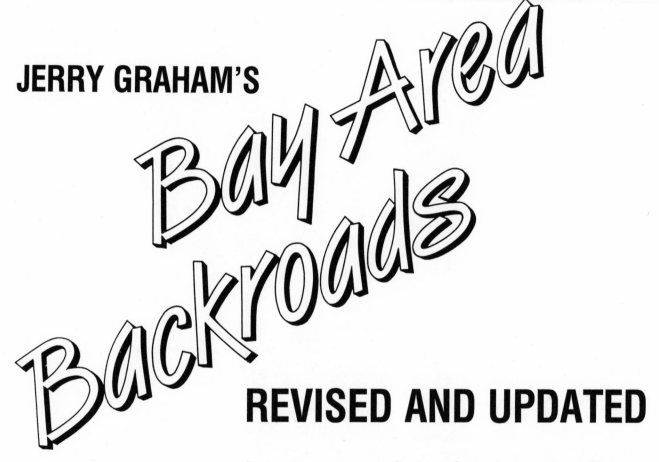

JERRY GRAHAM'S

Bay Area Backroads

REVISED AND UPDATED

by Jerry and Catherine Graham

PERENNIAL LIBRARY

HARPER & ROW, PUBLISHERS, NEW YORK
Grand Rapids, Philadelphia, St. Louis, San Francisco
London, Singapore, Sydney, Tokyo, Toronto

JERRY GRAHAM'S BAY AREA BACKROADS Revised and Updated. Copyright © 1990 by Jerry and Catherine Graham. All rights reserved. Printed in the United States of America. No part of this book may be used or reproduced in any manner whatsoever without written permission except in the case of brief quotations embodied in critical articles and reviews. For information address Harper & Row, Publishers, Inc., 10 East 53rd Street, New York, N.Y. 10022.

FIRST EDITION

Designed by Barbara DuPree Knowles

Maps by Ron Lang

LIBRARY OF CONGRESS CATALOGING-IN-PUBLICATION DATA

Graham, Jerry, 1934–
    Jerry Graham's Bay Area backroads/by Jerry and Catherine Graham.
    1st ed., rev. and updated.
      p.   cm.
    Includes index.
    ISBN 0-06-096470-7
    1. San Francisco Bay Area (Calif.)—Description and travel—Guide-books.   2. Automobiles—
Road guides—California—San Francisco Bay Area.   I. Graham, Catherine, 1955–   . II. Title.
F868.S156G7 1990
917.94'60453—dc20
                                                          89-45830

90 91 92 93 94 DT/RRD 10 9 8 7 6 5 4 3 2 1

Contents

South Bay

East Bay

Beyond the Bay

Acknowledgments

We are deeply indebted to many colleagues and friends for their contributions to this book.

First of all, thanks to Bob Klein, director of program development at KRON-TV, San Francisco. Bob had the original idea for a backroads show and in describing it to Jerry said, "You'll do a series, then write a book about it, then you'll make T-shirts and caps. . . ." He was kidding about the merchandising. Thanks also to the management of KRON-TV, including former general manager Jim Smith and current boss Amy McCombs, and former program director Dave Wilson and his successor, David Salinger.

On a daily basis, many thanks are due to the *Backroads* show staff, which literally gets the program on the air. Chris DeFaria was my original coproducer and, when Hollywood called, he was ably replaced by Jessica Abbe, the original researcher. Paul Ghiringhelli, Jeff Pierce, and Dave Vandergriff have all been with the show from the beginning, followed closely by Peter Hammersly and Stan Drury. Most recent additions to the staff have included Vicky Collins, Jim Morgan, and Claudia Gomez. Thanks to all the other folks at KRON-TV who have contributed to the success of the series.

Thanks, too, to the hundreds of thousands of viewers who embraced the idea of celebrating the glories of the backroads and have watched the program faithfully. Your response has been heartwarming.

Special thanks to our friend Gideon Bosker, who introduced us to Larry Ashmead of Harper & Row. Had that meeting not occurred, this book would still just be a dream of ours. Larry and his colleagues, John Michel, Eamon Dolan, Joseph Montebello, and Karen Mender, have taken care of us well, as has our eagle-eyed copy editor, Karla Billups.

Thanks to our agent, Peter Ginsberg of Curtis Brown Ltd., to Sayre Van Young for her indexing, Jean Haseltine for her invaluable research, Ron Lang for his maps, and Jeff Pierce for his photos on the front and back cover.

And finally, thanks to the man who opened America's eye to the backroads, Charles Kuralt.

Jerry Graham
Catherine Graham

OCTOBER 1989

INTRODUCTION: Read This First

As the earthquake of 1989 demonstrated all too well, things can change pretty quickly around here. The purpose of this book is to document the changes since our first edition, which was published in the spring of 1988. The changes come in a variety of ways. For some destinations, it may be simply a matter of new hours or new admission prices. For others, the story might be about expanded services, or relocation. Sadly some of our favorite people, such as Mickey McGowan of the Unknown Museum in Mill Valley, or Phyllis Lahargue of the Lakeville Marina, are no longer operating the attractions described in the first book. We are happy to report that the earthquake did not close any of our destinations.

Some background is in order for the first-time *Backroads* reader. This book grew out of a television series, *Jerry Graham's Bay Area Backroads*, which has been running since 1984 every Sunday evening on KRON-TV in San Francisco. It is based on the premise that most visitors and many residents are unfamiliar with the fascinating places and people that surround the city of San Francisco. We search for the offbeat location and the unforgettable character you can find only if you slow down and look around for a while. The same holds true for this book.

In our first edition, we included many of our most memorable locations up to the fall of 1987, arranged geographically. We also included a brief list of places to eat and stay on the backroads. As the television series continued to grow, so did the list of wonderful places to visit, prompting us to put together another book of new destinations, *Jerry Graham's More Bay Area Backroads*. In addition, we have expanded our food and lodging section into another complete volume, *Jerry Graham's Bay Area Backroads Food and Lodging Guide*. All three books are designed to be used interactively or separately.

The best way to use this book is to pick no more than two or three destinations per day and then head out. We recommend that you get a county map that will show you every road, no matter how small. Then take off and find some spots of your own. All you have to do is slow down and look.

We have included street addresses and phone numbers whenever possible. Some country locations have neither. *Always* check first before you make a long trip. Country property has a way of becoming prime real estate and charm has a tough time competing with potential profit. If you have your heart set on a specific destination, *please call first*.

Finally, a word or two about the writing of this book. The television series is about Jerry driving around in his convertible visiting places and meeting people. Though he is often the field producer of his stories, the show is always a collaboration with his coproducer, the crew, and the rest of the staff stuck indoors at the office. Writing the book was a similar collaboration between husband and wife. Our stories are not transcripts of television shows. We have tried to add a new dimension to each location and provide the kind of detailed information that television's time constraints prohibit. For simplicity, we decided that the book should follow the feeling of the show and use Jerry as the voice. Thus many of the stories are written in the first person, the "I" referring to Jerry. However, the book was a collaboration in the truest sense.

There is much to see out there, and we wish you well in your adventures. One last reminder: While you're out driving slowly to take in the sights, some motorists will be in a hurry. Pull over to let others pass, and drive defensively.

Sonoma

Napa

Yolo

Solano

Marin

Contra Costa

San Francisco

Alameda

San Mateo

Santa Clara

Santa Cruz

The Bay Area

JERRY GRAHAM'S BAY AREA BACKROADS
REVISED AND UPDATED

North Bay

In a recent survey of Bay Area residents, the North Bay was chosen as the place most people would like to live. This is the least populated region of the Bay Area and offers some of the most scenic country anywhere in California. When most Bay Area residents head out for an adventure on the backroads, we travel north from San Francisco. A drive across the Golden Gate Bridge is an attraction in itself, but it is where the bridge takes us that provides the real treat. What's more, the North Bay escaped the wrath of the World Series earthquake.

Marin and Sonoma counties feature unspoiled beaches, well-preserved parks, and hidden towns filled with interesting characters. Napa is famous as the center of the California wine country and also features some of the quirkier roadside attractions. And since one of the major industries is tourism, you will find an abundance of wonderful places to eat and spend the night.

If you only have time for a day trip, you can reach many points in Marin, Sonoma, and Napa and still return to San Francisco by bedtime. From San Francisco you can be in Marin in 15 minutes, in Napa and Sonoma in less than an hour. Of course, these times are based on ideal driving conditions. You might as well do yourself a favor and be prepared for a traffic jam at almost any time of the day, and most certainly during weekday morning and afternoon rush hours.

Route 101 is the main north-south road for Marin and Sonoma. Route 1 follows the coast. In Napa, the major road through the valley is Route 29. A good alternate road is the Silverado Trail, which is about a mile or two to the east.

CHAPTER **1** Marin County

AREA OVERVIEW

We'll begin by driving across the symbol of the San Francisco Bay Area, the Golden Gate Bridge, into Marin County. Just a few minutes from the city you can be in the famous waterfront town of Sausalito, and in an hour or so you can travel to the farthest points in the county. The two major roads are Highway 101, which is the freeway on the Marin side of the bridge that cuts inland until reaching the coast 300 miles to the north, and Route 1, which snakes its way along the coast.

Marin County has probably outlived its 1970s reputation as the land of rich hippies with hot tubs and peacock feathers. Certainly there are some residents who still fit that stereotype, but the real Marin is a diverse mixture of folks in stylish towns like Sausalito, in working-class cities like Novato, and in small, woodsy villages like Inverness and Point Reyes Station. Perhaps most important of all, it is a county of exceptional beauty, a place where you can go from the beach to the mountains to an unspoiled redwood grove to the fanciest Mercedes dealership around.

The main population centers are near Highway 101; the farther west you travel, the more countrified it gets. We will visit both sides of the county, starting in a part of Sausalito most visitors seem to miss.

BAY MODEL

This is a good place to begin a backroads tour of the entire Bay Area. In less than an hour you can walk around several counties, over bridges, and above tunnels from Sonoma to San Mateo. This is the Bay Model, a replica of San Francisco Bay and its interconnecting bodies of water. It's like a giant three-dimensional map that gives you a sense of where everything is in relation to San Francisco.

It is the size of two football fields, housed in a two-acre warehouse near the famous houseboat community in Sausalito. The building was originally constructed in 1942 for producing World War II Liberty ships; in 1955 the Army Corps of Engineers took it over and built this hydraulic model for the purpose of studying San Francisco Bay.

Today the Bay Model is used by engineers, scientists, and planners to see how

Point Reyes Station

Novato

Sir Francis Drake Blvd.

San Rafael

Mill Valley

Sausalito

Tiburon

Marin

changes proposed by the government or private enterprise can affect the salt-water flows and water quality of the region. Schoolchildren come here on field trips to learn how everyday life in the Bay Area is affected by the tides and other conditions on the area's waterways.

Tours are self-guided, with the help of plenty of descriptive material. But if that's not enough, there are more exhibits upstairs, including films and slide shows explaining life in and on the Bay.

THE BAY MODEL, *2100 Bridgeway, Sausalito. Phone: (415) 332-3871. Open 10 A.M. to 4 P.M. Tuesday thru Friday, 9 A.M. to 4 P.M. Saturday. Admission: Free. Be sure to call ahead; sometimes the model does not have water! It would still be open, but not as much fun. Wheelchair accessible.*

HOW TO GET TO THE BAY MODEL: *From San Francisco, take the Sausalito-Marin City exit off Highway 101, turn right off the ramp, and head south toward downtown on Bridgeway. At the third stoplight you will see a large supermarket called Molly Stone; turn left and follow the signs to the Bay Model.*

MARIN HEADLANDS
(2)

It's difficult to describe the dramatic beauty of the Marin Headlands without sounding evangelical. This area, just across the Golden Gate Bridge from San Francisco, is 15 square miles of open space—that's 10 times the size of Golden Gate Park. You will see rugged cliffs with knife-sharp drops to the ocean, beaches, and, depending on the time of year, your choice of lush valley, hillsides of blue and yellow lupine, orange poppies, eucalyptus, and sage, and maybe a fox or deer. And some of the best views of San Francisco are from the bluffs of the Headlands.

For nearly 100 years this was Army land; here and there you will stumble upon remnants of military bunkers and forts that helped defend the Golden Gate from 1870 through World War II.

In 1972 the land became part of the Golden Gate National Recreation Area (which we will refer to several times in this chapter, from now on as the GGNRA). Under the mantle of the National Park Service, the GGNRA includes 45,000 acres of recreation area on both sides of the Golden Gate Bridge, nearly 40,000 acres of which are in Marin County. This means that this land is your land, this land is my land, protected forever from development.

The military still occupies Fort Baker, down on the east side of the Headlands, facing the Bay. But down at Fort Cronkhite is a visitor's center where you can get maps and be introduced to all the Headlands has to offer. Park rangers and friendly volunteers like Irving Kernfeld will be on hand to direct you wherever you might like to go. Irving's story is typical of many Bay Area residents. He worked for 50 years running a neighborhood grocery in San Francisco. After he retired he got a chance to see what was in his own back yard. Now he's a volunteer, helping other people discover the place he wishes he had known about years before.

Let me recommend three other stops: the Point Bonita Lighthouse, Hawk Hill, and the Marine Mammal Center.

But first, a word of advice: Wherever and whenever you go, bring along a sweater or jacket; even on the warmest days it can get chilly out here.

✔ **Point Bonita Lighthouse.** If a Hollywood producer wanted to shoot a movie that takes place in a lighthouse, this is the one he'd use. The Point Bonita Lighthouse looks like everybody's image of the lonely beacon welcoming ships in the night. It is perched solidly on a craggy cliff with sea gulls circling overhead, and you can picture a grizzled Sterling Hayden character standing in its doorway.

Long before the Golden Gate Bridge was even dreamed of, the Point Bonita Lighthouse signaled sailors that they were entering the San Francisco Bay Area. Built in 1877, it was one of the West Coast's first lighthouses and is now one of its last.

Getting to the lighthouse is part of the fun. After parking the car, you follow a path that takes you through hand-dug tunnels and finally out to the point. The ocean breezes are invigorating, and if the sky is clear, you'll have the strange sensation of being in the middle of nowhere, where no one lives, and, by contrast, looking across the Bay at the bulging city of San Francisco. The final approach to the lighthouse is via a fairly new bridge. Before this was built, visitors had to risk life and limb by snaking around the cliff on a narrow dirt path, with nothing but a cold ocean below.

When you drop by, you might see a friendly looking man wearing a captain's hat. Not exactly Sterling Hayden, but a reasonable facsimile. He's Wayne Wheeler, founder of the United States Lighthouse Society. Like the 2300 members of his club, he is crazy about lighthouses (the society even has members in such un-nautical states as Kansas and Nebraska). Wayne says he doesn't mind being called a "lighthouse nut," though there are those who would take offense and would prefer to be known as "pharosologists," named after the first lighthouse on the island of Pharos, off Alexandria, Egypt. Wheeler explains the fascination with these unique structures: "They are romantic symbols of security, a picket fence against that dark, evil sea."

Wayne is a walking library of Marin Headlands lore. He told me about the West Coast's first foghorn, established nearby (this foghorn was a cannon that had to be fired every half hour in the mist). He also told me more than I thought there was to know about giant Fresnel lenses, which provide the light for the lighthouse.

If you can't find Wayne for a personal tour, just take matters into your own hands and stroll on your own as far as you can down the path to Point Bonita and its lighthouse, or catch up with a tour group; you can go inside only during regularly scheduled times, and it's a good idea to have a reservation. Inside or out, weather permitting, you'll get a wonderful view of San Francisco.

✔ **Hawk Hill.**   The very best view of the entire Bay Area can be found on Hawk Hill, high on a bluff looking down on the Golden Gate Bridge. On a clear day you can see Mount Diablo, more than 30 miles to the east, not to mention Alcatraz, Angel Island, Berkeley, San Francisco—in other words, you can see forever!

So why are so many people on the hill ignoring the view and looking up at the sky? They're looking for birds. This is also one of the best places on the West Coast for watching concentrations of birds of prey, as many as 11,000 spotted in a single season. Every year in the fall, the largest migration of predatory birds in the West heads over this bluff, which has been nicknamed Hawk Hill.

In addition to avid birdwatchers and school groups, you're likely to run into Alan Fish. He's head of the project studying the migration. Fish is aided by volunteers and other knowledgeable ornithologists who will tell you all you need to know about what you're seeing overhead.

All you need is a pair of good walking shoes, some warm clothes (in case the fog rolls in), and a pair of binoculars. It's also recommended that you bring something to eat and drink since you'll probably want to hang around once you get up there. The crowd you'll meet is fun and fascinating. Every now and then somebody has to look up and say, "Look it's a bird . . . " so someone else can chime in, "No, it's a plane. . . . " But soon, when a majestic hawk or a rare golden eagle flies by, the joking stops; the excitement is real and contagious.

On weekends in October, hawks are caught and banded for study, which is a chance to put down the binoculars and see the birds up close. And birds or no birds, there's always that spectacular view.

✔ **Marine Mammal Center.**   The California Marine Mammal Center is in a different section of the Headlands than the lighthouse and Hawk Hill. This is a hospital of sorts for sea lions, seals, and other oceanic creatures in need of medical attention. Wounded animals from as far north as the Oregon border and as far south as San Luis Obispo are brought there to be cared for until they are well enough to return to their natural environment.

At any given time you are likely to find 20 or more animals being nursed back to health. Some of the patients are cute and amusing as they recover from minor scrapes and bruises acquired while at play in the ocean. Other cases are heart-breaking, the victims of some act of human cruelty.

On a typical visit you will see volunteers cleaning cages, coaxing wounded animals to eat, encouraging them to play or get some needed exercise, and giving shots (this may sound simple, but it is no easy task to get a huge sea lion to sit still for a hypodermic needle, even if it is for its own good).

A trip to the Marine Mammal Center is a chance to get close to animals that grew up in the wild and will soon return there and to give encouragement to the center's staff and volunteers. Special tours can be arranged, particularly for school groups. It is a truly educational experience.

THE MARIN HEADLANDS, *just across the Golden Gate Bridge from San Francisco. The visitor's center is located at the end of Bunker Road, across from the Rodeo Beach parking lot and is open from 8:30 A.M. to 4:30 P.M. every day except Christmas. Phone: (415) 331-1540.*

HOW TO GET TO THE VISITOR'S CENTER: *From San Francisco, take the Golden Gate Bridge and continue on Route 101 north to the Alexander Avenue exit. Go back under the freeway and follow the sign to Fort Cronkhite. Go through the tunnel and continue on Bunker Road until you come to the visitor's center; it is well-marked.*

POINT BONITA *is open all year-round and worth a visit anytime. The lighthouse is open at irregular times and requires an advance appointment during certain times of the year. The best advice is for you to call ahead and get the current schedule. Phone: (415) 331-1450. You might want to join one of the walks conducted by park rangers at sunset and during the full moon. Admission to the lighthouse and all tours is free.*

HOW TO GET TO THE POINT BONITA LIGHTHOUSE: *Follow the directions to the visitor's center (above) but after going through the tunnel, turn left and follow signs to the lighthouse. (Note: The tunnel is called the six-minute tunnel because that's how long it takes for the light to change.)*

HOW TO GET TO HAWK HILL: *Follow the same directions to the lighthouse, but well before you get there look for an area where cars can pull off the road to park and a road marker for "Hill 129." You have a wonderful view of the Bay Area from the parking area. Hawk Hill is directly above and requires a steep climb. In the fall, that's where the experienced birdwatchers hang out.*

THE MARINE MAMMAL CENTER *is open from 10 A.M. to 4 P.M. daily. Admission is free, but donations are appreciated. Phone: (415) 331-SEAL. Wheelchair accessible.*

HOW TO GET TO THE MARINE MAMMAL CENTER: *From San Francisco, take the Golden Gate Bridge to the Alexander Avenue exit off Route 101. Follow the sign to Fort Cronkhite. Go through the tunnel and continue on Bunker Road until you see the sign for the center.*

TIBURON

Mark Twain is quoted as having said, "The coldest winter I ever spent was a summer in San Francisco." Well, when the summer fog cools the City, many San Franciscans head to the dockside restaurants of Tiburon where there is usually bright, warm sun. Sam's was the first and busiest of the hangouts, and it's now joined by Guyamas and other places. Others may have better food, but with its huge deck and ever-present population of sea gulls, Sam's is still *the* place. On a clear day, there's a marvelous view across the bay of San Francisco, and of people who have mastered the California art of "hanging out."

Sam's is located on Main Street, which in the 1800s was a tough waterfront strip of hotels, taverns, and heaven knows what else. Today it is a quaint little street with some buildings dating back to the Gold Rush, others constructed to look like they date back to the Gold Rush, and where you can find cafes, art galleries, and fine clothing stores. Much of that commerce has now spread out to adjacent streets, and Tiburon, which by the way means "shark" in Spanish, is bursting with new condos and shopping centers.

All this growth makes the work of the local Landmarks Society even more important. Members are preserving a past that comes as a surprise to the visitors of this most expensive of Marin neighborhoods. Old St. Hilary's Church is one of the nicest preservation projects, a souvenir of the days when Tiburon was a working-class community of railroad workers, lumbermen, and farmers.

It's a modest shrine built in what is called "carpenter's Gothic" style. In other words, they used whatever tools and materials were available to construct a Gothic-style church. A walk inside reminds you of the typical western-movie church on a set like the one where Gary Cooper tried to get the support of the townspeople in *High Noon*. The Landmarks Society has arranged some simple exhibits and can tell visitors about the history of the town and the church. For me, the major attractions were the setting, the simplicity of the building, and the acres of wildflowers that surround it. This is said to be the state's richest concentration of diverse wildflowers, with over 200 species unique to the Tiburon peninsula. Much attention is given to maintaining the botanical integrity of the site. Whenever non-native plants are found, they are quickly removed.

Spring is the best time of the year to visit to enjoy the color. During the late summer and fall you will see mostly lilies and various grasses. Still, it's a very restful site, with many trails and benches along the way.

For a nautical taste of Tiburon's past, you might also want to visit the China Cabin, a faithfully restored dining room from a luxury cruise ship. It too is cared for by the Landmarks Society and is located en route to the local yacht club.

OLD ST. HILARY'S CHURCH, *Tiburon, and* CHINA CABIN, *Belvedere. Phone: (415) 435-1853. Open Wednesdays and Sundays only from 1 P.M. to 4 P.M. beginning April 1 through the summer. Tours available by appointment. Admission: Free.*

For more information, call the Belvedere–Tiburon Landmarks Society, (415) 435-1853. Volunteers will answer the phone Monday through Friday, 9 A.M. to noon; the rest of the time you'll get an answering machine.

HOW TO GET TO OLD ST. HILARY'S AND CHINA CABIN: *From San Francisco, take the Golden Gate Bridge to Route 101 North. Take the Tiburon exit and follow Tiburon Boulevard toward town. When you come to Beach Road (the one stoplight in town), turn left to go to Old St. Hilary's, right to China Cabin.*

ANGEL ISLAND

From Tiburon, backroads travelers can leave their car behind and take a 10-minute ferry ride to Angel Island State Park. This is the largest and one of the least explored islands in San Francisco Bay.

This is not to say you'll be alone. During those cold San Francisco summers, the island is often as toasty as the Caribbean, and private boats and public ferries take sun worshipers out in droves. Most people, however, never get past Ayala Cove with its picnic areas, snack bar, and rest rooms. It takes some hiking over the hill to get to the really interesting parts.

On the island, there are 740 acres with hiking trails. You can hike around the perimeter in about three hours—it's a 5-mile, hilly jaunt. There are also Civil War barracks, the Chinese immigration center, and many nooks and crannies where you can find solitude, even on a day when the main cove is jammed with tourists.

Angel Island was discovered in 1775, when the Spanish first entered the Bay. Captain Don Juan Manuel de Ayala anchored at the island, which he named Isla de Los Angeles, and landed at the location now known as Ayala Cove. During the War Between the States, the Union Army built garrisons on the northwestern shore at Camp Reynolds. The purpose was to foil a Confederate plan to sail through the Bay to the Gold Country and steal gold to fund the war effort. The Confederates never made it, and there was never a cause to try the effectiveness of the many cannons, which still point out from land.

Near the turn of this century, Angel Island was called "the Ellis Island of the West" because on the eastern side of the island was the place where Asian immigrants would enter the United States. During World War II it was a detention center for Japanese and others considered "enemy aliens." Visitors can see the remains of this island's checkered past on foot or by bicycle.

The island's most significant recent development is the Angel Island Association, founded by Robert Noyes, a retired doctor from Palo Alto. The Association has been restoring buildings in the Civil War barracks area to provide access for the elderly and disabled. Their projects include special docking facilities and special buses for tours of the island.

TO GET TO TIBURON, *take Highway 101 North from the Golden Gate Bridge to the Tiburon Boulevard-East Blithedale Avenue exit. Turn right off the freeway and continue until you can go no farther. Turn right, and you will be on Main Street in the quaint, somewhat cutesy downtown of Tiburon. Parking is at a premium, so you will probably want to pull into a lot. The ferry entrance is on Main Street.*

TO GET TO ANGEL ISLAND FROM TIBURON: Park your car in town and head up Main Street to the pier. Look for the Angel Island State Park Ferry Company. The ferry leaves Tiburon every hour on the hour from 10 A.M. to 4 P.M. every day during the summer and on Saturdays, Sundays, and holidays during the rest of the year, weather permitting; always call ahead to check the schedule. The last ferry leaves Angel Island at 4:40 P.M. Round-trip price, which includes admission to the state park is $4 for adults, $3 for children 5 to 11; children under 5, free. Transporting a bicycle costs 50 cents for the round trip. Phone: (415) 435-2131; after 6 P.M. call (415) 388-6770.

TO GET TO ANGEL ISLAND FROM SAN FRANCISCO: Check the schedule of the Red and White fleet, (415) 546-2896 or 1-800-445-8880 in California. They usually run half-hour ferry trips from Pier 43½, which is at the Embarcadero, near the end of Powell. Phone for current schedules and rates.

OTHER USEFUL PHONE NUMBERS: Angel Island State Park Ranger Station at Ayala Cove: (415) 435-1915. Angel Island Association: (415) 435-3522; this is the group that organizes tours for the handicapped, plus many other activities.

MUIR WOODS
⑤

This preserve of majestic redwoods is on everybody's list of places to visit in the Bay Area, as you will quickly realize when you encounter all the tour buses in the parking lot.

But there are *Backroads* ways to avoid feeling like you're in the thick of a crowd, hints learned from Lawson Brainerd who is the "heart and soul" of the park. Now in his 90s, Brainerd still gives walking tours two days a week and can be seen greeting visitors and telling stories. He's a former park superintendent and the man responsible for establishing Muir Woods as a pristine environment, without beer cans, food litter, or honky-tonk attractions. To avoid the crowds, he says you should visit in the early morning or late afternoon when the crowds tend to thin out. Then, go where the busloads of tourists don't go. More about that in a second.

In the 550-acre park you'll walk among giant coast redwoods, some more than 200 feet high (be sure to bring a sweater; even on hot days the shade can be chilly). You'll find trout and salmon running in the brook; look closely and you'll spot some deer running free. There are 6 miles of paved paths for easy walking, including a braille trail for the blind. But leave the picnic basket in the car; no snacking is allowed in the park.

Now, about all those tour buses? Well, the drivers are on a tight schedule, so the tour groups rarely go farther than a half mile into the redwood grove before turning around. So if you really want to enjoy the quiet of the woods, start your private tour deep in the forest and discover the area the bus passengers never see. You can stay as long as you like, but if you are trying to schedule your time, plan on a visit of at least an hour.

MUIR WOODS NATIONAL MONUMENT, *Mill Valley. Phone: (415) 388-2595. Open 8 A.M. until sunset every day. Admission: Free. Wheelchair accessible.*

HOW TO GET TO MUIR WOODS: *From San Francisco, head north on Highway 101. Take the Highway 1–Stinson Beach exit and follow the signs to Muir Woods. The route is well marked. Muir Woods is 17 miles north of San Francisco.*

Just above Muir Woods is Mount Tamalpais, which everyone in the Bay Area knows as "Mount Tam." Many others call the mountain by its nickname "The Sleeping Lady"; with a little imagination you can see this mountain range as having the contours of a reclining maiden.

TOP OF MOUNT TAM

Most Bay Area residents view Mount Tam from below. Surprisingly few people know how easy it is to get to the top.

You can drive almost to the summit, which is nearly 3000 feet above sea level. A beautiful road takes you to about a quarter of a mile from the peak. You leave your car in the parking lot, then, in good walking shoes, you climb to the summit on a fairly steep dirt road to the 1937 stone building that houses the fire lookout. This building is not open to the public, but from the grounds below the lookout you will have a spectacular view. Quite conveniently, nature has furnished many boulders for sitting on what feels like the top of the world.

On one memorable trip to the top of Mount Tam, it was one of those summer days when the fog blanketed San Francisco and the normally sunny parts of Marin. But as I made the final turn up the hill to the summit parking area, the sun was shining brightly. This is par for the course; it's a rare day when it's not warm and sunny at the top.

The main activities at the top are boulder-sitting and hiking. If you enjoy the latter, you can take a fairly long hike to the old West Point Inn, which is a very secluded series of camplike buildings. Hikers can get fresh lemonade and rest in the shade; overnighters can get an inexpensive room if they're willing to forsake electricity and to bring their own provisions. A less vigorous trip would be simply to roam around the various paths near the top and wind your way back down to the parking lot. Or you may want to join a group led by the Sierra Club or the other organizations that offer nature walks.

When sitting or standing at the top, you can see the entire panorama of Marin County, from the densely populated areas around Highway 101 inland, past vast canyons and forests until you see the ocean. Even though I have traveled many of these roads, I was amazed to see how much of Marin is still undeveloped. Much of it is protected by either the state park system or the adjacent GGNRA.

In the early days of Marin, the Mount Tam summit was where the action was. There were grand hotels and taverns and a scenic railway to bring customers here. All this was before Prohibition. The rail line was abandoned in the early 1930s, and most of the structures have been removed; the previously mentioned West Point Inn is one of the few that remain from this era. Now all the action is down below in the towns, and the summit has become one of nature's hideaways. The treasures to be found are of a spiritual and sensual kind. There is a feeling of magic here, and the sights and smells are wondrous.

On a more prosaic level, you might want to know that the parking area has rest rooms, phones, and a snack bar.

Other points of interest on Mount Tam include the Mountain Theater, the outdoor site of a major musical production each spring, and, farther down, the Pantoll Ranger Station, where you can find a map and get your bearings.

TAMALPAIS STATE PARK, *open 7 A.M. to sunset daily. Admission: Free. For general information about the park and group hikes, call the Pantoll Ranger Station, (415) 388-2070; for information regarding West Point Inn, (415) 388-9955.*

HOW TO GET TO MOUNT TAM: *From San Francisco, take the Golden Gate Bridge to the Stinson Beach–Route 1 exit. Follow Route 1 until you come to Panoramic Highway, which is marked by a sign pointing to Muir Woods. Turn right and continue past the Mountain Home Inn to the intersection of Southside Road. Turn right onto Southside Road and continue uphill to Ridgecrest Boulevard to the parking lot.*

SLIDE RANCH
(7)

The Shoreline Highway (aka Route 1), which you will find off Route 101 in Mill Valley, is the quickest way to the area's most popular beaches, Muir and Stinson. Muir is closer to San Francisco and is also small and usually uncrowded. Situated in a cove, it doesn't have the long stretch of beach Stinson has, nor does it offer the amenities of a beach town like Stinson. It does, however, offer the curious contrast of a family beach (on the main section) with a nude beach (in an adjoining cove, out of view of the G-rated area).

If you continue north on Route 1 for a few miles, you will come to Slide Ranch, a unique demonstration farm where visitors can watch workers milk goats, shear sheep, pick vegetables, and—so that we have no romantic views of how we get our food—even slaughter chickens.

The director of the project is a warm, earnest man with the unlikely name Trout Black. His mission is to celebrate all forms of life and to help us understand all of life's interconnections. He is a joy to spend an afternoon with. When he took me into the chicken coop to show me an egg warm under its mother, he was thrilled as if it were his first time. And when he pointed out each new flower or vegetable in the Slide Ranch's many gardens, it was like meeting his children.

The experience is more that just visiting a farm. Trout and his staff challenge us to think about our relationship to other creatures, what we eat, and what we wear—"letting people know where the source of their lives comes from," as Trout puts it. The experience made me feel like a school kid again.

Trout, his wife, and four staff members live on the ranch, along with six farmhand interns. The activities range from afternoon visits to one-, two-, and three-day programs, for people of all ages, preschool to senior citizen, with a special emphasis on inner-city kids and the handicapped. Also, you can drop in just about any time during daylight hours to walk around the 164 acres of ranch property, which has hiking trails and tide pools and is adjacent to Mount Tamalpais.

SLIDE RANCH, *Muir Beach. Phone: (415) 381-6155. Open during daylight hours all year. No admission charge for hikes or wandering around the land. For demonstrations of the working ranch, groups of 10 or more people can arrange for a guided tour. The fee is $8 per person with a group, and you must call in advance. Wheelchair accessible.*

HOW TO GET TO SLIDE RANCH: *From Highway 101, take the Stinson Beach exit and follow the signs to Highway 1. This is a curvy road that winds through the hills and gives you a spectacular view of the ocean. Stay on Highway 1, about a mile past Muir Beach, and look to your left for the driveway. Go slow because this turn is on a curve.*

AUDUBON CANYON RANCH

As a transplanted Midwesterner, it took me a while to realize one essential fact about California life: Not all of the birds go away in winter. Birdwatchers get to enjoy looking through their binoculars all year-round in various parts of the state.

Birdwatchers are in paradise in West Marin. Several species of rare birds thrive on the lagoons and forests that are thankfully protected from development.

One of the best places of all for seeing and learning about our fine-feathered friends is at Audubon Canyon Ranch. This 1000-acre wildlife sanctuary bordering the Bolinas Lagoon is a unique spot for birdwatchers: you get to watch birds from above rather than below.

The land was originally purchased in 1961 as a cooperative effort of several environmental groups, including the Marin Audubon Society; in 1969 the ranch became a registered national landmark. Named in honor of the most famous bird lover of all, John James Audubon, Audubon Canyon Ranch is run by a private, nonprofit organization that supports itself from the gift shop in the visitor's center and from donations.

There are several ways to take advantage of this special place. You can spend an hour or so at sea level, picnicking in the meadows, wandering through the exhibits to learn about egrets, herons, and other natives, or browsing in the bookstore. There are several miles of hiking trails, each varying in length and difficulty, including the relatively eash ¾-mile Harwell Nature Trail and the more formidable 3-mile Griffin Loop (it is steep, narrow, and often slippery). But I recommend the ½-mile Rawlings Trail, rising 250 feet to the top of the canyon. It is worth the effort. Each spring the incredible great blue herons (which are 4 to 5 feet tall, with a 6-foot wingspan) come to nest in the tips of the redwood trees in Schwartz Grove on the east side of the ranch. By mid-March they are joined by their neighbors the great egrets (smaller creatures, with 4½-foot wingspan). From the overlook you will have a unique view of the nesting pageant of the birds.

Audubon Canyon Ranch offers weekend programs, some designed especially for families making use of the overnight accommodations in the bunk house, which boasts such alternative features as solar-heated water and wind-powered toilets (don't ask me how they work). Participants provide their own bedding and food. Free docent-conducted tours can be arranged for groups, and pamphlets for self-guided tours of the ranch are available at the registration desk.

AUDUBON CANYON RANCH, *4900 Shoreline Highway, Stinson Beach. Phone: (415) 868-9244. Open mid-March through mid-July 10 A.M. to 4 P.M. on Saturdays, Sundays, and holidays. Schools and other large groups can make arrangements to visit Tuesdays through Fridays; the ranch is closed every Monday. Admission: Free. For appointments and information, call the ranch office on weekdays 9 A.M. to 5 P.M. Wheelchair accessible.*

TO GET TO AUDUBON CANYON RANCH: *From Slide Ranch, continue north on Route 1 past Stinson Beach. Look for the Audubon sign 3 miles north of Stinson. From San Francisco, take the Golden Gate Bridge to Highway 101 North. Exit at Route 1–Stinson Beach and follow the road all the way. It's 28 miles from San Francisco and will take at least an hour by car.*

BOLINAS
⑨

One of the most intriguing towns in Marin County is Bolinas, a place made mysterious by the fact that there is no sign letting you know where to turn to get there or even if you've arrived. As soon as someone puts one up, somebody else tears it down. This is not an official policy, but, you see, a lot of locals would prefer we didn't know about the place.

Bolinas is a charming town, well situated on bluffs overlooking the Pacific.

There is not much in the way of public places—a bakery here, a cafe there; it's the physical setting that is its main attraction nowadays. However, near the turn of the century, it was the largest town in Marin, featuring 11 hotels and 9 saloons, and was both an artists' colony and a playground for Marin society. Its present character is reminiscent of the halcyon days of the 1960s. That's because much of its population migrated about that time from the famous Haight-Ashbury district of San Francisco. An oil spill off Bolinas threatened the environment and thousands of birds; the hippies answered the call of a San Francisco radio station and arrived in droves to help clean things up. Many of them never left. Today the town is a study in contrasts: the artists and craftspeople, wealthy retirees, authentic hippies, and just plain folks living quietly in a quaint town surrounded by incredible natural beauty.

And in spite of the town's reputation, a lot of locals welcome visitors. The welcome mat will surely be out at the Bolinas Museum, which specializes in collections of local residents. For example, during my first visit there was an exhibit of postcards and a collection of handkerchiefs on display. The idea behind the museum is to showcase personal memorabilia of real people, not impersonal artifacts of the distant past. It works. The good folks running the place will be glad to tell you all about the history of the town and direct you to other points of interest. The museum is small and intimate, although larger than the original site mentioned in our first book.

There's also a lovely little town park, a secluded beach that overlooks Stinson Beach, and some beautiful drives past impressive homes.

THE BOLINAS MUSEUM, *48 Wharf Road, Bolinas. Phone: (415) 868-1650. Open 1 to 5 P.M. Saturday and Sunday. Admission: Free.*

HOW TO GET TO THE BOLINAS MUSEUM: *From San Francisco, take the Golden Gate Bridge to Highway 101 North. Take the Stinson Beach exit and follow Route 1 past Stinson Beach. The Bolinas road is approximately 5 miles from Stinson. Since there is no sign pointing to the Bolinas turnoff, look for a large white farmhouse on the right. Immediately on your left will be a turn; that's the road you want. Continue to a T-intersection; turn left and head into the small commercial center of town. You will come to Wharf Road on the left.*

POINT REYES NATIONAL SEASHORE

Entire books have been written about this part of the world, so I won't try to compete. But by way of introduction, let me say that Point Reyes ("Point of Kings") National Seashore is a 65,000-acre park that should not be missed; you can spend days here and not cover all it has to offer.

Activities include beachcombing and swimming at the seashore's many beaches (though you'll most likely do more in the way of beachcombing since it tends to be cold and windy and the water temperature will make your bones ache). Campsites are available, but only for hikers, not drive-in campers. There is also horseback riding, nature study, hang gliding, bird-watching, fishing, and just getting away from it all.

Just as one brief description can't cover it all, don't expect to see all of Point Reyes in one visit. It is huge, and you can drive great distances simply getting from one beach to another. For example, it's a 22-mile drive from the entrance near Olema to the lighthouse at the end of Sir Francis Drake Road.

Among the many attractions are three separate visitors' centers, each offering maps, information, and educational exhibits. There's also a Miwok Indian village, an earthquake trail that traces damage on the fault line, and the lighthouse, which is a favorite spot for whale watchers in the winter. At the far northern end, near McClure's Beach, is the tule elk range. Here you can see scores of rare and majestic tule elk. Once on the brink of extinction with only two remaining, they have been nurtured and protected in their own range on the fringe of Tomales Bay.

Let me point out a few places I think deserve more detailed explanations:

✔ **Point Reyes Hostel.** Those who do not require luxury overnight accommodations might want to check out the Point Reyes Hostel, a part of the American Youth Hostel system. For $6 a night you can stay near Limantour Beach if you do not mind sleeping on a bunk in a room with as many as 40 other guests of the same sex and sharing the bathrooms, kitchen, and chores.

The positive side is that the accommodations offer a chance to meet people from all over the world, and you will probably eat very well (guests tend to pitch in to create wonderful communal meals). You will stay within walking distance of the beach and you can watch the sunset from the lodge room.

Clearly, hosteling is not for everyone, but the facility at Point Reyes is particularly inviting.

✔ **Morgan Horse Ranch.** The National Park Service operates this working ranch where you can learn about the Morgan horse. Rangers will tell you the history of this very versatile work animal—the first American-bred horse, in fact—and let you roam through the farm. More elaborate tours can be set up in advance, with riding and shoeing demonstrations, and you can observe firsthand the daily life on a ranch. Wait until you see the vet check the horses' teeth; you don't know what dentist phobia is all about until you've seen a horse get its teeth filed!

On most days there's a school tour in progress. I have found that a very entertaining way to learn about a new place is to simply join in with the kids, the younger the better. There is also a small visitor's center with historical photos and displays about the Morgan horse.

POINT REYES HOSTEL, *P.O. Box 247, Point Reyes Station, CA 94956. Phone: (415) 669-7414.*

HOW TO GET TO THE HOSTEL: *From San Francisco, take the Golden Gate Bridge to Highway 101 North. Take the Sir Francis Drake exit and follow it all the way to Olema. Turn right and look for the signs for the entrance to Point Reyes National Seashore. Head for Limantour Road and watch for the signs to the hostel.*

MORGAN HORSE RANCH, *near the Bear Valley visitor's center on Bear Valley Road. Open 9 A.M. to 5 P.M. daily, including most holidays (somebody's got to be there to feed the horses, and he or she can show you around). Admission: Free. Phone: (415) 663-1763. Large groups should call ahead. Most of the ranch is wheelchair accessible.*

HOW TO GET TO THE MORGAN HORSE RANCH: *Follow the directions to the Hostel, but after reaching Olema and turning right at the T-intersection, turn left when you come to Bear Valley Road.*

To get to the northern section of the Point Reyes National Seashore, you have to get back on Sir Francis Drake Road and drive through the town of Inverness, which borders Tomales Bay. It's a worthy destination on its own.

Inverness is one of my favorite towns in the Bay Area. It is lovely to look at all year-round and filled with interesting and unusual places and people. Although only an hour from San Francisco, it has escaped being turned into a crowded tourist trap, probably because of the efforts of townspeople to keep things the way they are. There are many contradictions surrounding Inverness that some-how add to its charm. Although its name is Scottish, three of the most notable buildings are two Czech restaurants and a domed Russian-style beach house. The town also offers several charming bed-and-breakfast inns, plus bayfront motels. There are probably more writers living in the hills around Inverness than in any other town its size in California, which may explain the importance of the Inverness Library.

As you drive through town, on your right you will see a tiny red building near the heart of town. For years this was the home of the world's smallest library.

But in late 1986 Inverness gave up this claim to fame, and the library moved to a building four times the size of the old one. It is in the former home of the town's most famous historian and writer, Jack Mason, the man everyone in Marin used to call when they needed to know a fact about the county's heritage. Mason died in 1986, and he willed his house to the community for use as a library and museum.

I never thought I'd wax enthusiastic about a branch of the public library, but librarian Nancy Hemingway (no relation) makes this place special. She has

INVERNESS

turned the library into an unofficial community center. Locals drop off their kids to read while they run errands or get information on who is available for house-cleaning or babysitting services; visitors can find out about the best places in the area to eat and spend the night.

Even if you're not a resident of Marin County, the library is a comfortable place to read, do research, or get to know the town. You will be surprised how much more you can learn about a town in a library than at a place that caters to tourists, especially in this library, where it's OK to talk. That's because if you're disturbing someone who's reading, all you have to do is walk into another room of this converted house and you're in a museum where you can chatter to your heart's content.

This library and museum are in one of the first houses in Inverness. Built in 1894, it was called "The Gables." Its previous occupant, historian Mason, self-published seven books on Marin County history. Mason's books and his files chronicled the rich lore of the town. In one room you can explore the history of the town through historical photographs and the private papers of one man's passion for his community.

INVERNESS LIBRARY AND JACK MASON MUSEUM, *15 Park Avenue, Inverness. Phone: (415) 669-1288. Open Monday 3 P.M. to 6 P.M. and 7 P.M. to 9 P.M.; Tuesday and Wednesday, 10 A.M. to 1 P.M. and 2 P.M. to 6 P.M.; Friday 3 P.M. to 6 P.M.; and Saturday 10 A.M. to 1 P.M. Closed Thursday and Sunday. Admission: Free. Wheelchair accessible.*

HOW TO REACH INVERNESS: *From San Francisco, take the Golden Gate Bridge to Highway 101 North. Take the Sir Francis Drake exit and continue all the way until you come to a T-intersection at Olema. Turn right, proceed for a few miles and look for a turn on the left to Inverness. You will be back on Sir Francis Drake, which takes you directly into town.*

OYSTER FARM
(12) Whether you say "oyster" or "erster," I am willing to bet you have never seen as many of these creatures in your life as you will find here. The Johnsons have been oyster farmers for generations. They cultivate the slimy delicacy using the traditional Japanese method of grafting tiny seeds onto shells, then taking them out into shallow waters of the Bay to hang them on racks. Eighteen months later, the Johnsons harvest them and sell them on the premises.

Papa Charlie Johnson is as crusty as one of those shells you'll see lying in a mound, and he's piled just as high with stories. He'll open one of his darlings for you with his knife and give you a lesson in eating them raw.

This is not a tiny operation. Several boats are being loaded and unloaded daily, and you have an opportunity to see quite a lot of action, such as watching work-ers haul oyster-filled nets out of the bay or visiting the incubation room to see how thousands of oysters are growing in huge tubs of warm water. After the cells have reached an appropriate size, they are ready to be taken out to the bay. Johnson's farm appears to combine the latest technology in a setting that looks perfect for an old seafarer's movie.

I'd like to note that several smaller "gourmet" oyster operations have sprung up around Tomales Bay, mostly to the north on Route 1 around the town of Marshall. At this writing, none of these operations is the size of Johnson's, nor are they set up for visitors to see the seeding operation. They also tend to be open at unpredictable and flexible times. However, some do offer tasting rooms and are worth stopping by if you like oysters. Weekends are your best bet for finding them open.

JOHNSON'S OYSTER COMPANY, *11171 Sir Francis Drake Boulevard, Point Reyes National Seashore. Phone: (415) 669-1149. Open 8 A.M. to 4 P.M. Tuesday through Sunday; closed Mondays. Admission Free.*

HOW TO GET TO JOHNSON'S: *Follow the directions to Inverness and continue through town on Sir Francis Drake. You will see signs to Johnson's Oyster Company once you enter the Point Reyes National Seashore.*

THE CLOCK THAT MOOS

If you're driving around West Marin and hear a very loud cow moo, don't be alarmed. That just means that it's high noon in Point Reyes Station. This lovely little town near the Point Reyes National Seashore has several claims to fame. One is the town clock. Instead of the usual chiming at noon and 6 P.M., the Point Reyes Station clock moos.

Judy Borello, who runs the Old Western Saloon in town, was the driving force behind the clock. She and several other locals wanted to preserve the cow-town image of the place lest it become yet another yuppified boutique town. She organized some supporters, and with the technical help of engineers from filmmaker George Lucas's company (whose headquarters at Skywalker Ranch is close by), a mooing clock was created.

The other major claim to fame is the local newspaper's Pulitzer Prize. In 1979 the *Point Reyes Light* was awarded the prestigious honor—not bad for a town that still has cattle stampedes down Main Street. David Mitchell, editor of the *Light,* took me on a tour of the town for the *Backroads* television program. He explained that the original town was the train station for the railroad bringing people to West Marin and the seashore, thus the name, Point Reyes Station. Main Street was the rail yard; what is now the post office was the depot.

Today Point Reyes Station has a population of 625 and is the economic hub for rural West Marin. Point Reyes Station is the place farm folks come to the bank and to shop. Toby's Feed Store is the biggest business in town. Toby sells hay from his own fields, plus many items appealing to both farmers and weekend city visitors; I was there once when they had a sale on baby chickens, and it was a great scene.

A tip: Most visitors descend upon this little town on weekends during the summer when the weather is its greyest and foggiest. Thus, a better time to visit is during the week in the fall. The weather is much nicer then, the streets, restaurants, art galleries, and bookshops are less crowded, the locals are in a better mood, and you can get a good idea of what day-to-day life in this town is like.

The clock that moos is located on the sheriff's substation, which is at Fourth and C Streets (nobody uses street addresses in Point Reyes Station); however, the moo comes from a speaker atop the Old Western Saloon two blocks away, on the main drag of town at Main and Second. The clock moos twice a day, at noon and at 6 in the evening. Don't worry about missing it if you're in the area; the town moo is LOUD.

TO GET TO POINT REYES STATION: *Follow Sir Francis Drake Boulevard-Highway 1 north from Olema. Just south of town the road crosses a small bridge and then makes a sharp turn left onto Main Street/Highway 1.*

MARIN MANSIONS ⑭

Back on the inland side of Marin County, San Rafael is Marin's "big city," though anywhere else it would be considered a small town. Its downtown was used, practically untouched, as the setting for George Lucas' film *American Graffiti.* Though San Rafael does resemble Modesto, circa 1962, or a typical small town in the Midwest, it is the county seat and the place where many people go to shop.

But just two blocks above the downtown area you can be transported into another era. You see, after the Gold Rush, San Rafael became a fashionable town, with ritzy resort hotels and "good" neighborhoods where bankers, railroad barons, and others who struck it rich built elegant homes. Thirteen historic buildings have been restored in this neighborhood, which makes for a nice walking tour.

You can begin at Falkirk, the centerpiece of the neighborhood. Located on Mission Avenue between E and D Streets, Falkirk is a gorgeous Queen Anne-style home that belongs to the citizens of San Rafael. Several years ago some developers tried to tear it down to put up condominiums; San Rafaelians rallied around the house and turned the 17-room historic mansion into a community cultural center. Built in 1888, Falkirk is the former residence of shipping magnate Robert Dollar. Today the elegant parlor where the Dollars entertained their guests is a community room, available for meetings, lectures, and weddings. The mansion also has three contemporary art galleries, open to the public during regular business hours. Throughout the house, the ornate wood paneling, elegant chandeliers and stained glass transport you back into an era of refinement and elegance.

Continuing east on Mission Avenue, you will see Maple Lawn, a Gothic-to-the-max mansion that is not open to the public but is nonetheless wonderful to gawk at. It was built in 1873 by two brothers who made a killing in the Comstock lode. Today it is an Elks lodge.

Next door to Maple Lawn is the Gate House, a guesthouse the brothers built for their dear old dad. Today it is the home of the Marin Historical Museum. Here you can find on display the items that defined the Victorian era: gloves, high-button shoes, satin gowns, and stiff collars. You can also pick up a map that will lead you to the other points of interest on your walking tour.

FALKIRK COMMUNITY CULTURAL CENTER, *1408 Mission Avenue, San Rafael. Phone: (415) 485-3328. Open 11 A.M. to 4 P.M. Monday through Friday, 10 A.M. to noon Saturdays. Admission: Free. Wheelchair accessible.*

MARIN HISTORICAL MUSEUM, *1125 B Street (at Mission), San Rafael. Phone: (415) 454-8538. Open 1 to 4 P.M. Wednesday, Saturday, and Sunday. Admission: Free. The Marin Heritage Group sponsors docent-led walking tours of Marin's mansions. Call the Historical Museum for current information.*

HOW TO FIND MARIN'S MANSIONS: *From San Francisco, take the Golden Gate Bridge to Route 101 North to the Central San Rafael exit. Turn left on Fourth Street for a look at San Rafael's American Graffiti street, then turn right on E Street to Mission Street. Park on the street and begin your walking tour at Falkirk.*

FRANK LLOYD WRIGHT'S LAST HURRAH

One of the most remarkable structures in Marin County is visible from the freeway. Heading north on Highway 101, on your right you will see the blue-tiled roof of the Marin County Civic Center, a long, low graceful building designed by Frank Lloyd Wright; as a matter of fact, it was his last major project before his death in 1959. It is a prime example of the architect's visionary obsession with circles, half circles, and shapes attempting to become circles.

Inside, the civic center itself is the nerve center for the county; it houses the main branch of the library, a post office, the jail, and the courthouse where, in 1970, a famous shoot-out involving a San Quentin inmate and smuggled guns took place; in 1985, fugitive attorney Stephen Bingham was tried here. Making your way around inside is a bit like Alice's adventures in Wonderland, so you might want to try to join a tour group; but if you would enjoy the challenge of finding your own way around, be forewarned that some sections of the building have three floors, others have four.

It is an amazing architectural feat. Exotic tropical and subtropical plants grow in many of the balconylike hallways which are illuminated by skylights. Architecture buffs might be interested in seeing Wright's original model, on display on the ground floor. You might want to visit the cafeteria, which is open to the public and has pretty good food (one of my viewers wrote recently to say he and his wife enjoy having a cup of coffee there); the cafeteria opens up to an outside patio with a fountain. Outside the fourth floor on the south side of the top wing is a water-conserving garden, a very attractive display of California native and other drought-tolerant plants. All the plants are labeled for your edification, and picnic tables are provided for your comfort.

The *Backroads* traveler will also find the grounds of the Civic Center worth a visit because they are so special. The Marin Civic Center sits on 140 acres that include a duck-inhabited lagoon and a hill with a panoramic view all the way to the Bay. You can walk around anytime and feel well removed from the hustle and bustle of the freeway. The annual county fair is held on the grounds each July.

Better yet, the Farmers' Market is held here twice a week. This is where the farmers of Marin and neighboring counties come to sell their produce directly to consumers. Not only can you buy tomatoes, carrots, and apples, but you will find rows and rows of vegetables you've never seen in your life: nopales, Lady Godiva squash (the ones with naked seeds), bok choy, 12 kinds of lettuce, 4 zillion kinds of peppers—all presented by the person who grew it. The food reflects the multicultural population of California. Here you can get an idea of what real California cuisine is all about.

MARIN COUNTY CIVIC CENTER, *San Rafael. Phone: (415) 499-7407. Open 8 A.M. to 5 P.M. Monday through Friday; closed on legal holidays. Tours led by docents —most of whom are devotees of Frank Lloyd Wright—are available between 10 A.M. and 3:30 P.M. daily. There is no charge, and tours last about an hour, including a visit to the drought-tolerant garden. You must make arrangements at least three days in advance. The tours and the civic center itself are wheelchair accessible.*

FARMERS' MARKET, *on the grounds of the Marin County Civic Center, in the parking lot of the Marin Civic Center Auditorium (also designed by Wright). Phone (415) 456-FARM. Open 8 A.M. to 1 P.M. Thursday and 9 A.M. to 1 P.M. Sunday. Admission: Free.*

HOW TO GET TO THE MARIN CIVIC CENTER: *From San Francisco, take the Golden Gate Bridge to Highway 101 North. Follow 101 past the main San Rafael exits and then turn right at the San Pedro Road exit. The civic center will be in full view, and there are signs directing you to the parking lot.*

At one time the Northern California coast was dotted with Chinese fishing villages. Like many fortune-seekers, the Chinese had come here for the Gold Rush in the mid-1800s. Unfortunately, many arrived too late and had to find something to do to make a living. Many of these immigrants were from the area around Canton, where they had fished the Yangtze and Pearl Rivers for shrimp. After importing nets from the old country, these fishermen and their families set up 30 villages around the bays of San Francisco, where shrimp flourished.

Their business flourished, too, much to the dismay of American fishermen, who pressured legislators to pass discriminatory laws designed to end the Chinese fishing boom. By 1910 many Chinese had returned to their homeland or become absorbed into nearby cities. One by one, the villages faded away.

Today, only one of these fishing villages remains. It is the main attraction in China Camp State Park. The state park service acquired the land in 1977 and has restored many of the buildings and piers and has set up a small museum that tells the sad history of the Chinese and their camps.

According to the 1880 census, China Camp was the largest of all the fishing villages in the Bay Area, with a population of 500 residents. Today China Camp has only one resident, Frank Quan. His grandfather had been a storekeeper in the village in 1890; his father and uncle found a way to fish legally and started the shrimp business that Frank now operates. Every day, Frank is up before the crack of dawn, pulls shrimp out of the bay, then cooks them in huge vats by boiling them in very salty water, according to methods handed down from his father. He also operates a snack bar on weekends where you can taste what really fresh shrimp is like.

The Chinese fishing village is only one section of the 1500-acre state park. Other activities include hiking and picnicking; campers can walk to the primitive campground area and stay for $6 a night (no trailers or RV amenities, though).

CHINA CAMP MUSEUM AND STATE PARK, *San Rafael. Phone: (415) 456-0766 or (415) 456-1286. Park is open 8 A.M. to sunset daily. Admission: Free. The Chinese fishing village opens at sunrise daily and closes at 5 P.M. from November through March; 6 P.M. in April, September, and October; and 7 P.M. May through August. The museum is open most weekends year-round, and rangers can arrange tours with advance notice.*

HOW TO GET TO CHINA CAMP: *From San Francisco, take the Golden Gate Bridge and follow Highway 101 to the San Pedro Road exit. You will see the Marin Civic Center on your right at the exit. Go on San Pedro Road approximately 3 miles and you will enter China Camp State Park. Continue on the main road until you reach the fishing village.*

The little town of Novato is fast becoming a bedroom community. During rush hours the freeway is jammed with Novatans going to and from work on the other side of the Golden Gate Bridge. The town joke is that Novato is a very safe place because so many San Francisco policemen live here. But long before Novato served the housing needs of San Francisco, it had its own long and colorful history. After the Gold Rush, Novato became an authentic frontier town. Americans and European immigrants settled in the area and built stores, hotels, and saloons. They raised chickens, beef, and dairy cattle. The climate was perfect for growing pears, cherries, and apricots; soon the world's largest apple orchard was growing in Novato. The timber industry supplied oak and laurel for the elegant Victorian homes in San Francisco.

Today several historic buildings have been put to good use by the community. City Hall is the town's original Presbyterian church (located at the intersection of De Long and Sherman Avenues); the interior has been remodeled for office space, though several pews are available for sitting in a foyer. The exterior is painted red with white trim. Nearby, the church parsonage is now occupied by the city finance department.

Across the street from City Hall, at 807 De Long Avenue, is the Novato Chamber of Commerce, located in a Queen Anne-style cottage built in 1905, with additional offices built into a three-story water tank next to the house; here you can pick up a colorful brochure explaining other points of interest in town.

And next door to the Chamber of Commerce is the Novato History Museum, where you can really get a sense of what life has been like in this community over the years. The Novato History Museum is set up in the oldest house in town, built in 1850 for the town's first postmaster, who was murdered outside in the horse trough. The museum opened in 1976 as a temporary exhibit, but when the old-timers assembled their personal collections of memorabilia, they realized they were on to something too good to let pass. Today the place is stocked like an antique store. Along with photographs depicting life through the decades, you'll find antique tools and artifacts, from branding irons to the old school bell. There are only a few rooms to visit, so you won't need to spend more than an hour.

But the best thing about a visit is the chance to chat with Jacqueline Moore, a lovely lady who looks and talks like everybody's favorite school teacher. She takes her role of curator seriously and breathes life into the exhibits of old photos and mementos of the days when Novato was a Wild West town.

If you happen to visit the museum with fidgety youngsters, just ask Ms. Moore to tell them the story about the postmaster's mysterious demise. She'll keep them entertained.

NOVATO HISTORY MUSEUM, *815 De Long Avenue, Novato. Phone: (415) 897-*

4320. Open 10 A.M. to 4 P.M. Thursday and Saturday; groups admitted by appointment Monday through Saturday. Admission: Free.

HOW TO GET TO NOVATO: *From San Francisco, take the Golden Gate Bridge to Highway 101 and continue north past the city of San Rafael. Take the De Long exit and you will come to the museum before you reach the center of town.*

MIWOK MUSEUM

Long before the hot tub and BMW came to symbolize the Marin lifestyle, the area had another lifestyle, one that bore little resemblance to the way the present inhabitants live in this beautiful county.

For centuries, Marin was the land of the coastal Miwok Indians, and the museum dedicated to their existence—past and present—is a must-see for all of the county's public schoolchildren; the local school board mandates that all its students be brought here as part of the curriculum. But don't assume that this is just a place for kids. This tiny museum, tucked into the outskirts of Novato, is a real find for people of all ages.

Several things make this place special. First, the story of the Miwoks and how they lived is amazing. Their ability to live in harmony with nature and to live off the bounty of the earth is inspiring; they ground acorns for flour, tied strands of tule (an abundant type of bulrush) to make boats, and made coats for the chilly Marin nights out of rabbit pelts. The museum features hands-on displays where you can perform traditional activities with acorns, shells, stones and antlers, play a game of chance—sort of a Miwok version of pick-up-sticks—and even ride in a boat made from tule.

Second, since it is a small museum with a very interested staff, you are almost guaranteed a personal guide as you wander through the small but well-presented exhibits. Program director Marilyn Englander guided me through; the holder of a Ph.D. in Native American studies, she regaled me with interesting stories, and I left feeling connected to the history of the area in a way I never had before.

Finally, the museum is important because it emphasizes that this is not a lost culture. To the contrary, you'll learn that many Miwoks still live in Marin and that they have an active role in setting up the exhibits.

MARIN MUSEUM OF THE AMERICAN INDIAN, *2200 Novato Boulevard, Novato. Phone: (415) 897-4064. Open all year, 10 A.M. to 4 P.M. Tuesday through Saturday, noon to 4 P.M. Sunday. Admission: Free.*

HOW TO GET TO THE MUSEUM: *From San Francisco, follow the directions to the Novato History Museum. On De Long Avenue, continue west until you come to Novato Boulevard. Turn right and follow the road to the Miwok Park and Museum.*

MARIN FRENCH CHEESE COMPANY

From the Miwok Museum, if you take Novato Boulevard out of town, you will find yourself on one of the most beautiful roads in Marin. This is an area of rolling hills and lush dairy farms, very green most of the year, brown in the summer.

Just 9 miles south of Petaluma, at the junction of Novato Boulevard and the Point Reyes–Petaluma Road, you will be at a good place to stop for a picnic or a little bite to take on the road: the showroom and factory of the Marin French Cheese Company. You have probably seen or tasted their product, sold in stores all over the country under the brand name Rouge et Noir.

A French cheese company in Marin? It surprised me, especially since there are so few French people in the area. As it turns out, the Gold Rush attracted a contingent from France. They failed to strike it rich in the mother lode and eventually settled in these hills because they were reminded of Normandy. Louis Cantel started making camembert in his small dairy in Petaluma (believed to be the first to manufacture this soft-ripening cheese in the United States). In 1865 his neighbors, the Thompson family, started their own cheese factory, now operated by the fourth generation of cheese-making Thompsons.

In addition to camembert, three other types of cheeses are produced here: brie, schloss (sort of a pungent cross between limburger and camembert), and "breakfast cheese," a buttery, soft white cheese to be sliced thin on toast or cut into cubes for salads.

When I went on a tour of the plant, I expected to see vats of boiling cheeses. Instead I saw a succession of spotless chilled rooms. As it turns out, these cheeses are not cooked; the process involves small round molds of cheese being turned and aged until ready to eat.

The tours are offered every day, ending with the opportunity to sample each kind of cheese. There is also a large retail outlet where you can purchase sandwiches, wine, fruit drinks, and more cheese for a picnic.

MARIN FRENCH CHEESE COMPANY, *7500 Point Reyes–Petaluma Road, Petaluma. Phone: (707) 762-6001. Sales room open 9 A.M. to 5 P.M. daily, though closed on some holidays; tours available from 10 A.M. to 4 P.M. daily, closed on some holidays. Admission: Free.*

HOW TO GET TO THE CHEESE COMPANY: *From Novato, follow Novato Boulevard to the intersection of Point Reyes–Petaluma Road. From San Francisco, take the Golden Gate Bridge to Highway 101 North. Exit on Lucas Valley Road to Nicasio Valley Road. Turn right to the Point Reyes–Petaluma Road. Turn right and follow this road to the cheese company. This is a very scenic drive.*

CHAPTER **2** Sonoma County

Sonoma County is directly north of Marin, bordered on the east by Napa County and on the west by the Pacific Ocean. The closest destinations to San Francisco, such as Petaluma, can be reached in less than an hour from the Golden Gate Bridge; some of the more distant stops, such as Fort Ross, require about a two-hour drive. As in Marin, Highway 101 provides the most direct inland route, and Route 1 takes you along the coast.

Sonoma is one of the great playgrounds of the Bay Area. While next-door neighbor Napa draws visitors from around the world to its famous wine country, Sonoma goes about its quieter, less chic ways. There are just as many wineries and good places to eat in Sonoma as in Napa; they're just more spread out in Sonoma. In fact, there is probably a little bit more of just about everything in this large and scenic county, including ocean beaches, mountains, parks, resorts, farms, and boomtowns.

Santa Rosa, a solid hour's drive from San Francisco, is the major city; the towns of Sonoma, Petaluma, Sebastopol, Healdsburg, and Occidental highlight unique facets of Sonoma life.

In almost any town, you can stop off at the local Chamber of Commerce or visitor's center to pick up a Sonoma Farm Trails map—a list of the farms in the county that are open to visitors and feature everything from animals you can pet to produce you can pick yourself.

Aside from a few chic resorts like the Sonoma Mission Inn, this is still "jes' plain folks' territory." Restaurants tend to be informal, towns a bit rustic, and inns and hotels a bit cheaper than similar accommodations in Napa. In the three years of shooting television stories on the Bay Area's backroads, no one county has provided such fertile material.

This is the first winery we present in this book, so let's celebrate with champagne. Gloria Ferrer is one of the newer wineries in Sonoma Valley, though the Ferrer family has been making wine in Spain since the twelfth century. The family owns the company that makes Freixenet (pronounced "fresh-a-net"), the champagne that comes in a black bottle, and is one of the largest producers of wine made by the method champenoise, the time-honored way champagne is made in its namesake region in France.

With so many wineries in the Bay Area, I try to find places that offer something unique. Gloria Ferrer Champagne Caves fills the bill in several ways. First of all, it is the first Spanish winery in the area since the mission days. But even more important is the tour, which includes the opportunity to see the unusual caves wedged in the mountainside and a collection of antique winemaking tools on display. This machinery, used 100 years ago, was 20 times slower than the modern operation you see today, yet the actual process of making the champagne remains much the same.

The winery building is an elegant structure, designed to create the feeling of Barcelona. Flags of California and Catalonia fly out front. The facility, which opened in September 1986, sits on 250 acres planted with several sparkling wine varieties, including pinot noir and chardonnay.

The wine produced here is Gloria Ferrer Brut, named for the wife of Freixenet president José Ferrer (not the one who played Cyrano). Tours are free, but to sample the wine it will cost $2.50–$3.00 for a full flute of Brut and some snacks. Then you can relax and enjoy it in their Sala de Catadores or on a patio overlooking the hills of Sonoma.

GLORIA FERRER CHAMPAGNE CAVES, *23555 Highway 121, Sonoma. Phone: (707) 996-7256. Open 10:30 A.M. to 5:30 P.M. daily; last guided tour begins at 4:30 P.M. Admission: Free; tastings cost $2.50 for a flute of nonvintage champagne, $3.00 for vintage.*

HOW TO GET TO THE CHAMPAGNE CAVES: *From San Francisco, take the Golden Gate Bridge to Highway 101 and follow it north to Route 37. Turn right onto Route 37 to Route 121. Turn left and head north on Route 121 approximately 5 miles. The entrance is well marked on the left of the road.*

WORLD OF EXOTIC BIRDS
(2)

It's one of those nondescript places I've driven by dozens of times, so nondescript I eventually had to check it out. What you see from the road is just an average one-story building with a parking lot and a sign with the slogan "Our business is for the birds." Inside, you are suddenly overwhelmed by the sight and sound of hundreds of birds of every size, shape, and color.

Even if you have little interest in feathered fauna, it's worth a visit to meet owner Pat Barbera. The license plate on her car says BIRD MA. Sure enough, Pat hatched most of the gang you will find here, and she stays up all night with them when they are sick, feeding them with eyedroppers. If you play your cards right, she'll talk with them while carrying on a clear and concise conversation with you at the same time.

Let me make it clear that Pat takes no guff from her brood. While telling me how friendly and harmless a favorite parrot of hers is, the bird kept chewing on her sleeve. She simply looked the bird in the eye and warned, "Parrot soup, parrot soup . . ." The bird behaved.

Sonoma

Save some time for a visit here. There are so many birds to see and Pat has so many stories you'll want to hang around for a while. Be sure to go into the back room to see the prize macaws with spectacular plumage. There is also a pond with swans (for sale), and out back on the 10 acres that surround the place, you'll see a herd of llamas (also for sale).

The birds come in all sizes, colors, and prices—from $22 to $9000. If that sounds like a lot of dough for one pet, just remember: it will probably outlive you and me.

WORLD OF EXOTIC BIRDS, *23570 Highway 121, Sonoma. Phone: (707) 996-1477. Open 10 A.M. to 5 P.M. daily. Admission: Free.*

TO GET TO THE WORLD OF EXOTIC BIRDS: *From San Francisco, follow the directions to the Gloria Ferrer Champagne Caves, but enter on the right almost directly opposite the winery.*

HISTORIC SONOMA PLAZA ③

One of the most intriguing figures in California history is General Mariano Guadalupe Vallejo. A gentleman, a scholar, and an entrepreneur, Vallejo was born in Monterey in 1807 and became an influential statesman. When Alta (Northern) California was under the rule of Mexico, he was put in charge of San Francisco's Presidio, with civil power that extended north to Sonoma.

A mission was established in Sonoma in 1823; Vallejo was not far behind with a garrison and plans to build himself a lovely home. The Sonoma Plaza was where all the action was: the Mission San Francisco Solano de Sonoma; barracks for the soldiers; a hotel called the Blue Wing Inn, owned and operated by Vallejo (and visited by such nineteenth-century superstars as Kit Carson, Ulysses S. Grant, and William T. Sherman); and La Casa Grande, Vallejo's home.

In June 1846 the Plaza was the site of the famous Bear Flag Revolt. Rebellious settlers captured General Vallejo in his Casa Grande (the legend is that he took this intrusion in stride and offered them cognac); then they hoisted the flag of the new Bear Republic above the Plaza as a declaration of independence from Mexico. California remained an independent nation for only a few months before joining the United States, living happily ever after as a state. Meanwhile, Vallejo continued to enjoy a long and prosperous life. He bought an estate just a few blocks from the Plaza and built a home that looked like a place you'd find on Cape Cod, with a steep-pitched roof, ornamental eaves, and dormer windows. He lived there with his wife and 10 of their 16 children until his death in 1890.

Today a visit to the Sonoma Plaza and General Vallejo's estate is a wonderful way to spend the day. The Plaza itself is a grassy park with shade trees and picnic tables. It's also the largest town plaza in the state. It is bordered by wonderful places to buy picnic supplies and historic settings that include the mission, the Blue Wing Inn, and the monument where the rebellious settlers raised the Bear Flag.

One ticket is good for admission to the Sonoma Mission and three surviving creations of Vallejo: the Sonoma Barracks, what's left of Casa Grande (most of it was destroyed in a fire), and Lachryma Montis, General Vallejo's bucolic retirement estate. This estate was 20 acres that came with an abundant water supply and an Indian legend about a jilted princess who cried so long and hard that her tears created the springs of water. Always the scholar, Vallejo gave his estate a Latin name, Lachryma Montis, "Tear of the Mountain." Always the entrepreneur, Vallejo sold his water to the city of Sonoma; in fact, he owned all the water rights to the area. From this estate he would send the townspeople their H_2O via redwood pipes.

Visitors can go inside the Atlantic seaboard-style dwelling, complete with the furnishings, antiques, and clothing used by the Vallejo family; in fact, were it not for the iron railings that bar entry into the rooms, you might believe that the family still lives here. On the grounds is a Swiss chalet-style building that was used for storing olives, wine, and produce and is now a museum of General Vallejo's history.

But the grounds are the best part of the visit. Vallejo was fond of flowers—he was a member of the state's first horticultural board—so today you can walk and picnic in a lively garden that is no doubt watered by the tears of the mountain.

LACHRYMA MONTIS, *Sonoma. Sonoma Park and Recreation Department. Phone: (707) 938-1519. Open 10 A.M. to 5 P.M. daily; closed Thanksgiving, Christmas, and New Year's Day. Admission: Adults, $1.00, children, 50 cents. Ticket also good for admission to the Sonoma Mission, Sonoma Barracks, and La Casa Grande in Sonoma Plaza. Tickets for sale at the Sonoma Mission, Spain Street at First Street East.*

HOW TO GET TO SONOMA: *From San Francisco, take the Golden Gate Bridge to Highway 101 North. Exit at Route 37 and bear to the right (east). Follow Route 37 to Highway 121. Turn left on Route 12, and continue to the town of Sonoma.*

HOW TO GET TO LACHRYMA MONTIS: *From Sonoma Plaza, head west on Spain Street until you get to Third Street West. Turn right and continue about a half mile. Signs will direct you into the parking lot.*

If you glance at the names of most of the wineries in the Sonoma and Napa valleys, you would logically assume it was the Italians or the French who started this booming industry in Northern California. But would you believe it was actually the Hungarians?

CALIFORNIA'S OLDEST WINERY
④

Colonel Agoston Haraszthy is credited as "the father of California viticulture." It says so on a plaque in downtown Sonoma. Haraszthy, a career diplomat, migrated from Hungary in 1840 and had a colorful career before arriving in Sonoma, where he founded the Buena Vista Winery. Arriving with grapevines from the old country, Haraszthy first founded a settlement in Wisconsin; his crop did not fare well there, so he moved on to the sunnier climes of San Diego, where he was elected county sheriff and became a member of the state legislature. Then in 1857 the colonel moved north and planted the first large vineyard in Northern California. The crop thrived, and the rest is history.

Today California's self-proclaimed oldest premium winery is owned and run by one of the youngest teams in the Sonoma Valley. The owners and their winemaker are barely in their thirties. The winery and the surrounding grounds are beautiful, with an ivy-covered, cavelike tasting room and plenty of outdoor tables for picnicking. Even though it's just a few minutes from Sonoma Plaza, there is a feeling here of being miles away, in gorgeous country.

By the way, the colonel's colorful history did not stop with the founding of the Northern California wine industry. After both his sons married daughters of General Vallejo, the elder Haraszthy moved to Nicaragua and became a successful sugar manufacturer. According to legend, he died attempting to cross a stream near his plantation; the alligators left not a trace.

BUENA VISTA WINERY, *18000 Old Winery Road, Sonoma. Phone: (707) 938-1266. Open 10 A.M. to 5 P.M. daily; tours around the historic cellars are self-guided. Admission: Free.*

HOW TO GET TO BUENA VISTA: *From San Francisco, follow the directions to Sonoma Plaza. At the plaza, turn right onto East Napa Street and continue until you come to Old Winery Road. Turn left and follow the signs to Buena Vista.*

CALIFORNIA'S UNPRONOUNCEABLE WINERY ⑤

Another of the oldest wineries in the Sonoma Valley is also one of the hardest to pronounce. For me, the fact that Jim Bundschu has resisted all temptation to change the name and make life easier for everyone makes the place worth a visit. But even better, I find Gundlach-Bundschu a very pleasant stop.

Jim is the young, personable boss of the operation. He is a member of the fifth generation of Bundschus to operate the vineyard at this very location. His ancestor, Charles Bundschu (pronounced "bund-shoe") came from Bavaria with his friend Jacob Gundlach (pronounced "goond-lock") to strike it rich in the California Gold Rush. However, they arrived in 1856, a bit too late. Like the Chinese and French in Marin, they decided to stay and do what they knew best. They found a spot in Sonoma that reminded them of the Bavarian hills and began making wine.

If this is what Bavaria looks like, I'm going there soon. The winery overlooks a small lake, with rolling hills in every direction. After you park your car, you walk down a lovely flower-lined stone path to a stone-and-wooden building that houses the winery. It's a small operation, much smaller than its neighbor, Buena Vista, and appearing even smaller than Hacienda. One look inside will reveal the tasting room to the left, the storage barrels to the rear. It's not uncommon to find Jim's wife and daughter labeling bottles in the corner.

Everything is informal and folksy. Outside the winery building is a shaded picnic table, plus more secluded picnic areas up on the vine-covered hillside.

The tasting room has a big drain in the middle of the floor. Jim encourages visitors to taste the wine and then spit it out into the drain. Like many other winemakers, he is concerned about tourists overindulging on winery tours by trying to take in too many wineries in one day. His advice: Stay in the area for a few days, take time to see other attractions the area has to offer, and visit only a few wineries each day. When tasting, avoid swallowing. Look for a dump bucket or drain, and don't worry about not appearing chic or elegant. Highway patrol officers are out there waiting.

GUNDLACH-BUNDSCHU, *2000 Denmark Road, Sonoma. Phone: (707) 938-5277. Open 11 A.M. to 4:30 P.M. daily; closed on major holidays. Admission: Free. Large groups should call in advance.*

HOW TO GET TO GUNDLACH-BUNDSCHU: *From San Francisco, take the Golden Gate Bridge to Highway 101 North. Exit at Route 37 and bear to the right (east). Follow Highway 37 to Highway 121. Turn left on Route 12 and continue to the town of Sonoma. At the town plaza, turn right on East Napa Street. Turn left at Eighth Street and go 1 mile. Turn right on Denmark Road and follow for about a mile to the winery. There are now clearly marked signs for all of the local wineries in Sonoma.*

JACK LONDON STATE PARK

Once upon a time—at the turn of the twentieth century, to be exact—Glen Ellen was the place to bring your family for the summer. Two railways chugged into town, bringing fashionable people from all over the Bay Area to the lovely hotels, quaint cabins, and lively saloons.

One summer, Jack London, "America's first millionaire author," came up from Oakland and decided to stay. He started buying parcels of land, eventually totaling 1400 acres, that he named Beauty Ranch. Jack's dream was to build a house for himself and his wife, Charmian, and to create a utopian community for the ranch workers; each worker would get a parcel of land to call his own, and there would be a school on the property so that each ranch child would be educated. London's dream never came true. In 1910 he started construction on

Wolf House, a 26-room, four-story mansion, complete with accommodations for London's 18,000-book library. Shortly before construction was completed in 1913, a mysterious fire destroyed the house. The cause has never been determined; some say it was a tragic accident, others that an arsonist destroyed the place in angry response to London's socialist politics. Jack and Charmian spent the next few years traveling and writing; Jack died in 1916.

Fortunately for us, 49 acres of London's Beauty Ranch have been preserved as a state historic park. It is one of the loveliest and most accessible parks in the Bay Area, complete with a hilltop lake, riding stables, and picnic tables. There are beautiful nature trails, ranging from a difficult 3.3-mile trek up to the summit of Mount Sonoma to the easy 1-mile stroll on a path through the woods, which can take you to the ruins of Wolf House.

I recommend that you begin your visit to Jack London State Park at Wolf House. The foundations are still intact, and diagrams show the construction plans; you can see the grandeur of the plan and the kind of life the writer had in mind for himself. Enough of a structure remains to give you an idea of the layout and scope of the project. Walkways take you to second-level overlooks, which provide good views of the ill-fated dream house. Being a contemporary California homeowner, I was stunned to learn that the house cost only $80,000 to build; but then, that was in 1910. . . .

On your way back, you can take a slight detour along the way to visit Jack's grave, a lovely hillside spot where you can take time to pay your respects and to admire the peaceful and untouched surroundings (may we all end up in such a spot!).

Above the parking lot where you left your car is the House of Happy Walls, the place the widowed Charmian built in honor of her late husband. The house is full of memorabilia from their global travels and contains such items of interest as Jack London's desk and files. The house is now operated by the state parks department as a museum featuring displays of original manuscripts. Upstairs, Charmian's belongings are also on display; for someone with socialist ideals living in the woods of Northern California, this lady had some fine dresses!

JACK LONDON STATE HISTORIC PARK, *Glen Ellen. Phone: (707) 938-5216. Open 8 A.M. to sunset daily. Museum open 10 A.M. to 5 P.M. daily. Admission: $2 parking fee.*

HOW TO GET TO THE PARK: *From San Francisco, take the Golden Gate Bridge to Highway 101 North. Take 101 to Route 37 East and continue to Route 121. Turn left on Route 12 and follow it into the town of Sonoma. When you reach the plaza, turn left on West Napa Street, which is Highway 12. Continue about 6½ miles to the town of Glen Ellen and follow the signs to the park.*

The sign may seem routine, but you will quickly realize that this is no ordinary bookstore. First of all, you will be greeted by Brewster the Rooster, a friendly bird that strolled into the bookstore about seven years ago and decided to stay. Nobody's bothered to tell him he's not human (he probably wouldn't listen anyway).

Then you might see an elderly woman exploring the bookshelves. She's Becky London, the 86-year-old daughter of the author; Becky lives with the remarkable couple who runs the bookstore, Russ and Winifred Kingman.

Russ Kingman has devoted his life to knowing everything about Jack London. He even has a card file, cross-referencing every single day of the writer's life between 1904, when he met his wife, Charmian, and his death in 1916. Ask Kingman what London was doing on July 17, 1907, and he'll tell you. Russ used to be an advertising man in the Bay Area. One of his accounts was a tourist attraction in Oakland called Jack London Square. While doing some research to promote the place, Russ got hooked on the subject. In 1973 he quit the advertising game and moved to Glen Ellen to run his bookstore.

But as I said before, this is no ordinary bookstore. It is also a museum dedicated to the art and life of Jack London, with research materials that attract literary scholars from all over the world. If it was written by or about Jack London, you'll find it here.

JACK LONDON BOOKSTORE, *14300 Arnold Drive, Glen Ellen. Phone: (707) 996-5288. Open 11 A.M. to 5 P.M. daily.*

TO GET TO THE BOOKSTORE: *From Jack London State Park, the bookstore is about 1½ miles south on Arnold Drive.*

JACK LONDON BOOKSTORE

While driving through Sonoma County, particularly in the area near Penngrove, you can get the paranoid feeling that there are highway patrol cars everywhere. Look again; what you're seeing out of the corner of your eye might be highway patrol cows.

Dick Gray bred this unique type of cattle that look painted to Highway Patrol specifications: black at the front and rear, white in the middle. Actually, they are a crossbreed of Holstein and a kind of dutch cow. Gray says he bred them not for their looks but for the milk they produce. If you would like to see a lot of highway patrol cows, and maybe take a snapshot for the folks back home, drive down Roberts Road off Route 101 north of Penngrove. That's the site of the main Gray farm, but the cows are also grazing in several other locations in the general Petaluma area.

HIGHWAY PATROL COWS
(8)

Heading toward Santa Rosa on Petaluma Hill Road near Rohnert Park, you will notice that the name Crane is prominent in these parts: Crane Road, Crane Hill,

CRANE MELONS

Crane Farm Stand. This is the home of the Crane melon, developed by the Crane family, which has been farming this land for six generations.

Today fourth-generation George Crane is the patriarch of the family. His great-great-grandfather was a pioneer who came to Sonoma from Missouri on a wagon train in 1852; his grandfather developed the melon bearing the family name. The Cranes still live in the family house, built in 1868, with the melon patch next door, plus 80 more acres down the road.

So if it's melon season, which is mid-August through November, you ought to stop to try some of the best fruit you've ever tasted. Outside, Crane melons look like a cross between a giant cantaloupe and a honeydew. Inside, they have a soft orange flesh. Folks come from all over the Bay Area just to buy them, and they're shipped all over the world.

George says the secret is dry-land farming. Other melons are irrigated, which he says reduces the flavor. The Cranes water their seed only once, and from then on they're on their own. Apparently, it works.

At the family farm stand, the Cranes sell various items raised on their ranch, including string beans, corn, tomatoes, and a special yellow-fleshed watermelon. Years ago, a relative brought one seed of this unusual fruit from Texas; today the yellow melons of Texas thrive in Sonoma.

CRANE MELON BARN, *4947 Petaluma Hill Road, Santa Rosa. Phone: (707) 584-5141. Open 10 A.M. to 6 P.M. from approximately August 10 through the week of November 15, depending on the readiness and availability of the melons.*

HOW TO GET TO THE CRANE BARN: *From San Francisco, take Golden Gate Bridge and follow Highway 101 North, pass the Petaluma exits to the Rohnert Park exit. Turn right and go to the end of the road. Turn left on Petaluma Hill Road, and the barn will be on the left, 2½ miles down the road.*

LUTHER BURBANK'S HOME AND GARDENS ⑩

I remember learning about Luther Burbank in school. I knew that he was America's most famous fruit and vegetable man, inventing new plants by crossbreeding. What I didn't realize is what a giant he was in his day. I came to appreciate this fact when I stopped at the Luther Burbank home and gardens in Santa Rosa. Burbank was regarded as the Henry Ford of horticulture, the Thomas Edison of the tomato. Burbank moved to Santa Rosa from Massachusetts; he thought the area offered the ideal climate for growing things.

Burbank would probably be shocked to find that Santa Rosa is now a bustling city—in fact, one of the fastest growing in Northern California. But he'd be pleased to discover that the folks haven't forgotten their man of many roots.

Burbank arrived in Santa Rosa in 1875 and lived here for 50 years. Though the town was devastated in the famous 1896 earthquake that rocked San Francisco, his greenhouse withstood the shake. The home, however, did not and had to be rebuilt. While living in Santa Rosa, Burbank created over 800 varieties of fruits, vegetables, and flowers, including the russet potato, the Santa Rosa plum, the Shasta daisy (which took him 17 years to perfect), and the spineless cactus, which he developed with the help of his friend, writer Jack London, who was interested in producing a new kind of cattle feed.

The house itself is a modest, two-story dwelling, furnished with the belongings Burbank brought with him from "back East." It is filled with photos and memorabilia that illustrate the scientist's fame. It's a warm and cozy home, nicely decorated, but hardly the mansion one would expect of someone of Burbank's standing. The greenhouse, included in the tour of the home and gardens, is where Burbank started his plantings; for larger experiments he had an 18-acre farm in Sebastopol. But the highlight of the visit is the beautiful outdoor garden, filled with the plants developed by Burbank.

LUTHER BURBANK'S HOME AND GARDENS, *204 Santa Rosa Avenue (at Sonoma Avenue), Santa Rosa. Phone: (707) 576-5115. Gardens open 8 A.M. to 5 P.M. daily all year. Home and museum open 10 A.M. to 4 P.M. from the first Wednesday in April through the second Sunday in October only. Admission to the gardens is free, but it costs $1 to visit the house. The gardens, greenhouse, and downstairs of the home are wheelchair accessible.*

HOW TO GET TO LUTHER BURBANK'S HOME AND GARDENS: *From San Francisco, take the Golden Gate Bridge to Highway 101 North and continue all the way to Santa Rosa. Take the Third Street exit and follow the signs to the Burbank Home and Garden Center.*

THE CHURCH BUILT FROM ONE TREE

Believe it or not, just a few blocks from the Burbank home is a place dedicated to Santa Rosa's most famous native son, Robert Ripley. The building that houses the Robert L. Ripley Memorial Collection is itself like an item out of Ripley's famous "Believe It or Not" column: a church built entirely from just one redwood, felled in nearby Guerneville. This is the church Ripley attended as a young boy.

However, let me make it clear that this is not a "Believe It or Not"–type tourist attraction, like the kind you can find on San Francisco's Fisherman's Wharf. This museum is dedicated to the man himself: his life, his career, his writing. Ripley was an avid sports fan; he even played semipro baseball in his hometown. He was a shy man and an eccentric; for example, he owned several automobiles, yet never learned to drive. He collected oddities (such as the famous fur-bearing trout).

He also liked to draw, and he started his career as a sports cartoonist for a New York paper. For his own amusement he collected odd facts about sports. The first "Believe It or Not" column came about on a slow day, when nothing very interesting was happening in the wide world of sports. To break the doldrums, Ripley drew and published a series of cartoons called "Champs and Chumps." The editor loved the cartoons but hated the name. On display in the museum is the original drawing with the title "Champs and Chumps" crossed out and replaced by the title that became famous, "Ripley's Believe It or Not."

While you're here, see if you can find curator Shirley Carter. She really knows the life of Ripley and wrote her doctoral dissertation on the man.

THE ROBERT L. RIPLEY MEMORIAL COLLECTION, *located in the Church Built from One Tree, 492 Sonoma Avenue, Santa Rosa. Phone: (707) 576-5233 or (707) 576-5268. Open 11 A.M. to 4 P.M. Wednesday through Sunday, March through October. Closed November through February. Admission: Adults $1; seniors 75 cents, children .50 cents, children under 8 free.*

HOW TO GET TO THE ROBERT RIPLEY COLLECTION: *From the Luther Burbank Home and Gardens, cross Santa Rosa Avenue and go down Sonoma Avenue approximately one half block to the Church Built from One Tree. I recommend walking from the gardens, where there is better parking for visitors.*

SNOOPY ON SKATES

If Luther Burbank and Robert Ripley were Santa Rosa's most famous citizens of the past, Charles Schulz is surely the most famous citizen of the present. In case you can't place the name, think "Peanuts." That's right, Charles Schulz is the father of Snoopy, Charlie Brown, and the rest of the gang.

Schulz is also one of America's most published creators. For nearly 40 years he's drawn the "Peanuts" gang for newspaper strips, books, drinking cups, sweatshirts, and the like. Schulz lives and works in Santa Rosa but spends every spare minute he can visiting the site of his true love, his Redwood Ice Arena. It must be love; the place loses a fortune every year, and the cartoonist must work like crazy just to keep the doors open.

Schulz, whose studio is located in a small cottage behind the ice arena, has his breakfast every day in the coffeeshop. He also plays hockey at the rink as many nights as he can, a holdover from his childhood days in Minnesota. He bought the arena in the late 1960s when he learned it was about to go out of business. He refurbished the place, so now it is an entertainment complex. Inside are the ice rink and a coffeeshop, which have become an unofficial community center; outside there are picnic grounds. It's one of those rare places where you can find both young and not-so-young people enjoying themselves.

Every year Schulz and skating champion Karen Kresge write the script for an ice show that is produced at the Redwood Ice Arena. According to "Sparky" (which is what Schulz's friends call him), this is one of the most impressive shows on ice. Not only does it attract big-time skating stars like Scott Hamilton, but the show is made more special by the intimacy of the 1000-seat theater;

unlike going to a show at a giant arena, there isn't a faraway seat in the house.

Next door to the rink is a large gift shop which features what I assume is everything ever made with the likenesses of the "Peanuts" character: neckties, golf tees, stuffed Snoopys, and tiny Linuses. But if you're more of a historian than a shopper, go upstairs to the gallery—a graphic museum of Schulz's career. You can see the evolution of the character, magazine spreads, and correspondence from some of the most famous people of our time, giving you an idea of the wide range of lives Sparky and his "Peanuts" gang have touched.

REDWOOD ICE ARENA AND "PEANUTS" MUSEUM, *1667 West Steele Lane, Santa Rosa (on the northwestern side of town). Hours vary each day and each season; it is best to call ahead: (707) 546-7147. The arena complex, including galleries and gift shop, is wheelchair accessible.*

HOW TO GET TO THE ICE ARENA: *From San Francisco, take the Golden Gate Bridge up Route 101 North to the West Steele Lane exit, past the town of Santa Rosa. Stay in the middle lane and turn left off the freeway; stay in the right lane after the turn and continue past two stoplights. The road will fork; stay to the right. After you cross Range Avenue, the Redwood Ice Arena will be the third driveway on your right.*

Just a few minutes' drive from the Redwood Ice Arena you can have another cultural experience, as far removed from the Americana of an ice arena and the "Peanuts" gallery as you can imagine.

Like the Redwood Ice Arena, the Kyoto Koi Garden is the fulfillment of a dream. But this time the dreamer is a burly former real estate developer named Paul Pattingale. A couple of years ago Paul bought a house, and while clearing away overgrown foliage he discovered a Japanese garden on his property. He became curious about the little bonsai trees and about the Japanese culture that created the art form. Curiosity led to obsession, and Paul opened the Kyoto Koi Garden as both a business and a place of serenity to share with others.

From the parking lot, you may think you're about to enter a plant nursery. You will see hundreds of bonsai trees, plants that are dwarfed according to the bonsai master at work. Hiroshiko Suzuki gives demonstrations daily. He sits on a pedestal, surrounded by attentive students, and snips a branch here, binds a limb with wire there. Without the master's attention these trees would grow to be 60 to 80 feet tall; by careful shaping, pruning, and binding, the trees are allowed to grow only a foot or so high, and the result is all the energy of a full-grown tree packed into a beautiful miniature.

After taking your time admiring the trees, you can visit the *koi* tanks. *Koi* are orange, white, black, and gold fish, descendants of Japanese carp, and are as prized as the bonsai trees. They are another of Paul's obsessions, on display in

JAPANESE GOLDFISH AND GARDENS

several waist-high tanks. For a quarter you can buy a handful of fishfood and feed the koi; they will swim up and nibble from your hand. The larger and older the fish, the more it is worth; the jumbos sell for $500 to $10,000 and often live to be 200 years old.

You get to top off the visit with a stroll around the formal Japanese garden, complete with stone paths, ponds, footbridges, statuary, and dramatic waterfalls that completely mask the sound from the road just over the wall. Though the bonsai trees and the fish are for sale, there is nothing for sale in the garden. It is provided for tranquility and peace, a place of refuge from the hustle and bustle of the city, and you are invited to simply enjoy it.

KYOTO KOI AND GARDEN CENTER, *2783 Guerneville Road, Santa Rosa. Open 9 A.M. to 5:30 P.M. daily. Phone: (707) 575-9223. Admission: Free.*

HOW TO GET TO KYOTO KOI AND GARDEN CENTER: *From San Francisco or any point north of the Golden Gate Bridge, take Route 101 to the Guerneville Road exit. Take Guerneville Road west until you come to Kyoto Koi.*

THE GOAT CHEESE REVOLUTION STARTED HERE
(14)

One of the staples of California cuisine is goat cheese, and Laura Chenel is the person responsible, or guilty, depending on your opinion of goat cheese. In the late 1970s Laura moved to a farm where there were several goats. She tried making some cheese, and by her own admission, it was dreadful. So Laura went to France to learn from the masters. Four years later she was back in Northern California peddling her product to a few choice restaurants. It was such a hit that not only was her cheese served at Chez Panisse and other California gourmet meccas, but these places even included her name on the menu.

Today at least seven or eight other goat cheese makers have set up shop in Northern California to keep up with the demand. But Laura was the first, and she has customers nationwide. She is also the first to take a cue from the wine industry and set up a tasting room.

An attractive, bubbly woman who looks like she'd be just as comfortable at a chic cocktail party as she is working on the farm, Laura makes her famous cheese in a modest little building in a residential neighborhood outside Santa Rosa. From these cramped quarters, 13 varieties of Laura Chenel chevre (aka goat cheese) are made. It's a fairly simple process. After the milk is pasteurized, a culture and coagulants are added. The mixture sits overnight to thicken. The next day the yogurtlike substance is ladled into molds, some roundish, others tubelike. As the excess liquid drains out, the cheeses are turned each day by hand and individually handled until they achieve the right age and consistency. When ready, some are rolled in pepper or herbs; others are preserved in olive oil or grated like parmesan.

Unfortunately, the current manufacturing area is too small for organized tours. But since so many people seem interested in seeing the process, Laura has plans to open a larger showplace somewhere in Sonoma. In the meantime, she has set up the informal tasting room in a little building outside the manufacturing plant where you can sample a variety of goat cheese, ask questions about the process, and purchase an attractive package or two for an afternoon picnic. Laura also does a brisk mail-order business, so you might want to add your name to her mailing list.

Be advised to call ahead for an appointment; Laura buys her milk from about a dozen goat farmers in the area and is often out on a run.

LAURA CHENEL CHEVRE, *1550 Ridley Avenue, Santa Rosa. Phone: (707) 575-8888.*

HOW TO GET TO LAURA CHENEL CHEVRE: *From San Francisco or any point north of the Golden Gate Bridge, take Route 101 to the Steele Lane-Guerneville Road exit. Take Guerneville Road west approximately 1½ miles and turn left on Ridley Avenue. Continue on Ridley past Jennings Street, and turn into the driveway between the fourth and fifth houses on the left. The tasting room is in a little shack next to the main building.*

HOP KILN WINERY

Long before a bottle of wine was sold in this part of Sonoma, this was beer country. Up until World War II, hops were grown on farm after farm near Healdsburg, then sent to breweries for the production of beer. All that changed in the 1950s when a disease hit the crop and large breweries switched to rice instead of hops. This produced a lighter beer that not only sold well but was cheaper to produce. And so marked the end of the hop-growing industry in this region. The hop farms dried up and the land was put to other use, but many of the old buildings remain. One of the most striking has been turned into a winery.

Though I had never seen a hop kiln in my life, I knew I had arrived at Hop Kiln Winery when I saw from the road three huge chimneys growing out of a barn. As I soon learned, these towers were for drying the hops. They would be hung near the top of the chimney. Inside the building, at ground level, fires would burn in huge furnaces with grates carrying the heat outside. This hot air would rise up through the hops for the drying process. It took eight hours to dry a load of hops.

The source of this information was Marty Griffin, owner and chief storyteller at Hop Kiln. He is also a practicing physician who runs the winery as a way to unwind, though he'll be the first to tell you that the wine business is basically farming and involves hard work and long hours. But as you will learn from visiting any small winery in California, there is something about the business that hooks people. A look at Marty's home may provide a clue. Right behind the winery is his marvelous two-story frame farmhouse, complete with a huge porch overlooking acres of vineyards and a pond filled with ducks and geese. It was built in 1873 and used to be 20 miles away; in order to move it to its present location, it had to be cut into four sections and rebuilt. It is an official Sonoma County landmark building.

The home is not open for public tours, but it is in clear sight when you visit the property, and there are public picnic tables in front of it (and more around the pond). The winery/hop kiln/barn, originally built in 1905, has been restored nicely and features photographs showing the old days of hop farming.

Tours are self-guided, and you will see basically the same things you see at any small winery: storage tanks and bottling lines; if you happen to be there at harvest time in the fall, you will see a crush. Most people make a quick circuit and end up at the wine-tasting bar where you can sample several of the Hop Kiln varietals. One specialty is a rare German Christmas wine called "weihnachten"; try it if you like sweet wine or have the spirit of Christmas.

For your edification, you may wish to know that *The Magic of Lassie* with James Stewart, Mickey Rooney, Alice Faye, and America's favorite canine was filmed here in 1977. Stewart is said to have become quite fond of the winery's French colombard; Lassie abstained. You may also wish to know that Westside Road, where Hop Kiln is located, is one of my favorite drives in the wine county; plan to spend several hours in the area.

HOP KILN WINERY, *6050 Westside Road, Healdsburg. Phone: (707) 433-6491. Open 10 A.M. to 5 P.M. daily.*

HOW TO GET TO HOP KILN: *From San Francisco, take Golden Gate Bridge to Route 101 North. Follow Route 101 to the town of Healdsburg and take the downtown Healdsburg exit. Make an immediate left turn onto Mill Street, which becomes Westside Road. Follow Westside Road approximately 6 miles to Hop Kiln Winery.*

LIVE FROM JOHNSON'S OF ALEXANDER VALLEY WINERY ⑯

As I said earlier in this section, with so many wineries in the area, I always try to find those that are one of a kind. The Johnson's place certainly fits that description. As far as I know, it's the only winery in the world with a pipe organ in its tasting room. And this is no ordinary pipe organ. Built in 1924, it was originally intended for use in a theater. It is the prize possession of the Johnson brothers, who own this small, family-run business. They owned the organ long before they went into the wine business in 1975; when they decided to open a winery, the brothers had the tasting room built around the musical instrument.

Once a month, Joan Shaffer comes from Santa Rosa and performs a Sunday matinee concert. She plays pop standards with a bounce, including a rousing rendition of "Beer Barrel Polka." Joan will also play requests and has the patter of a lounge performer. As you can imagine, the workings of such an instrument take up a lot of space, and you can get a close view of the various pipes and percussive devices in operation through glass windows in the walls.

The winery is also located in one of the least crowded valleys in Sonoma County. The Alexander Valley is said to have a climate similar to that of the Bordeaux region of France. It is quite warm in the summer and mild in the winter when it's not raining. The winery is in a barn with lots of antique farm equipment casually decorating the grounds. It's a small operation, so there is no organized tour; your visit here will be to enjoy the scenery, relax on the picnic grounds outside, and maybe catch an organ concert.

If your timing is right, you might have an additional treat. On one of my visits, I was entertained by a dozen playfully rambunctious basset hound puppies. You see, the Johnsons also breed bassets and sometimes display the latest litter on the winery grounds.

I should mention that there is another Alexander Valley winery down the road. It's also a nice place to visit but not the one with an organ.

JOHNSON'S OF ALEXANDER VALLEY WINERY, *8333 Route 128, Healdsburg. Phone: (707) 433-2319. Open 10 A.M. to 5 P.M. daily. Admission: Free.*

HOW TO GET TO JOHNSON'S: *From San Francisco, take the Golden Gate Bridge and continue north past Santa Rosa to the town of Healdsburg, approximately a 90-minute drive from the bridge. Exit onto Healdsburg Avenue and continue to Alexander Valley Road. Turn right. The winery is another 20 to 30 minutes from Healdsburg. From the Napa Valley: Take Route 128 West all the way from Calistoga. This is a long and beautiful drive.*

HORSE AND BUGGY RIDES

Another way to Johnson's of Alexander Valley Winery is by horse and carriage. A business called Five Oaks Farm Horse-drawn Vineyard Tours offers rides around the Alexander Valley in a genuine surrey with red fringe on top. It's a lot of fun. You can get off the backroads onto the back dirt roads of the wine country with somebody else doing the driving. This operation is run by Greg and Sue Hannan, a married couple who are both emergency care nurses at a local hospital. Plodding along and holding the reins of their Percheron draft horses is their idea of a perfect way to relax. Though the Hannans offer moonlight rides and dinner-time tours, their main business is daytime wine-tasting excursions that can either begin or end with a picnic at Johnson's Alexander Valley Winery.

I should mention that there are two other similar businesses servicing Sonoma County. Another is Carriage Charters, headquartered in Sebastopol, and the rides are tailored to individual interests; so if you don't give a hoot about wine but want to see apple orchards, the driver will take you there in a 100-year-old surrey. The third carriage charter company is called Stage-a-Picnic, which features rides in an antique milk wagon or an 1882-vintage stagecoach made by

Studebaker; rides begin and end at the Hope-Bosworth House, a beautifully restored Victorian bed-and-breakfast inn in Geyserville.

How to choose one? Well, prices are competitive (around $40 a person for a daytime excursion that includes food), so the only advice I can offer is to look for a driver who doesn't talk much; out here, silence is golden. I found the sound, or rather the lack of motor noises, to be one of the most soothing and hypnotic parts of the ride; you can always ask questions and have a conversation at lunch. Take note that reservations are necessary and you are expected to pay in advance; you must cancel at least seven days in advance for a refund.

FIVE OAKS FARM, *Alexander Valley. Phone: (707) 433-2422. This service operates from April 1 through December 1; the rest of the year, weather permitting.*

CARRIAGE CHARTERS, *Sebastopol. Phone (707) 823-7083. Open all year, weather permitting.*

STAGE-A-PICNIC, *Geyserville. Phone: (707) 857-3619. Open May through October.*

SALLIE'S ATTIC

One of the most appealing antique stores I've ever come across happens to be run by the Salvation Army. It's not like any other Salvation Army store you've ever seen. This one is situated in one of the most beautiful spots in all Sonoma County, on the site of a farm and former hot springs resort. There are three Salvation Army-run stores on the property, but Sallie's is the real find.

Sallie's Attic is not really an attic. There are no stairs to climb. It is an old building with several rooms, which are filled with old furniture, clothing, books, glassware, china, and other vintage treasures—the cream of the crop of all donations made to the Salvation Army of Sonoma. The stock changes often; regular customers who come from as far away as San Jose and Eureka see to that. Proceeds from the store help operate the farm, which is a rehabilitation center for men addicted to alcohol or drugs. The men enrolled in the rehab program care for the several acres of beautiful grounds, which include a public fishing pond. They also tend the cows that are later sold for beef at auction.

In case you're wondering how the Salvation Army ended up with such a paradise, the property was acquired for a song after the hot springs resort went belly up. At first it was used as a home for boys, but recently it was converted to an adult center.

By the way, though she sounds like somebody's lovable old grandmother, the "Sallie" in Sallie's Attic is a pet name for the Salvation Army. The other stores on the property are a thrift store and an as-is shop. If some members of your party get tired of browsing, they can roam the property or go fishing while the others rummage through the shops.

SALLIE'S ATTIC, 200 Lytton Springs Road, Healdsburg. Phone: (707) 433-5177. Open 10 A.M. to 5 P.M. Monday through Saturday; closed Sunday.

HOW TO GET TO SALLIE'S ATTIC: From San Francisco, cross the Golden Gate Bridge and take the Lytton Springs Road exit off Highway 101 (it is the first exit north of Healdsburg). Cross under the freeway and look for the signs for Sallie's. You will actually see the grounds on the left from the freeway before leaving Highway 101.

In the fabulous 1960s, thousands of people seeking a new lifestyle came to San Francisco, literally or figuratively wearing flowers in their hair. Today the city streets that once were a haven for the flower children now feature croissants, cappuccino, and haute cuisine, and many of the hippies have become yuppies. But there are havens for those who have not forsaken the New Age, and one is nestled in the little town of Geyserville. The sign that greets you at Isis Oasis tells most of the story. It advertises bed and breakfast, with therapy, massage, tarot readings, past-life excursions, dance, theater, and the availability of various spiritual and corporeal experiences.

ISIS OASIS

The "oasis" was founded by Lora Vigne, who must be the world's most unusual innkeeper. She calls herself an artist, New Age minister, and tarot reader, wears her hair à la Elizabeth Taylor in Cleopatra, and wears clothes that evoke a feeling of Egypt. She is particularly devoted to the Egyptian goddess Isis, goddess of fertility.

Her partner, Paul Rames, is equally interesting. He is a gestalt therapist and past-life guide. Together Paul and Lora have created "a retreat for body and spirit" on 8½ acres of woods and meadows where exotic animals (including an ocelot, a llama, and an emu, a huge flightless South American bird) mingle with artists, New Age spiritualists, and curious visitors.

Folks who spend the night or a week here have a choice of accommodations. The main lodge has several common rooms and individual bedrooms; guests share a large bathroom with showers. There are also tepees; the wine barrel room, which is a tiny bedroom in an actual barrel; and last but not least, yurts. (At the risk of underestimating your housing knowledge, I will explain that a yurt is a large, round Afghan structure, similar to a tepee.)

Food in the dining hall tends to be along the health food line, with mostly vegetarian and herbal tea-type offerings, although chicken and fish are served. The place might make you think you've been transported to the Age of Aquarius, since Lora and Paul believe they are very much a part of the future. There is in fact a very quiet and peaceful feeling about the place. You can be part of a group or be by yourself. You can spend all your time alone by the swimming pool or hot tub, or just take part in the activities that appeal to you.

Room rates are cheap for this neck of the woods. The top rate is $90 a night for two, including a country breakfast; lodge rooms are $60 with a shared bath. Massage, readings, and various therapies are all extra.

ISIS OASIS LODGE AND CULTURAL CENTER, 20889 Geyserville Avenue, Geyserville. Phone: (707) 857-3524. If you're planning to drop by, call first so that someone can come down and open the gate.

HOW TO GET TO ISIS OASIS: From San Francisco, take the Golden Gate Bridge to Highway 101 North. Continue for about 90 minutes to the town of Geyserville. Take the Geyserville Avenue exit at the northern end of town and turn right. Geyserville Avenue is the frontage road that parallels the highway. Continue south on Geyserville Avenue, drive through the small commercial area of town, and you will come to a sign for Isis Oasis on the right. Near the entrance is an obelisklike mock street sign designating the intersection of "Isis" and "Goddess."

LAKE SONOMA

When visitors to the Bay Area are in the mood for the water, they usually head to the Pacific Ocean. These beaches are indeed beautiful, but here's one problem —even during the warmest weather, the water is usually freezing cold. Those who like to take a dip and linger awhile are advised to visit one of the several lakes close to the Bay Area, the newest being Lake Sonoma.

This artificial lake and recreational area has been in operation since 1982, with the completion of the Warm Springs Dam. With each rainfall, what was once the Dry Creek Valley fills up higher and higher. It is a lovely body of water, with one major wide area and five fingers each leading to more secluded spots. Most of the use now is for fishing and water skiing; as for swimming, the water is brisk but much more tolerable than the ocean, especially in summer, when the air temperature at the lake hovers around the 100-degree mark.

Nearly 50 years passed from the time the dam and lake were first proposed until the dam was finally completed. Plans call for resort hotels, fancy restaurants, theaters, and other tourist-oriented attractions but at last check, the facilities were minimal. There are a few boating docks for launching motorboats and sailboats, a snack bar and deli, and, high above the lake, an overlook with a spectacular view. The overlook is in a parklike setting, with picnic tables, rest rooms, and a pay phone.

LAKE SONOMA MARINA, headquarters for the various activities. For information about launching boats, swimming, and other facilities, call (707) 433-2200. There is a $3 parking fee.

HOW TO GET TO LAKE SONOMA: From San Francisco, take the Golden Gate

Bridge to Route 101 North to Healdsburg. Exit at Dry Creek Road and follow the signs to the lake.

When visiting Lake Sonoma, you might want to stop next door and see an example of our new awareness of responsibility when we alter the course of nature.

Thanks to environmental protection laws, to build the Warm Springs Dam that created Lake Sonoma, the Army Corps of Engineers also had to build a fish hatchery. You see, before the dam, migrating salmon and steelhead came to the fresh water of Dry Creek to deposit their eggs. Since the dam would block Dry Creek and its tributaries, a new environment for spawning had to be created; hence the hatchery. It's probably not the salmon's idea of a romantic honeymoon setting, but it works, and the public is invited to see the operation.

After parking in the ample lot, you cross over a bridge to the visitor's center, a very attractive structure that looks like a museum. Inside you are given an illustrated brochure for the self-guided tour. This is a large operation, and you can spend a few hours here or just breeze through after a bit of salmon sex education.

I won't attempt to tell you everything you'll see if you go through the entire process, but some of the various stations on the tour show fish being tranquilized and workers from the California Fish and Game Service removing eggs and sperm from the drugged salmon and steelhead. Depending on the time of year you visit, you can witness live artificial insemination, incubation, and finally tanks of baby fish awaiting release back into the creek as soon as they're large enough. You can watch the entire process on video all year.

The hatchery's goal is to produce a million fish per year. Though the tour is self-guided, state park rangers are on hand to answer any questions you may have.

WARM SPRINGS FISH HATCHERY, *Lake Sonoma. Phone: (707) 433-6325 at the hatchery or (707) 433-9483 for visitor's information from the Army Corps. Though spawning season is November through March, the visitor's center is open all year-round. Open from 9:30 A.M. to 4 P.M. Monday, Thursday, and Friday and from 10 A.M. to 5 P.M. Saturday and Sunday; closed Tuesday and Wednesday. From Memorial Day to Labor Day the hatchery is open from 10 A.M. to 6 P.M. seven days a week. Admission: Free. Wheelchair accessible.*

HOW TO GET TO THE FISH HATCHERY: *From San Francisco, take the Golden Gate Bridge to Route 101 North to the Dry Creek exit, north of Healdsburg. Follow Dry Creek west (left) until it ends at the dam. An alternative is to take Canyon Road out of Geyserville, which intersects with Dry Creek Road. This is at least two hours from San Francisco.*

FISH HATCHERY
(21)

RUSSIAN RIVER AREA

The Russian River is the name given to the large resort area centered around the community of Guerneville. The river itself runs from just south of Healdsburg and empties into the Pacific just below the town of Jenner.

The only constant in this area is change. Perhaps the central community of Guerneville should have been called Phoenix, because it keeps rising from the ashes of one disaster after another. There have been three town-destroying fires and two floods, but still the town and the area keep coming back.

This used to be redwood forest country until major logging companies moved in. Their rail lines went throughout western Sonoma, first for logging, then for bringing tourists up from San Francisco. While the superrich went to Marin and Tahoe, working-class families came to the Russian River. In fact, it used to be called "Little Mission," named after the modest neighborhood in the City. When the trains stopped coming to town in the 1940s, tourism died. In the 1960s the hippies discovered they could live a less hassled life here than in the City and moved up. Then in the late 1970s the Russian River resorts became a haven for San Francisco's gay population.

But just as the area was coming back to life, two disasters struck. The first was the devastating flood of 1986, destroying many homes and businesses. Then the growing concern about AIDS frightened many customers away from the area, forcing some facilities catering to gay clientele out of business.

Still, the area keeps bouncing back and is worth seeing. A drive on River Road will show you the remnants of all the above-mentioned cultures. You will see old hotels, modest cabins in the woods, and new condos designed for an influx of yuppies. You will see middle-class families and people who look like the cast of *Easy Rider,* and you will see men walking hand in hand with other men and women walking hand in hand with other women.

The town of Guerneville is the best place to begin a visit to the Russian River resorts. The visitor's center in the downtown section is a good place to stop for a map and information about the latest developments in the area. Downtown you'll find the year-round residents mingling with the tourists, supermarkets and shoe repair stores next to the shops catering to the tourist trade.

In town you might even happen upon a world leader or two. That's because in the summer the most powerful men in the world flock to nearby Bohemian Grove, a private and well-guarded club, a sort of summer camp for elected officials, stars, corporate leaders, and other kinds of millionaires. The stories of what really goes on at the Grove are legion. You can probably pick some of them up by stopping for lunch or a drink at the Northwood Gold Club restaurant, between Guerneville and Monte Rio on River Road. Many of the "Bohemians" are rumored to hang out there at night, hoping to meet some ladies looking for, let us say, part-time work. Boys, even old rich ones, will be boys.

The Russian River has its share of wineries to visit, too. The most famous and appealing of these is the Korbel Champagne Cellars, also on River Road in Guerneville. Korbel is located in a 120-year-old ivy-covered building, surrounded by redwoods and a beautiful rose garden, with the Russian River flowing by. Free tours of the winery are given daily, every 45 minutes, and the garden is in bloom from April through June. You can picnic on the grounds with supplies of your own, and you can purchase drinks and snacks from a small store next to the tasting room.

Heading toward the ocean, west on Route 116, there is a town that looks like a movie set for an old lumber town. This is Duncan's Mills, population 20, elevation 26 feet. In fact, it was once a thriving lumber town with one claim to fame: Black Bart robbed a train here. An enterprising developer has restored the old downtown village, practically creating a stage set of a village of shops in hopes of catching some of the tourists coming around to taste wine and bask in the Russian River.

Duncan's Mills *is* a charming place to stop. The centerpiece of the town is a small museum located in the old railroad depot, the last remaining depot from the once-active Western Pacific Coastal Line, which ran from Sausalito to Cazadero. The depot doubles as a reception office for the town campground. The town's original general store has been restored so you can pick up various and sundry items in a historic setting, and nearby are several buildings built to look like they existed in the late nineteenth century. Here you can shop for everything from tourist-oriented T-shirts ("Where in the hills is Duncan's Mills?" is a favorite) to fine leather and jewelry. Duncan's Mills is also the site of one of the few nightspots in the Russian River area, The Black Bart Tavern, where you can see historic photographs of "The Gentleman Robber" and be served an alcoholic concoction named in his honor. Behind the tavern is The Blue Heron, a restaurant that features live music on selected nights.

RUSSIAN RIVER VISITOR'S CENTER, *14034 Armstrong Woods Road, Guerneville. Phone: (707) 869-9009.*

KORBEL CHAMPAGNE CELLARS AND ROSE GARDENS, *13250 River Road, Guerneville. Phone: (707) 887-2294. Tasting room hours: October 1 through April 30, open 9 A.M. to 4:30 P.M.; winery tours 10 A.M. to 3 P.M. May 1 through September 30, open 9 A.M. to 5 P.M.; winery tours 9:45 A.M. to 3:45 P.M. Rose gardens open the second weekend in April; tours Tuesday through Sunday, 10 A.M. to 4 P.M.*

HOW TO GET TO GUERNEVILLE: *From San Francisco, take the Golden Gate Bridge and follow Route 101 North to the River Road exit. Follow the signs all the way to Guerneville. Plan on at least a two-hour drive from the bridge.*

HOW TO GET TO DUNCAN'S MILLS: *From Guerneville, take 116 West (toward the ocean) until you come to Duncan's Mills.*

THE RUSSIANS WERE COMING

The more you explore Northern California, the more it becomes apparent that some of the best real estate is owned by the military. The Presidio in San Francisco and Fort Ord in Monterey are certainly prime examples. And you will discover that this was true even as far back as 1812, when the Russians held forth in this neck of the woods.

Many visitors to the area are surprised to learn that there was a considerable Russian presence in these parts (hence, the name Russian River). Near the turn of the nineteenth century the Russians expanded their Alaskan fish and fur interests as far south as Fort Ross, an oceanfront outpost about 11 miles north of the modern town of Jenner. Within the wooden fortress walls was an active community of 700 colonists led by a Russian commandant and his princess wife. While this history may come as a surprise to Americans, it is well known in Russia. A docent and researcher at Fort Ross, Nicholas Katiansky, told me that the Soviets are very proud of Fort Ross and that its history is well catalogued there. He has made many trips as a guest of the Soviet government to help in joint study projects.

The Russians' original plan was to stick around awhile. However, they unexpectedly killed off the sea otter population (valued for their silky pelts), gophers ruined their crops, and the Mexicans who got there first were making them feel unwelcome. In 1841 the Russians sold the land and buildings to Captain John Sutter (of Gold Rush fame) and went home. Katiansky points out that the Soviets got along very well with the Native American population, accepting them as they were instead of trying to convert them.

A visit to Fort Ross, which is now a state historic park, is a low-key stop along the way up or down the coast. The tour of the grounds is self-guided and involves the use of white telephonelike objects that sit on stakes in front of various points of interest; you listen to a recorded message, complete with background music, that tells the story of Russian life in these parts. You will see the stockade, a Russian Orthodox chapel, a tower with a cannon, and the officers' barracks, which is also an information center where you can ask questions not answered by the telephones. A recent addition is a large library and museum, which is the only modern building at the Fort. It's also the warmest, information you will be glad to know if the wind is whipping off the ocean.

FORT ROSS STATE HISTORIC PARK, *on the ocean north of Jenner. Phone: (707) 847-3286. Open 10 A.M. to 5 P.M. Admission: $2 per car.*

HOW TO GET TO FORT ROSS: *From San Francisco, take Golden Gate Bridge to Route 101 North. Past Santa Rosa, take the River Road exit and follow River Road all the way through the Russian River resort area until you connect with Route 1 heading north at Jenner. Follow Route 1 to Fort Ross.*

If you're making your way back to Route 1 and it happens to be between late May and early July, you're in for a treat. Seaview Road will take you north to the town of Plantation, where you will catch Kruse Ranch Road down to the ocean. Suddenly you will be in the midst of a huge rhododendron preserve. If so inclined, you can pull off the road and take a walk on trails through 317 acres of lush fern canyons and redwoods, amid clusters of white, pink, red, and purple rhodo blossoms. Before you take this route, be advised that the road is rough, long, and winding. Don't take it if you're in a rush.

KRUSE RHODODENDRON STATE RESERVE, *at the intersection of Highway 1 and Kruse Ranch Road, about 8 miles south of Stewart's Point. Phone: (707) 865-2391. Open sunrise to sunset all year. Admission: Free.*

KRUSE RHODODENDRON STATE RESERVE

The only town in America to be named Occidental lies just a few miles from the Pacific Ocean, the gateway to the Orient. The main street is the hub for the roads leading to the Russian River resorts to the northwest, Bodega Bay to the west, Petaluma and Sebastopol to the southeast, and Santa Rosa to the northeast. Just outside of town on Coleman Valley Road there are several lovely attractions, including Bodega Bay.

But what brings people to town? Food.

Yes, Italian food, and lots of it. For years, family-style restaurants have been drawing folks to Occidental. There are three big restaurants in town, each one capable of seating the entire population of permanent residents with plenty of seats left over. This is not the sort of fare you will find in the pages of *Gourmet* magazine, nor is it what you would call "spa cuisine." The meals are down-home affairs, often starting with a big bowl of minestrone, followed by mounds of homemade ravioli, then a meat or chicken course served with vegetables, followed by dessert. Everything is served family-style, and the portions are huge. It is also inexpensive.

The Union Hotel on the main drag is the oldest establishment in town. But it's not a hotel at all, it's a 500-seat restaurant with a saloon and the Bocce Ballroom with even more tables and a place to hear live music. The Gonella family runs the Union Hotel; in fact, they pretty much own the whole side of the street, including the town grocery, and a Christmas wreath-making business outside of town. The family patriarch, Dan Gonella, is known as Dan Mahoney. That's because when he was a kid, there were two Dan Gonellas in town, this Dan and his cousin Dan. So that everybody could keep them straight they got nicknames that stuck: Dan McGee and Dan Mahoney.

Across the street from the Union Hotel you'll find Negri's, where 500 more people can sit down for dinner all at once. A sign proclaims it to be the town's

OCCIDENTAL

"original" Italian restaurant. You'll probably find Joe Negri behind the bar and his mother, Theresa, will probably be in front of the bar watching a TV quiz show along with the regular customers. Joe looks like he could be the bouncer at the toughest club in New York City, but his mom says he's just a shy pussycat. Joe's wife does the talking for both of them. She comes out of the kitchen, wisecracking, "You marry an Italian, you do all the work."

The Negris also own racehorse stables down the road and Negri's Occidental Lodge, a motel with a swimming pool. The Gonellas also own a motel, the Union Hotel Motel, and it, too, has a pool (I should mention that it gets very warm here in the summer, and after pasta and wine at Union Hotel, Negri's, or the town's third competitor, Fiori's, many people feel like turning in for the night or taking a dip.)

In case you haven't guessed, there's an atmosphere of rivalry in this town. The Gonellas stay on their side of the street, the Negris stay on theirs. For the rest of us, that means both are competing for our business.

There are a few other things to do in town: A lovely bed-and-breakfast place called Heart's Desire has opened, you can shop at some nice local crafts stores, and a few places in town serve espresso drinks and light meals to those who don't feel like a major mealtime production. If you enjoy botanical gardens and nurseries, you can take Coleman Valley Road a few miles out of town toward the ocean and you will come to Western Hills Nursery, over three acres of winding paths where you can see and purchase a wide variety of hard-to-find plants.

But the town's main attraction continues to be the dueling Italian restaurants. Reservations are recommended for weekends during the summer months especially.

UNION HOTEL, *Occidental. Phone: (707) 874-3662.*

NEGRI'S, *Occidental. Phone: (707) 823-5301.*

FIORI'S, *Occidental. Phone: (707) 823-8188.*

WESTERN HILLS NURSERY, *16250 Coleman Valley Road, about one mile west of downtown. Phone: (707) 874-3731. Open Wednesday through Sunday, 10 A.M. to 5 P.M.; closed Monday and Tuesday.*

HOW TO GET TO OCCIDENTAL: *The easiest way from San Francisco is to cross the Golden Gate Bridge and take Route 101 North to Route 116 West, an exit you pick up after you pass the Petaluma exits (it seems a bit confusing, but Route 116 West is several miles beyond the turnoff for Route 116 East). Take 116 West to the town of Sebastopol; then follow the signs to Bodega until you come to the Bohemian Highway and the town of Freestone. The Bohemian Highway will lead you into Occidental. An alternative route is to take 116 from Sebastopol to Graton Road and turn south; this will also lead into Occidental.*

A few weeks before Easter, I noticed a small ad in a Sonoma County newspaper offering a rent-a-bunny service. This sounded like an interesting idea worth investigating.

RENT-A-BUNNY

As it turns out, the service is the brainchild of a schoolteacher, Sharon Cahn of Buzzard's Roost Ranch. The idea is simple. Sharon feels that taking care of an animal is a serious responsibility. Sometimes around the holidays, families will buy a cute little bunny for the kids, but when the novelty wears off, or the rabbit grows up (whichever comes first), pets often fall victim to neglect. So Sharon decided to rent her rabbits; if family and beast turn out to be compatible, she will sell the bunny so everyone can live happily ever after.

But a visit to Buzzard's Roost Ranch offers even more. This is a working farm with sheep, chickens, pigs, organically grown vegetables, and herbs. Sharon loves to show people around (once a teacher, always a teacher) to let city slickers see what life on the farm is like close up. Because this is a small, family-run farm, operated just by Sharon and her husband, Gene, you can imagine what your life might be like if you lived here. But Sharon really loves her rabbits. Her prize pets are Angoras, from which she makes scarves and sweaters (which are for sale, by the way). She will set up a spinning wheel on the deck of the farm-house and you can watch her pluck the rabbit and spin the yarn right there; it is quite a sight. The rabbits need plucking every two weeks anyway, so it is a happy marriage of necessity and enterprise.

BUZZARD'S ROOST RANCH, *1778 Facendini Lane, Occidental. Phone: (707) 823-2799. Open by appointment only.*

HOW TO GET TO BUZZARD'S ROOST: *From San Francisco, take the Golden Gate Bridge to Highway 101 North to Route 116 West. Take 116 West into the town of Sebastopol. Continue on 116 and a few miles from Sebastopol, turn left on Occidental Road and continue for several miles to Facendini Lane on the right. If you reach the town of Occidental, you've passed the turn. From Occidental Road ride a few minutes out of town to Facendini Lane and turn left.*

THE BODEGAS
(27)

The Bodega Highway winds through rolling hills dotted with sheep and cattle as you head from Sebastopol or Petaluma toward the ocean and to the "twin towns" of Bodega and Bodega Bay. These twins are "fraternal" rather than identical; in fact, the only things they have in common, really, are the similarity in name, phone area code, and the fact that Alfred Hitchcock used both places to film *The Birds* in 1963. There the similarities end.

Bodega is a small, quiet town, and everybody there likes it that way. Visitors are welcome, but they are not actively pursued. This is not a tourist town. There are a few stores along the main highway, businesses that cater to the many farm families that live in the area. The big event around here is the annual spring auction of the town quilt. Ladies from town work all year to make the huge bedspread; the proceeds from the auction benefit the volunteer fire department.

Just before you round the curve into town, you will notice an old schoolhouse on a hill to the left. If you're a movie buff, you will probably recognize it as the place the birds attacked the schoolchildren in Alfred Hitchcock's thriller. Now it's a bed-and-breakfast inn; upstairs is a common room with a spectacular view of the lush Bodega countryside. Downstairs a couple of the rooms are adorned with the chalkboards seen in the film; another room has one of the town quilts hanging on the wall.

The scariest thing you're likely to find in Bodega is the ghost story told by a lady named Charlene, who operates the only business in town geared for visitors. She's easy to find. Right on the highway, on the right side of the road before entering town, you will see a sign for Charlene's Country Treasures. Behind her home is a long garden and several buildings jammed to the rafters with stuff for sale. "I keep what Grandpa threw away," says Charlene, who appears to have cleaned out several flea markets. Visitors are invited to roam and can regard her collection as either a store or a museum. Her motivation is to preserve a part of America's past.

Now, about that ghost story. I was told by people in town that Charlene has a ghost living in her house. She was glad to talk about it. She says that it's not a bad ghost, it's just there. Charlene loves to tell visitors what she's seen and heard and then watch the reactions. She says everybody is interested in ghosts, and everyone has a ghost story to tell her.

Bodega Bay is another story entirely. This is fast becoming a tourist destination, with a small Fisherman's Wharf, at least two large inns and lodges, and a country club with a golf course. Within easy driving to the north are several beaches with access from the coastal highway (Route 1). More than 200 fishing boats port here; in the afternoons you can watch the catch of the day being unloaded.

The ocean is just beyond the spit of land called Bodega Head. Residents like to boast that Bodega Bay is the town with a hole in its head. That's because the citizens blocked a planned nuclear power plant on Bodega Head, even after the power company had dug the hole for the foundation. Now the hole remains as a reminder that the town chose to grow with tourism rather than nuclear power.

In addition to seeing many new motels and inns, the main street, which is Route 1, features several tourist-type shops. There is also camping nearby at the Bodega Dunes.

HOW TO GET TO BODEGA AND BODEGA BAY: *From San Francisco, take the Golden*

Gate Bridge to Highway 101 North to the Central Petaluma exit. Take Washington Street through the center of town and continue until it becomes Bodega Avenue. Continue west to Valley Ford Road, which eventually goes into Route 1 and on into Bodega Bay. To get to Bodega, turn right before you get to Bodega Bay and onto the Bodega Highway. The town of Bodega is only a few minutes away. Charlene's Country Treasures is on the Bodega Highway, as you head out of town, traveling east.

KOZLOWSKI FARMS

If you like jams, jellies, mustards, fresh fruit, and unusual chocolate surprises, chances are you've come across the name Kozlowski. Supermarkets across the country sell this family's sugarless preserves, made only with fruit and fruit juice. When you visit their headquarters, you will quickly see that the Kozlowski operation is a far cry from Smucker's.

The Kozlowskis live and work in the heart of Sonoma apple country, on the appropriately named Gravenstein Highway. For years the family had sold the berries and apples raised on their farm at a little stand in front of the family house. One year they were overwhelmed by raspberries. Mrs. Kozlowski made a batch of jam in the kitchen and sold it at the family fruit stand. Another year they were overwhelmed by apples, so Mrs. Kozlowski used them instead of sugar to sweeten her jam. As it turns out, many of her regular customers were cutting down on sugar anyway, and soon she had a popular product. Sometimes she didn't get the chance to put a batch onto the shelves; people were buying it still warm from the kitchen. Now production has expanded to include a wide variety of Kozlowski products, including vinegar, juices, and syrups. But Mrs. Kozlowski insists her jams and jellies are still made the old-fashioned way. Despite their success and wide distribution, the farm still has the look and feel of a family operation.

As you drive in, you pass by Gravenstein apple orchards and berry patches on the long driveway that leads to the farm buildings. On one side is the modest but comfy-looking farmhouse; on the other side is the huge barn, which doubles as the retail outlet. You can roam the grounds, but most people make a beeline for the barn. Inside, you are likely to meet Mrs. Kozlowski and several of her children, all of whom work in the family business. Depending on the season, there will be fresh berries or apples for sale, plus the various Kozlowski products. They even have a tasting room, but instead of wine you get jam or mustard on a cracker, or perhaps a spoonful of Mrs. Kozlowski's chocolate sauce sweetened with fruit juice.

KOZLOWSKI FARMS, *5566 Gravenstein Highway (Route 116), Sebastopol. Phone: (707) 887-2104 or (707) 887-2105. Open 9 A.M. to 5 P.M. daily, closed major holidays. Spring and summer are the best times of the year to get fresh berries, but frozen berries are available all year.*

HOW TO GET TO KOZLOWSKI FARMS: *From San Francisco, take Golden Gate Bridge to Highway 101 North. Follow Route 101 to the Route 116 West exit, which is several miles past the exit for Route 116 East. Turn left off the exit and take Route 116 West past the town of Sebastopol. After several miles, look on the left for the entrance to Kozlowski Farms.*

PET-A-LLAMA RANCH

Many futurists say that national trends start in California. If that's true, then, no matter where you are, there's probably a llama in your future. I know of at least three llama farms that have cropped up in the past year or so and the llamas are selling like tortillas, or whatever it is they use for pancakes in Peru, where these creatures come from.

Why llamas? Well, one of the best people to answer that question is Chuck Warner, who runs the Pet-a-Llama Ranch in Sebastopol. It used to be in Petaluma, which made for a more euphonious name, but Warner moved to a place with 50 acres rather than 5. Anyway, he's an entertaining character who became fascinated with the Andean work animals and decided to make his fortune in llamas. A transplanted New Englander (as you can quickly tell by his accent), Warner seems to like nothing more than to talk llama. He'll tell you that they are a great investment as well as a versatile work animal or pet. He can tell you their history—that they originally thrived near Lima, that the Incas domesticated them, that their wool is good for clothing and making rope, that William Randolph Hearst was the first to bring them to the United States, and that they seem to adapt to all altitudes and climates (you can find them in Alaska, Florida, and Texas, too).

As for the animals themselves, they are intriguing: friendly, big-eyed, with sweet faces and long necks. Believe me, growing up in Indiana, I for one never saw anything like them. They spend most of the day peacefully munching alfalfa, hay, and other native California cuisine. Trained to kneel, they are easy to load for use as pack animals. They are also relatively quiet and very strong. In fact, if you make arrangements in advance, Chuck will take you for a ride in a buggy pulled by a pair of llamas.

Also on the premises is a gift shop (much larger than in the original Petaluma location) featuring sweaters and other apparel made from llama wool.

For the record, the proper pronunciation of "llama" in Spanish is "yama"; most Americans call them "lamas," though.

PET-A-LLAMA RANCH, *5505 Lone Pine Road, Sebastopol. Phone: (707) 823-9395. Open Saturday and Sunday from 10 A.M. until 4 P.M.; by appointment only during the week. Visitors can roam the grounds and join in feeding the animals. No admission charge on weekends; minimal group charge during the week.*

HOW TO GET TO PET-A-LLAMA RANCH: *From San Francisco, take Highway 101 North to the Route 116 West exit and continue toward Sebastopol. When you come to Lone Pine Antiques, turn left on Lone Pine Road. Continue about one-quarter of a mile; Pet-a-Llama Ranch will be on your left.*

CINNABAR THEATER

Petaluma is not an internationally known cultural center. However, it was once an internationally known chicken center, nicknamed Chick-a-luma, the poultry capital of the world. Then developers convinced the farmers that the dollar came before both the chicken and the egg and the population boomed.

For a long time, Petaluma's main claims to fame were its annual arm wrestling and ugly dog competitions. Recently a statue honoring the arm wrestlers and a town character named Bill Soberanes was erected near downtown at the corner of Washington Street and Petaluma Boulevard North. Soberanes, "Mr. P-Town," as he's affectionately called, has been a columnist for the local paper since 1952. His trademark is his collection of photographs of himself with famous people. He claims he's the world's number one people-meeter, and his collection includes shots of him with Jayne Mansfield, Jimmy Hoffa, and The Beatles. Bill came up with the idea for the arm-wrestling championship during one such photo session.

These days, Petaluma has a lot going for it. Though Main Street still has the look of Smalltown, Anywhere, USA, fancy and imaginative restaurants have opened, the local high-school kids dress as stylishly as their San Francisco counterparts, the historic buildings of the downtown area have had attractive face-lifts, and—the ultimate in modern civilization—you can get good espresso coffee in the cafes. And last but not least, you can attend live theater almost year-round at the Cinnabar Theater.

What makes the Cinnabar so charming is that at any moment you expect Judy Garland and Mickey Rooney to pop out of the woodwork and say they've got the barn and the talent, so why not put on a show! Here at the Cinnabar, the Mickey Rooney part is played by Marvin Klebe, a former singer with the San Francisco Opera. Years ago he decided to leave the bureaucracy of a big company and move to the country to start his own place.

Marvin and his family moved to Petaluma, buying the old Cinnabar School building, high on a hill a few blocks from the main part of town. With the help of his wife and four sons, Marvin converted the classrooms into an unusual combination of living quarters and 150-seat theater. With a small staff and many volunteers, Marvin now fulfills his artistic dreams, offering programs ranging from Wagnerian opera to an updated version of Menotti's "Consul" (in which the setting is changed from a Soviet bloc nation to Latin America). There are also frequent showcases for new talent and a wide variety of ambitious productions. Because of Marvin's eclectic programming, reasonably free of the economic restraints of most big-city theaters, the Cinnabar draws an audience from around the Bay Area. It's a good idea to check on ticket availability before making the trip.

CINNABAR THEATER, *3335 Petaluma Boulevard North, Petaluma, near the intersection of Skillman Lane. Phone: (707) 763-8920.*

HOW TO GET TO PETALUMA AND THE CINNABAR: *From San Francisco, take the Golden Gate Bridge to Route 101 North to the Penngrove exit, above Petaluma. At the exit, go left over the freeway and continue south on the Old Redwood Highway approximately 1½ miles. The theater is on a hill to your right.*

MILLIE'S CHILI
(31)

There is a trend around the country to re-create diners of the 1950s and suddenly people are rushing to stand in line for meat loaf sandwiches, mashed potatoes with gravy, and BLTs. Well, in Petaluma, just south of the main drag, is such a place that is not a re-creation; it is the real thing.

I first heard of Millie's Chili from the film crew working on Francis Coppola's film *Peggy Sue Got Married.* They used the place as a 1950 doughnut shop, changing the name and the food. Pity; you can't improve on the genuine article, and you could probably make the most entertaining movie ever made just by watching Millie and her twin sister Vickie in action.

Millie and Vickie live in back of the diner. They're in their late sixties, maybe early seventies now. They're up by 5:30 A.M., getting the chili on the stove, making salads, peeling onions. By opening time (11 A.M.), you'd better be ready to operate at their pace. Millie stands behind the little cooking area, flipping burgers and stirring her chili; Vickie's right there, order pad in hand, ready to take your order. All the time, they go at each other, bickering, teasing, laughing, and having the time of their lives. If they're really busy they'll tell you not to bother them; they have to concentrate!

It seems that no matter what you order, it's going to have chili on it. I'm not going to tell you this is the best chili in the world, but I promise you won't ever forget a visit with these memorable people. By the way, make sure you eat everything on your plate or else Vickie will give you the dickens.

MILLIE'S CHILI BAR, *Petaluma Boulevard South, at H Street, Petaluma. Better hurry. They may not stay open much longer. Their hours are now down to three days a week, Monday through Wednesday, from 11 A.M. to 3 P.M. No phone.*

HOW TO GET TO MILLIE'S: *From San Francisco, take the Golden Gate Bridge to*

Highway 101 North to the South Petaluma Boulevard exit in Petaluma. Millie's is a mile or so from the exit, on the left.

While trying to come up with an unusual angle for our first Thanksgiving show, the staff and I decided to look for a backroads alternative to the frozen supermarket turkey. That's how I happened upon Krout's, a delightful place to visit anytime from late summer to early winter.

Verna and Jack Krout run their farm, which is north of Petaluma, with the help of their friendly and talented dog, Max. The Krouts originally started raising pheasants more than 30 years ago as a hobby and as a way for their children to have the experience of watching an animal grow up. In 1960 the Krouts purchased the farm where they live now. The previous owner had 24 pheasants he didn't know what to do with. The Krouts said to include them in the price of the property and they'd take care of them; after all, if they had done it once, they could do it again. The sideline grew into a full-time business. Last year the Krouts hatched more than 200,000 pheasants, most of them sold to consumers right from the premises.

When I arrived at the Krouts', I was greeted enthusiastically by Max, of the wagging tail. Past the picture-book, white frame farmhouse to the back, I was suddenly confronted by thousands of birds in pens: pheasants, chukar partridges, guinea hens, wild turkeys, and, in special cages, some gorgeous birds with multicolored plumes from Southeast Asia and Latin America.

Even if you do not happen to be shooting a television show, you are invited to roam around, or you can get right down to business and choose a bird for dinner. You are also invited to try to catch it yourself, which is no mean trick. Verna will show you how to take a net and swoop down to capture your prey, then hold its feet to pull it out of the net. After that, the Krouts will take the bird inside to prepare it for the oven, a process you may not care to watch. The Krouts are well aware of the difference between the realities of farm life, such as the butchering of the food we eat, and the romantic fantasies that many city dwellers have. They told me that when they moved to this farm, it really was the country. Now they are surrounded by prime real estate purchased by neighbors who are often not prepared for country life. The message to all of us, I think, is that living in the country means the smell of manure, the night-long sound of sick animals, and the early morning sounds of farm equipment. The Krouts would like visitors to return home with an appreciation of real country living.

As for that Thanksgiving program, I ended with the rather obvious question, "What are you going to have for dinner?" Jack said he would like partridge, they ought to have pheasant, but they would probably have turkey.

KROUT'S PHEASANT FARM

KROUT'S PHEASANT FARM, *3234 Skillman Lane, Petaluma. Phone: (707) 762-8613. Open to 1 to 5 P.M. Tuesday through Saturday, September 15 through January 1; closed Sunday, Monday, and holidays. It's a good idea to call ahead.*

HOW TO GET TO KROUT'S: *From San Francisco, take the Golden Gate Bridge to Route 101 North. Exit at Washington Street, about 45 minutes from San Francisco. Turn right on Petaluma Boulevard and continue north to Skillman Lane, then turn left.*

PETALUMA ADOBE

In Northern California you can see just about every style of architecture imaginable. But at one time the dominant style was the adobe. Today only a few remain, and none is so striking or important as the Petaluma Adobe, now a state historic park.

Remember our friend General Vallejo of Sonoma Plaza and Lachryma Montis fame (see earlier entries). Well, this was the headquarters of his enormous ranch, some 66,000 acres of farmland with nearly 2000 inhabitants. The adobe was a community center of sorts, where workers and their children would gather and make clothing, tools, flour, and candles for use on the ranch and for export. The original quadrangular adobe was huge, with the foreman of the ranch occupying one wing, Vallejo's living quarters on the second floor, and, on the ground floor, kitchen and eating areas, a milling room, and yet another wing for tanning leather and making tallow.

Only about half of the original two-story structure remains now, but it is still an imposing hillside edifice with 3-foot-thick adobe walls and balconies that run the entire length of the second floor. This is the sort of historic spot that could be drab and lifeless, the tourist-stop equivalent of taking medicine. Fortunately, the Rangers on duty have devoted their energies and talent to making the historic park into a living place. It's a wonderful destination to bring children because there is lots to do and acres of hillside parkland for burning off all that energy they store up sitting in the back seat of the car. There are also loads of farm animals roaming freely; in fact, you may be greeted by a sheep or two in the parking lot.

The best time to visit is on weekends or holidays, when you will encounter ladies dressed in costumes of the 1850s working at spinning wheels or baking bread as they did in Vallejo's day. Many hands-on activities are set up, allowing you to try your hand at dipping candles, churning butter, or performing whatever other activities are featured that day. Though most of the action is outside in the courtyard, the inside of the adobe is interesting, too. You can get a good idea of what life must have been like in the community.

PETALUMA ADOBE STATE HISTORIC PARK, *3325 Adobe Road, Petaluma. Phone:*

(707) 762-4871. Open 10 A.M. to 5 P.M. daily, though weekends are when most of the action takes place. Admission: adults, $1; children, 50 cents.

HOW TO GET TO THE PETALUMA ADOBE: *From San Francisco, take the Golden Gate Bridge to Highway 101 North toward Petaluma. Exit at Route 116 East. At Frates Road, turn left and continue for a few minutes to Adobe Road. Turn left, and the adobe is on your right. Directions are well marked from Route 101.*

CHAPTER **3** Napa County

AREA OVERVIEW

Napa County is sandwiched between Sonoma County on the west and Solano County to the south and east. The closest destination from San Francisco is the city of Napa, about an hour's drive from the Golden Gate Bridge. It will take another 45 minutes in moderate traffic to get up to Calistoga, home of popular hot springs and health spas. The county includes a few lakes and valleys to the east and, to the west, a small mountain range that separates Napa from the Sonoma Valley. Most of the action, however, is concentrated along the center of the Napa Valley. Catherine has even devised a system for remembering the order of towns along the main road through Napa, Route 29. Just remember that the Napa Valley is YORS; between the city of Napa and Calistoga, you come to Yountville, Oakville, Rutherford, and St. Helena.

The Napa Valley is the place you're most likely to run into a crew from a show like *Lifestyles of the Rich and Famous*. They're interested in some of the more expensive resorts and restaurants in the area, as well as the wealthy winery owners who entertain lavishly. Don't be intimidated. There are plenty of places that cater to all tastes and price ranges.

Route 29 is winery row. You can't drive very far without bumping into yet another little old winemaker. Pace yourself; there are more places than you can visit in one day. The major tourist draws are the large and famous operations like Domaine Chandon, Robert Mondavi, Beringer, and Sterling. These places offer tours through beautiful and interesting facilities. At Sterling, for example, you take a tram ride up to their hillside headquarters. By all means visit all the wineries that appeal to you, but don't miss the smaller operations or some of the other attractions available. In this chapter we will concentrate on the latter, with a unique winery thrown in here and there.

Despite the size of its international fame, Napa is one of the smallest counties in the Bay Area. Because it's little and because the wineries are concentrated along one main road, Napa is also one of the easiest places to visit. Unfortunately, there are times it seems that everyone in Northern California is on the road (Route 29), but fear not; there are backroads that can take you away from the crowds.

A few general tips: As you travel north and south through the valley, you can avoid the crowds by taking the Silverado Trail, which runs parallel to Route 29. You can pick it up by heading east on any major crossroad, such as the Yountville or Rutherford crossroads. Then you can wander through the many backroads that are between Route 29 and the Silverado Trail. The best time of the year to visit is the fall, when the weather is ideal and the annual grape crush is on. This is when the wineries are bustling with energy and the grapevines themselves light up the roadside with brilliant reds and yellows. Finally, as we mentioned in the Sonoma County chapter, if you're tasting wine and planning to continue behind the wheel, don't swallow the samples. Each winery provides buckets or drains so you don't have to drink and drive.

THE NAPA VALLEY SHOW

The town of Yountville is named for George Yount, a former trapper who hung out with Kit Carson and became Napa Valley's first pioneer settler. He is also the father of the local wine industry, the first to plant grapevines in the area. Yountville exists now primarily for tourists. The biggest crowds will be at Vintage 1870, a huge shopping center fashioned out of an old winery building. Don't be discouraged by all the cars; there is an attraction here that is a great introduction to the valley.

The attraction is called the Napa Valley Show, a slide presentation of beautiful photographs accompanied by classical music. There is no narration; the images tell you all you need to know for preparing your own exploration of the valley. With the help of Vivaldi, this is photographic evidence that there are indeed four seasons in Northern California. The Napa Valley Show is the creation of Keith Rosenthal, a photographer who spends much of his time combing the valley for his shots. He is on hand to answer questions from the audience and is happy to provide photo tips for your own snapshots. He also has a gallery on the premises to sell his photographs.

Keith himself is an interesting story. Originally from Pennsylvania, he spent 10 years as a long-haired, unshaven nomad named "Boof" (which was an acronym for "brain out of focus"), working his way around the world doing odd jobs and taking pictures. This was during the 1960s and 1970s, when a lot of young people were trying to find themselves. He found himself in the Napa Valley, and now there is not a grandmother around who wouldn't agree Keith is a clean-cut, attractive young man. Keith's beautiful photography is enjoyed by hundreds of

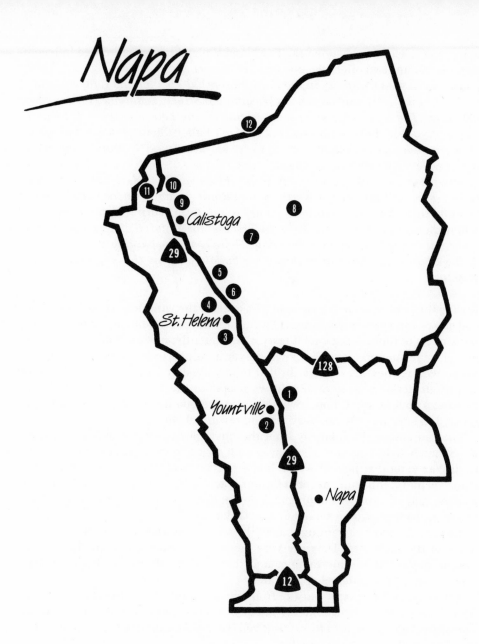

Napa

Calistoga
St. Helena
Yountville
Napa

appreciative viewers every week. The Napa Valley Show is presented in a comfortable theater and offers the opportunity for rest and reflection.

THE NAPA VALLEY SHOW, *in the Keith Rosenthal Theater and Gallery, located in the Vintage 1870 Building, 6525 Washington Street, Yountville. Phone: (707) 944-2525. The 15-minute slide show begins on the hour and the half hour, 10 A.M. to 5:30 P.M. daily. Admission to the Napa Valley Show: children 5 to 12, $1; children under 5 free; seniors, $2.50; everyone else, $3.00. No admission charge to the gallery. Wheelchair accessible.*

HOW TO GET TO THE NAPA VALLEY SHOW: *From San Francisco, take the Golden Gate Bridge to Highway 101 North. Exit at Route 37 and head for Vallejo, which is to the east. Route 37 eventually comes to Route 29. Turn left on Route 29 and follow the signs to Calistoga. Take the first exit for Yountville, turn left, and you will come to the Vintage 1870 Building. There is a huge parking area. The Napa Valley Show is on the eastern side of the building, facing the Napa Valley Railway Inn.*

VETERANS' HOME ②

During the peak seasons, the people who operate the wineries, restaurants, inns, and stores can get pretty swamped by curious and demanding tourists, and even the kindest of them can get a bit testy. Consequently, it is possible for the visitor to feel a bit unappreciated. This will never be the case at Yountville Veterans' Home, where they are always thrilled to have visitors. I realize this is not the sort of attraction that normally draws people to the Napa Valley, but it is as inviting a spot as you'll find anywhere, and the buildings are of historic importance. I'm sure you will be surprised and rewarded here.

Located across the highway from the busy tourist attraction Vintage 1870, the Spanish-style Veterans' Home was built over 100 years ago to accommodate Civil War veterans; later it would house survivors of the two world wars. The chapel is now a museum, devoted primarily to World War I memorabilia: bugles, posters, and newspaper clippings, all lovingly assembled and cared for by the residents, some of whom served in the "Great War."

Indeed, the most rewarding part of the visit is the reaction you will get from many of the residents. They are very happy to see someone actually take the time to detour from wine tasting, and they will regale you with stories from "Over There." You will feel appreciated.

YOUNTVILLE VETERANS' HOME, *Highway 29, Yountville. Phone: (707) 944-4000. The grounds are open to the public 8 A.M. to 4:30 P.M. seven days a week. The museum is open noon to 4 P.M. If you would like a guided tour, call 24 hours in advance. Wheelchair accessible.*

HOW TO GET TO THE VETERANS' HOME: *From San Francisco, follow the direc-*

tions to Yountville (preceding entry), but at the exit, go back under the highway and follow the signs to the Veterans' Home. It's well marked.

As you drive through Napa Valley, several homes will remind you of Jane Wyman's place on the TV show *Falcon Crest*. A prime example is the beautiful Beringer showplace on Route 29 in St. Helena. And the actual place used on *Falcon Crest* is tucked away on Spring Mountain Road outside the town of St. Helena. The house has a history even more interesting than anything the writers of *Falcon Crest* have dreamed up. This grand Victorian mansion was built in 1885 by a young wag named Tiburcio Parrot, the bastard son of a wealthy San Francisco businessman. Tiburcio was the black sheep of the family, which owned much of downtown San Francisco. To keep Sonny out of the way, Dad gave him 800 acres on Spring Mountain, and Sonny lived the life of an eccentric bachelor on his $5,000 a month allowance, a very tidy sum in the late 1800s (and not bad now). Tiburcio called his home Villa Miravalle. After Tiburcio died in 1894, the mansion was abandoned for years. Kids from town would break in to roller skate on the hardwood floors, occasionally stumbling on a possession of one of Tiburcio's many lady friends.

The place didn't have a permanent resident until 1974, when a wealthy San Francisco builder named Michael Robbins bought the crumbling mansion and renovated it. In addition to sprucing up the house, Robbins built a winery and began making premium chardonnay and cabernet sauvignon bearing the label Spring Mountain. Then location scouts from Hollywood came to the Napa Valley to find the perfect setting for a new TV series about a winery dynasty. You can probably predict the rest. Soon Spring Mountain Winery became better known as the "*Falcon Crest* House" than for its cabernet. So many winery visitors were sneaking up to the home where the Robbinses live that regular tours of the grounds were organized.

The house itself is not open to the public; the Robbinses prefer keeping their home to themselves (and, anyway, the TV show uses only the grounds; interiors are shot on a set in Tinseltown). The winery building, the first place you see, has a tasting room and many historical photos. It's also the business quarters for Spring Mountain, as well as where the wine is stored in barrels. You can taste the many varieties of Spring Mountain wine, including one called Falcon Crest. There are actually two ways to see the place. If you want simply to see the winery operation and taste some of the product, there is no charge. If, however, you want a guided tour of the 259-acre estate, complete with an outside look at the home used on *Falcon Crest,* including the swimming pool, gardens and the guide's stories about the making of the series, there is a $4 charge.

FALCON CREST **HOUSE**

If watching a TV crew at work is your interest, the series shoots occasionally at the location in summer; the rest of the year the series is shot in studios in Los Angeles. You might get lucky and bump into Lorenzo Lamas or Jane Wyman, but don't plan your trip around it.

SPRING MOUNTAIN WINERY, *2805 Spring Mountain Road, St. Helena. Phone: (707) 963-5233. The tasting room is open 10 A.M. to 4:45 P.M. daily; grounds tours are held between 11 A.M. and 4 P.M. daily. The tours are popular, so be sure to make an appointment in advance.*

HOW TO GET TO SPRING MOUNTAIN WINERY: *From San Francisco, take the Golden Gate Bridge to Route 101 North of the Vallejo—Route 37 exit. Take Route 37 until it connects with Route 29. Route 29 then goes all the way through the Napa Valley and is the main thoroughfare of St. Helena. When you reach St. Helena, turn left on Madrona Avenue. Go three blocks and look for Spring Mountain Road. Turn right and you'll come to the Spring Mountain entrance on the left.*

SILVERADO MUSEUM

If Sonoma Valley is the province of Jack London, Napa is Robert Louis Stevenson country, and the Silverado Museum is dedicated to the works of the Scottish author. As you enter this small and comfortable building, you will probably be greeted by the curator, Ellen Shafer. The first thing she'll do is put you at ease by explaining that the price of admission is your signature on the guest register. After that, you can browse on your own or engage Ms. Shafer in conversation. I recommend the latter since she is a storehouse of stories and information.

According to Ellen, although Stevenson lived for less than two months in Napa Valley, he made an enormous contribution to the history of the area through his writing. In 1884 Stevenson published a book called *The Silverado Squatters,* an account of his honeymoon in an abandoned bunkhouse near the Silverado Mines of Mount St. Helena. Unlike the well-paid Jack London, Stevenson was broke; he and his bride could not afford to stay at one of the warm spring spas in Calistoga. Instead they carved out an idyllic, albeit humble, little vacation spot on the slopes of Mount St. Helena. *The Silverado Squatters* turned out to be one of the best histories of life in early Napa, and it includes Stevenson's observations about the fledgling wine industry and his visit to the nearby Petrified Forest (see item 11). After Napa, the Stevensons headed for the South Pacific, where Robert Louis continued to write until his death in 1894.

Today the author is remembered in Napa County with Robert Louis Stevenson State Park and the Silverado Museum in St. Helena. The museum was started by an advertising titan, Norman Strouse, who was chairman of the board of the world's largest agency, J. Walter Thompson. Strouse read *The Silverado Squatters,* loved it, and began collecting Stevenson's writings. When he retired,

Strouse moved to St. Helena to create a Stevenson museum and a foundation to support it. He also recruited Ellen Shafer from Philadelphia to manage the place. On display are personal belongings of the author, including original manuscripts and toy soldiers from his childhood (the same toy soldiers that were immortalized in *A Child's Garden of Verses*). It's a good bet you'll come across a book or two that played an important part in your childhood. Remember *Treasure Island*? *Dr. Jekyll and Mr. Hyde*?

THE SILVERADO MUSEUM, *1490 Library Drive, St. Helena. Phone: (707) 963-3757. Open noon to 4 P.M. Tuesday through Sunday; closed Monday and holidays. Admission: free.*

HOW TO GET TO THE SILVERADO MUSEUM: *From San Francisco, follow the directions to St. Helena. Turn right when you get to Pope Street, then left on Railroad and right again on Library Lane. The Silverado Museum is next to the town library.*

BY THE OLD MILL STREAM ⑤

Route 29, the main road through the Napa Valley, can get pretty hectic during the peak tourist times with wine tasters bouncing from winery to winery. Fortunately, two adjoining parks between the towns of St. Helena and Calistoga offer a chance to get away from the action, with activities for the whole family.

Bothe-Napa Valley State Park offers picnicking, hiking, camping, and even a good-sized swimming pool, which can be very welcome during the summer when the valley temperature hovers in the 90s. The 50 campsites are often in great demand, so it's a good idea to reserve as far in advance as possible.

There's a trail in the park that leads next door to the Bale Grist Mill State Historic Park. Here you get an idea of what this valley was like before the first grapevine was ever planted. Back in General Vallejo's time, this area was the breadbasket of Northern California and wheat was the valley's biggest cash crop. Wheat and corn fields flourished, and an English doctor named Edwin Bale (who also happened to be Vallejo's brother-in-law) built a huge mill for grinding flour. The Bale gristmill became a community center; while farmers ground their flour, they'd exchange gossip and get to know one another. The mill was used until 1905. Over the years time and neglect took their toll and the old mill fell into abandoned disrepair. Then in 1974 the mill was taken under the wing of the State Parks Department and an ambitious restoration project began.

Today the 150-year-old water wheel turns again. It is an impressive sight, as large as a ferris wheel, turned by water spilling over the top from a trestle-supported flume. Inside the mill, the motion of the wheel turns two millstones, each weighing about a ton. These are set atop two stationary stones; the action of the moving stones against the fixed grinds wheat and corn into flour—not quite as exciting as a video game but just as fascinating. For now, the wheel runs on weekends only, and you can purchase a little souvenir sack of freshly ground flour for a dollar. Adjacent to the mill is the granary, where in the olden days the huge sacks of grain waiting to be ground were stored. It is now a bookshop and museum with historic photographs and artifacts from turn-of-the-century Napa life.

Today folks still gather down by the old mill stream, although the gossip tends to be about which winery offers the best tastings and restaurants where you can get a good meal for less than 20 bucks. The grounds are quite lovely. While restoring the mill, the Parks Department added a easy-to-walk pathway complete with wheelchair ramp. You will feel like you are miles away from the busy highway when in fact you are just minutes away from bustling Route 29.

BOTHE-NAPA VALLEY STATE PARK, *3601 St. Helena Highway North, St. Helena. For camping reservations and more information, call (707) 942-4575. Open 8 A.M. to sundown daily. Admission to the park: Free.*

BALE GRIST MILL STATE HISTORIC PARK, *adjacent to Bothe-Napa State Park. Phone: (707) 942-4575. Open 10 A.M. to 5 P.M. daily; water wheel in operation on weekends only. Admission: $1 adults, 50 cents for children. Wheelchair accessible.*

HOW TO GET TO THE MILL: *From San Francisco, take the Golden Gate Bridge to Route 101 North. Exit at Route 37 for Vallejo and Napa. At the intersection of Route 29, turn left, and stay on Route 29 until a few miles north of St. Helena. Look for the entrance on your left. There are separate entrances to the parks, but they are connected by trails.*

HURD'S CANDLE FACTORY ⑥

When you're driving up Route 29 in the Napa Valley, there is never any doubt you're in wine country. From Yountville to Calistoga there are countless wineries along the road, from the big and famous like Mondavi and Beringer to boutique wineries like Frog's Leap and Grgich Hills Cellars.

OK, now what goes with wine? Cheese? Yep, you'll find several cheese shops along the way, and some wineries even sell cheese to accompany any spirits you might purchase. How about candlelight? For that there is a very inviting shop and "factory" located in the Freemark Abbey winery complex between St. Helena and Calistoga.

The Hurds started making candles in their garage in the East Bay town of Concord. When the business got big enough, the family moved the operation to the Napa Valley. There they hired a team of local candlemakers and spend their own time in partial retirement.

As you enter Hurd's Candles, it looks like your typical tourist gift shop, except almost all the items are beeswax candles of varying sizes, shapes, and colors. Continuing into the next room there are still more candles, plus a friendly group of women at work making candles. This is the "factory," which looks more like my image of Santa's workshop. At one station, a worker will take a sheet of parchment beeswax, which resembles a lasagne noodle, soften it in an electric fry pan, then hand-roll it into the desired thickness. At another station, six or seven women will be adding decorations to the candles, using such implements as hair curlers and eyedroppers. At yet another table, another group is adding leaves to the candles, making a candle tree. It's a very homey operation.

You are welcome to come and watch. I chatted for quite a while with the staff, and they genuinely get a kick out of their work, each other, and showing others how they make their wares. It makes for a nice visit. They have more candles than you can shake a wick at. (And, if you need another stupid pun, you can always use "It's none of your beeswax.")

HURD'S CANDLES, *in the Freemark Abbey complex, 3020 St. Helena Highway North, St. Helena. Phone: (707) 963-7211. Open 10 A.M. to 5 P.M. daily; closed on major holidays.*

HOW TO GET TO HURD'S CANDLES: *From San Francisco, follow the directions to St. Helena or Calistoga. The Freemark Abbey complex is clearly marked on the east side of Route 29, north of St. Helena.*

**ELMSHAVEN
AND ANGWIN**

Up in the hills to the east of the Napa Valley, you are a world away from the tourist-oriented towns below. If you take Deer Park Road to Angwin, you will come to one of the few towns in the nation populated almost exclusively by Seventh-day Adventists. It is a quiet town, where much of the activity centers around Pacific Union College, a religious school whose students are quite different from those you might find at, say, U.C. Berkeley. For example, tune your car radio to the campus station, KCDS ("Christ Died for our Sins"), and you will hear "The Inspirational Top 40." It's the only FM station that will come in loud and clear in Angwin.

The supermarket in the center of town is worth browsing, if only to notice the absence of items like meat, alcoholic beverages, cigarettes, and other items forbidden by the faith.

Another point of interest is Elmshaven, the Victorian estate of Ellen G. White, one of the founders of the Seventh-day Adventist religion. She is said to have had 2000 visions and nine prophetic dreams, upon which the teachings of the church are built. Ellen White lived in this house, ironically situated in one of the best wine-growing regions of the world, from 1900 to 1915. Today it is a must stop for Adventist pilgrims on their way to Angwin, but the Victorian home and bucolic estate are also of interest to many people regardless of faith.

Whatever your religious inclinations, there is a peaceful, refreshing quality to Elmshaven and Angwin, sort of like stepping onto the set of a Frank Capra movie, a small town where everybody knows everybody, tips their hats, and tries to do good. Just don't look for a pub to hang out in.

ELMSHAVEN, *125 Glass Mountain Lane, St. Helena. Phone: (707) 963-9039. Open 10 A.M. to 5 P.M. Sunday through Thursday; 10 A.M. to 1 P.M. Friday; 2 to 6 P.M. Saturday. Admission: Free, though donations are requested.*

HOW TO GET TO ELMSHAVEN: *Take Highway 29 through St. Helena. One mile past town, turn right on Deer Park Road; there will be a sign pointing to Angwin. Pass the flashing red light, then bear left at the Y in the road (the sign will point to the hospital). Turn left on Glass Mountain Road. Elmshaven will be on the right at the white bridge.*

HOW TO GET TO ANGWIN: *Take Highway 29 through St. Helena, but instead of bearing left on Glass Mountain Road, keep to the right and go up the hill, following the signs to Angwin.*

HUBCAP RANCH ⑧

Outside of Angwin and over the hill, you will enter the rural and picturesque Pope Valley. In such a serene setting, it is a jolt to be greeted by the sight of one of the greatest folk art collections in the world.

At first it looks like a giant glare in the distance. As you get closer, you realize you are seeing hubcaps, thousands and thousands of hubcaps displayed in an endless variety of patterns. This is Litto's Hubcap Ranch. Name the car or a year, and the hubcap is there somewhere.

The collection belonged to Litto Diamonte, an Italian immigrant who settled in this valley to farm. When he started collecting hubcaps and arranging them in an artful manner, his family was at first amused, then amazed, then embarrassed, and finally accepting. The patriarch passed on in 1983 at age 93, but the Diamonte family has come to appreciate the folk art treasure they have on their hands and is doing everything possible to preserve it.

Although the family is not in the tourist attraction business, they maintain the property, keep those hubcaps shining, and welcome the curious who want to stop and have a look. You can either stare from the road or get out of your car and wander around to have a closer look at the hubcaps, plus Litto's collection of birdhouses, which are placed around the property. This collection simply sits in the yard and driveway of the family house. Though visitors are welcome, this is not an amusement park. There are no official greeters. No admission is charged, and last time I checked there were no souvenirs. It's simply there for all to see and to marvel at one man's dedication and ingenuity. Litto's has been established as a registered California landmark.

LITTO'S HUBCAP RANCH, *Howell Mountain Road, Pope Valley.*

HOW TO GET TO THE HUBCAP RANCH: *From San Francisco, the direct route is to follow the directions to St. Helena. On Route 29, north of St. Helena, turn right* on Deer Park Road and follow the signs up the hill to Howell Mountain Road. Take Howell Mountain Road until it intersects with Pope Valley Road and turn right. You can't miss Litto's. This is about a 30-minute drive from St. Helena. A more scenic route is to exit Route 29 earlier at Rutherford, turning right onto Route 128. Take Route 128 to Chiles-Pope Valley Road, turn left, and follow it all the way until you are blinded by the hubcaps. Litto's is 45 minutes to an hour from the Rutherford turnoff.

Calistoga is one town in Napa Valley famous for something other than wine. Its claims to fame are an abundance of mud baths and health spas, and it is the home of Calistoga mineral water. Tourists come in droves to visit the various spots offering rest, relaxation, and various "cures." They also come to see a very attractive little town with many lovely bed-and-breakfast places on the outskirts, a historic hotel downtown, and lots of good places to eat.

SHARPSTEEN MUSEUM

Calistoga has a special place in the history of the development of Napa County, which brings us to the Sharpsteen Museum. From the outside it looks like a small house, hiding the fact that this is a very large and well-designed museum worthy of your attention. As you enter, you might think you've walked into the wrong place. A room full of drawings of Mickey Mouse and Donald Duck? That's right, because this is the room honoring Ben Sharpsteen, founder of this museum, who was also one of the original Walt Disney animators. For many years Sharpsteen vacationed in the area, and he later retired to Calistoga. He wanted to help preserve the rich history of the area, so he personally paid for the museum project. One thing he had learned from Disney is that audiences want to be entertained, so he set up the museum accordingly.

One of the highlights of the visit is the glass-enclosed diorama showing in great detail the master plan of the original town. Calistoga was intended to be a grand spa, similar to New York's Saratoga. The man behind the plan was a fascinating figure named Sam Brannan, reputed to be California's first million-aire. He also performed the first American marriage ceremony in California, published the state's first American newspaper, and was the man credited with starting the Gold Rush. As the legend goes, he ran up Montgomery Streets in San Francisco with a vial of gold in his hand, shouting that gold had been discovered in the foothills of the Sierras (of course, he did this only after corner-ing the market on supplies to miners, hence Sam Brannan's millions).

To kick off his grand resort scheme, Brannan threw a large party. He may have had too much to drink, for during the ground-breaking ceremony for Sara-toga, California, he proclaimed the founding of "Calistoga, Sarafornia." The name stuck. Brannan's resort never really captured the loyalties of the very rich, but it did lead to the development of the town and the valley. Part of the museum is one of the cottages from the original spa. It is lavishly decorated with the original piano, Oriental rugs, and decorative Victorian furniture. In 1882 the cottage rented for $10 a week. This was too expensive for a newlywed writer named Robert Louis Stevenson, who had to go further up to Mount St. Helena for his honeymoon (see item 4, Silverado Museum).

You can be your own tour guide at the Sharpsteen Museum, although there are docents on hand to answer questions. Plan to spend at least an hour here enjoying the diorama, Wild West displays, stagecoaches, firearms, costumes, and artifacts of Messrs. Sharpsteen and Brannan.

SHARPSTEEN MUSEUM AND SAM BRANNAN COTTAGE, *1311 Washington Street, Calistoga. Phone: (707) 942-5911. Open 10 A.M. to 4 P.M. April through October, noon to 4 P.M. the rest of the year. Donations requested. Wheelchair accessible.*

HOW TO GET TO THE SHARPSTEEN MUSEUM: *From San Francisco, take the Golden Gate Bridge to Highway 101 North. Exit to the right (east) at Route 37, heading for Vallejo. Turn left on Route 29 and follow it all the way into the town of Calistoga. You will be on the main street, which is Lincoln. When you get to Washington Street, turn left and you will come to the museum.*

OLD FAITHFUL GEYSER (10)

Remember back in school learning about Old Faithful, the geyser in Yellowstone National Park? Well, for some reason the textbooks and teachers didn't seem to know about the Old Faithful geyser outside of Calistoga, California. This Old Faithful is, well, different from the famous one. For one thing, it's smaller and less crowded.

After following the several road signs pointing to the geyser, you see what looks like a national park entrance arch. But behind it is a little ticket booth, not far from a modest frame home. You buy your ticket and park the car. You walk around a fence and some trees until you come to a few picnic benches overlooking a pond that is sort of bubbling, then a voice on the loudspeaker announces when the next eruption is expected (usually it's every 40 minutes). While you're waiting, you can read the yellowed magazine articles that are posted on a wooden fence leading to the rest rooms. In December 1948 *National Geographic* published an article about this place. *Life* magazine did a spread in the 1950s; various newspaper headlines proclaim that this phenomenon you are awaiting is indeed "stranger than fiction."

Then you turn your attention to the bubbling pond. By George, it starts spouting, just like they promised. A huge stream of water shoots 60 feet or so for a few minutes. Then the eruption dies down, and the pond gurgles until the next eruption. That's about all there is to it, but there is a very compelling charm about the place, as if stepping back to a more innocent time. Part of that is due to the

operator, Olga Kolbek. She lives in the house near the ticket booth; having retired to this 26-acre property in the early 1970s. Olga loves it, and her enthusiasm is infectious. She even heats her hot tub with steam from the mysterious
underground waters. Olga keeps running records on eruptions and will gladly
tell you everything they know about geysers. She told me she loves to watch
people's reaction to the geyser. Her favorite is when a little girl said to her mother
at nightfall, "Look, mommy, it's washing the stars."

OLD FAITHFUL GEYSER, *1299 Tubbs Lane, Calistoga. Phone: (707) 942-6463.
Open 365 days a year, 9 A.M. to 6 P.M. during daylight savings time, to 5 P.M.
during the winter months. Admission: $3.00 for adults, $2.00 for children 6 to
12; under 6 free.*

HOW TO GET TO OLD FAITHFUL GEYSER: *From San Francisco, take the Golden
Gate Bridge to Route 101 North. Follow Route 101 to Route 37 and turn right
toward Vallejo. When you come to Route 29, turn left and go all the way through
the Napa Valley to Calistoga. Go through town, and after leaving the main part
of Calistoga, look for Tubbs Lane on the left. Turn left and you will soon come to
the entrance for the geyser.*

PETRIFIED FOREST

If you are overwhelmed by the excitement of Old Faithful, you can calm yourself
at another natural wonder of the world just down the road. The Petrified Forest
is also another example of private enterprise at its best, a roadside attraction
that is such a throwback to 1930s Americana that it doesn't even matter that not
much happens here.

As you might expect from the name, the Petrified Forest is a collection of tree
logs that have fossilized over the eons. Frankly, one tree that has turned into a
rock doesn't look all that much different from the next tree that has also turned
into a rock, but there's still something appealing about wandering through the
well-marked paths that meander through the forest.

This has been a tourist attraction much longer than the wineries peddling
their chardonnays (Robert Louis Stevenson wrote about it in 1883), and it is
apparently an item in tourist guidebooks for Europeans because you will see
people from all over the world strolling around, knocking on petrified wood. The
place was discovered by a Swedish seaman who retired and was looking for a
field for his cow, so the legend goes. Six million years before that, Mount St.
Helena had erupted, belching ash that engulfed the forest, which in turn seeped
all the water from the trees and turned them into stone.

Some major changes for the better have taken place since my first visit. The
management has cleaned the petrified trees by blasting them with a high pres-
sure hose, ridding them of dirt and moss. Now you can see colors and crystals

that add a touch of beauty to the logs. New walking trails have opened, and the small gift shop has been expanded to include several interesting displays of the geologic phenomenon.

By the way, if your image of a petrified forest is the classic Humphrey Bogart film, forget it. That was another part of the forest.

PETRIFIED FOREST, *4100 Petrified Forest Road, Calistoga. Phone: (707) 942-6667. Open 10 A.M. to 5 P.M. daily; closed Christmas and Thanksgiving. Admission: Adults, $3; children 4 to 11, $1; under 4 free. Wheelchair accessible.*

HOW TO GET TO THE PETRIFIED FOREST: *From San Francisco, follow the directions to the town of Calistoga. In town, Route 29 and Route 128 separate. Take Route 128 to the left until you come to Petrified Forest Road. Turn left and you will come to the forest, approximately 6 miles outside Calistoga.*

LILLIE LANGTRY SLEPT HERE ⑫

Driving north of the Pope Valley, you will cross over into Lake County, with Clear Lake as a major attraction. This is the largest lake entirely in California. Tahoe is larger, but part of it is in Nevada. Lake County also boasts a growing new wine industry, with one winery offering an unequaled bit of history. It's the house where Lillie Langtry lived, her hideaway when she needed a quiet place to be by herself. In case you don't know about Lillie, she was a turn-of-the-century entertainer as big in her day as say, Barbra Streisand is today. Nicknamed the "Jersey Lily" (after her home island off the English Coast), she was said to be the most beautiful woman in the world. Oscar Wilde said he would have rather discovered Lillie than America; the legendary Judge Roy Bean named a town in Texas for her, even though they never met. She was mistress to King Edward VII.

Lillie spent her weekends in this house from 1888 to 1908; she even started a winery here. A few years ago the property was purchased by a family that made a fortune farming in California and Hawaii. Son Orville Magoon lives in Lillie's house and runs things. He has lovingly restored the home to give it the look and feel of the Langtry era. Orville can tell you more about Lillie and her times than Lillie herself probably would have remembered. He has also put her picture on the label that graces the wine made here. The winery is called Guenoc, named for the valley in which it rests, and it produces a very fine chardonnay and other varietals.

The house is used for special occasions, which includes an annual open house each spring. Even if you can't be there for the big party, it's worth a trip to visit Guenoc. The setting is quite beautiful, with a shaded picnic area outside the tasting rooms, overlooking a pond and the hillside. You will want to linger and get the feeling of being out in the middle of nowhere, much as Lillie was when she sought her refuge from hordes of fans and suitors. Someday the Lake County region may be as popular as Napa and Sonoma counties, so you might as well see the area while it is still comparatively pristine. For now, there are no traffic jams, no souvenir shops or boutiques, and no restaurants, just quiet and wonderful scenery.

GUENOC WINERY, *21000 Butts Canyon Road, Middletown. Phone: (707) 987-2385. The winery is open 10 A.M. to 4:30 P.M. Thursday through Sunday; closed major holidays. Open house is held just once a year, usually in May. Call to find out when it is; admission is free.*

HOW TO GET TO THE GUENOC WINERY: *From San Francisco, take the Golden Gate Bridge to Highway 101 North. Exit onto Route 37 toward Vallejo and Napa. At Route 29, turn left and continue through the Napa Valley, past Calistoga to Middletown. Just past town, turn right at the Guenoc Valley sign onto Butts Canyon Road. Go 6 miles to the winery. The trip from Calistoga can take close to an hour if there is any traffic.*

From Pope Valley, continue on Pope Valley Road all the way to the Guenoc Winery.

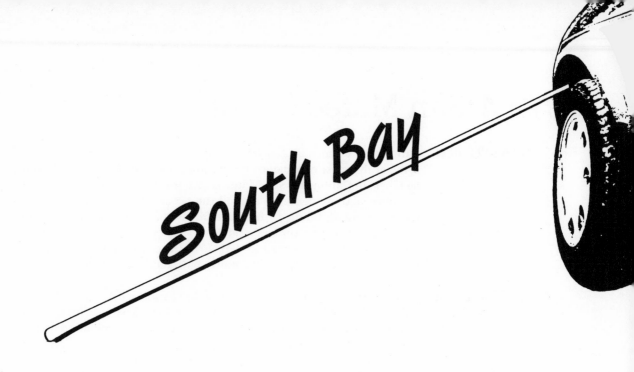

The largest population growth of the Bay Area in recent years has been to the south. This was once a valley of orchards and farms that was changed almost overnight as the computer chip became the area's most important product. Whole towns were practically created out of intersections, and a new wave of immigrants came in, speaking a new language of "techno-speak." Some predict that we will eventually see one continuing city between San Francisco and San Jose.

And yet, despite all this growth, there are several surprises that await a back-roads explorer in San Mateo, Santa Clara, and Santa Cruz Counties. Even though people who live in this area seem to head north for their leisure, there is much to see and do in the South Bay.

Routes 101, 280, and 680 are the north–south main routes to San Jose. From there, Routes 17 and 1 are the main roads to Santa Cruz. Figure on less than an hour to reach most destinations between San Francisco and San Jose; an hour and a half to reach Santa Cruz.

CHAPTER **4** San Mateo County

AREA OVERVIEW

San Mateo County begins where the city of San Francisco ends and includes some of the most expensive communities, as well as some of the most secluded beaches, in California. San Mateo is also the flower capital of the Bay Area, with the most activity centered around the ocean at Half-Moon Bay. Further down the coast, along Route 1, there are farms that grow such California cuisine as artichokes, Brussels sprouts, and kiwis. Along Route 101 are the county's heavy population centers as well as San Francisco International Airport. Route 280 takes you to the woodsier hill country with its tony suburbs.

ACRES OF ORCHIDS

①

Just a few minutes outside the city of San Francisco is a place I can wholeheartedly recommend for anyone who loves flowers. The industrial section of South San Francisco is a rather unlikely location to find such an abundance of flora. But that's where you'll find Rod McLellan's Acres of Orchids, and once you drive into the parking lot you are in another world entirely.

The name Acres of Orchids is no exaggeration. McLellan is the largest supplier of orchids in the world. Many varieties are grown here, in an area that includes over a million square feet of greenhouses. There are other flowers on display, too, including a fragrant gardenia section (in fact, Rod's father, who started the family floral business in the late 1890s, takes credit for developing the gardenia corsage) and roses in a greenhouse three times the size of a football field. The big attraction, though, is the orchids, and a public tour is offered that will teach you not only about the incredible variety of the exotic flora but also how they are cloned to produce perfect new plants. I was particularly intrigued by this cloning process, whereby a tiny seed is placed in a solution in a bottle. As the seed sprouts, the bottles are rotated to give each plant uniform growing conditions. Eventually the plant is moved to a larger bottle, then to a pot and soil. All this is done in a laboratory-like situation, easy to see as the guide takes you through the operation.

While you're here, the McLellans would not be displeased if you stopped in their salesroom where you can buy plants to take home or just browse in what feels like a lush tropical garden. This is a high-volume orchid factory, and it's a fascinating place.

ACRES OF ORCHIDS, *1450 El Camino Real, South San Francisco. Phone: (415) 871-5655. Gift shop open 8 A.M. to 5 P.M. every day, except major holidays. Tours*

San Mateo

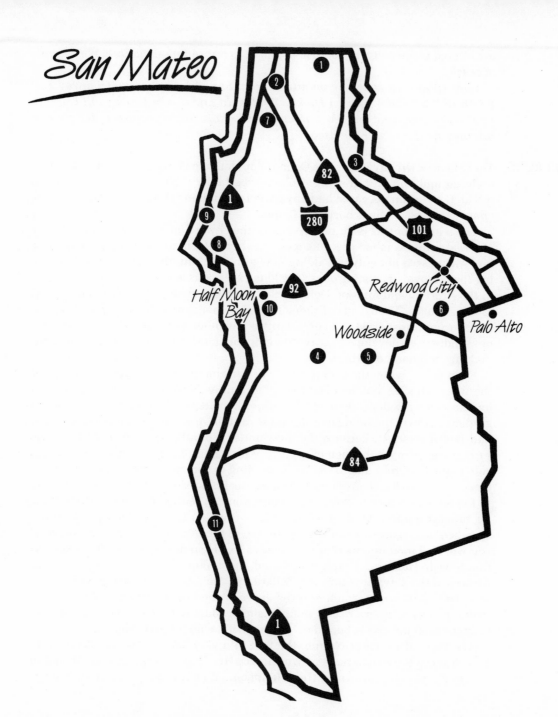

are offered twice daily, at 10:30 *A.M. and 1:30 P.M. Admission: Free. Wheelchair accessible.*

HOW TO GET TO ACRES OF ORCHIDS: *From San Francisco, take Highway 101 South to Route 280. Exit on Hickey Boulevard and proceed east to El Camino Real. Turn right and one block later, start looking for the entrance. It's just 15 minutes south of San Francisco.*

COLMA, DEAD OR ALIVE

There is no town anywhere like Colma. Population 731 above ground, 1,500,000 underground and still growing. Colma is certainly the cemetery capital of the world. If a certain deceased had any part of the making of San Francisco history, chances are he or she is buried in Colma.

The reason for this is that in the 1920s, the city of San Francisco declared that city real estate was too precious a commodity to be used as burial ground. So a law was passed not only forbidding new graves within the city limits but ordering the removal of existing ones. The lone exceptions were the military cemetery in the Presidio and Mission Dolores. So began the great exodus of the deceased to the suburbs. Thousands of memorial monuments and the accompanying remains were transported to a community a few miles south of the city limits, and new industries developed: grave digging, memorial garden care, monument making, and floral offerings.

Even today, when the backhoe has cut back on the need for gravediggers and the weed whacker has reduced the opportunities for lawn workers, Colma still has an economy dependent on the life of cemeteries. There are 14 memorial gardens in town, including ones for those of Italian, Japanese, Chinese, Serbian, and Jewish descent. Perhaps the most unusual of all is Pet's Rest, where some 11,000 graves mark the memory of dogs with names like Ferocious and Pepi and cats named Sabrina and Marcello. According to cemetery insiders, the pet cemetery gets more floral offerings daily than the final resting places of people.

For a crash course in Bay Area history, you can search the various cemeteries for famous names. At plush Cypress Lawn, which features duck ponds and a spectacular display of stained glass in one of the huge cremation mausoleums, you will find monuments that bear names like Hearst, Crocker, and Matson. At the Jewish Home of Peace, you'll find the group nicknamed the Merchant Princes of the City: Levi Strauss, Zellerbach, Magnin. At another Jewish cemetery, Hills of Eternity, you'll find the grave of the famous lawman Wyatt Earp, which comes as a surprise to many visitors. Marshall Earp lived out his later years in Oakland and is buried next to his wife, who was Jewish.

The revered Emperor Norton, the first in a very long line of famous only-in-San Francisco characters, is at Woodlawn. His final resting place is the site of an annual shindig thrown by the self-appointed guardians of Bay Area history,

E. Clampus Vitus; this organization of hard-drinking, party-loving men spends its nonparty time placing very authentic-looking metal plaques as historical markers all around the Bay Area. The Emperor, who proclaimed himself king after he lost all his money and part of his mind in the Gold Rush, is the patron saint of the "Clampers."

You can visit the various cemeteries just about any time during daylight hours simply by driving through the gates. Each cemetery has a large parking lot, and you can drive through the grounds of some of them. If you're feeling adventurous and want to hear some old-time stories about the town, drop in at Molloy's Bar, a century-old Irish bar where the locals always seem to be having a wake. It's at 1655 Mission Road; phone: (415) 755-9545.

TO GET TO COLMA: *From San Francisco, take Highway 101 South to Route 280. Exit at the Junipero Serra Boulevard exit and head east, which is to the left away from the Serramonte Shopping Center, then down the hill to El Camino Real. This is Colma, and the cemeteries are on both sides of the road. From Acres of Orchids, continue south on El Camino Real to the town of Colma.*

COYOTE POINT MUSEUM

Practically in the shadow of San Francisco International Airport, on the Bay side of what is known as the Peninsula, is a large and appealing park at Coyote Point. The 670-acre recreational area offers biking and walking paths, a picnic area, golf, and a marina, all under the shade of fragrant eucalyptus trees.

The highlight of the park is the Museum for Environmental Education, which is one of the best museums of its type that I've seen anywhere. The San Mateo County Park System has done a wonderful job in designing a facility that is entertaining and informative, one that effectively illustrates an important fact: that the earth is very fragile and we need to take care of it. The exhibits are presented in such a way that if this place had been around when I was in school, I think I would have been a more willing participant in field trips.

It is an ambitious presentation, with exhibits on four descending levels, representing the areas of the Peninsula from the mountains to the ocean to the Bay. There is a light and airy quality to the place; you feel like you are outdoors much of the time. Almost everything that lives in the Bay and on the Peninsula is shown here in a way that reveals its connection to our daily life.

The museum is set up for a self-guided stroll through descriptive exhibits. The one that fascinated me most shows the relationship of predators to the ecological balance by displaying what a hawk eats in one year. On a facsimile of a tall tree you see representations of more than 1000 mice plus birds, squirrels, gophers, snakes, weasels, and the rest of the hungry hawk's diet. It's a graphic demonstration that one man's killer is another man's pest control, or vice versa. I'm sure you'll find your own favorites and draw your own conclusions on your quick and entertaining lesson about the environmental balance of the Bay at the Coyote Point Museum.

COYOTE POINT MUSEUM FOR ENVIRONMENTAL EDUCATION, *Coyote Point County Park. Phone: (415) 342-7755. Open 10 A.M. to 5 P.M. Wednesday through Friday, 1 to 5 P.M. Saturday and Sunday. Admission: Park entrance fee, $3.00 per car; museum admission: adults, $2.00; children, $1.00 . Free admission on Fridays. Wheelchair accessible.*

HOW TO GET TO COYOTE POINT: *From San Francisco, take Route 101 South to the Poplar Avenue exit. Follow signs to Coyote Point Drive and the park entrance. When you pay the entrance fee, the person at the gate can direct you to the museum.*

DYNASTY HOUSE

The suburban communities of Atherton, Hillsborough, and Woodside are among the wealthiest in the nation. Here you will find estates owned by families like the Hearsts, the Davies of San Francisco Symphony Hall fame, heirs to Levi Strauss, and other names synonymous with the Bay Area society. You will also find Blake Carrington's mansion. Though the exterior of the house is shown every week on television, the *Dynasty* folks don't really hang out here, except to shoot an occasional scene outside. No matter, the history of the house known as Filoli is better than anything TV writers can come up with.

The name is a combination of the words Fight, Love, and Life. This was the motto of one William Bourne, a gold-mining millionaire and the original water baron of the Peninsula. He's the one who saw that the expanding San Francisco suburbs would need lots of water, so he figured out a way to bring it down from the melting snows of the Sierra. That's still the way the Bay Area gets its water, often in competition with Southern California for the rights.

In 1916 Bourne commissioned the noted architect Willis Polk to build him the 43-room Georgian mansion on the 654-acre estate that would become known as Filoli. Though he paid $109,000 for it—a very tidy sum in those days—there's no point in trying to guess what it would cost now. This kind of place simply isn't built anymore, not even for the Carringtons. It is spectacular.

Among the many features are 20-foot ceilings, priceless Oriental rugs, rare antiques, and a bank vault for storing family china and silver. Each room has a distinct character, from the massive book-lined library to the elegant "French Room," all powder blue with white trim and very delicate. The centerpiece of the house is the grand ballroom, complete with a stage, crystal chandeliers, and impressive murals. However, the main attraction for many visitors is the garden. This 16-acre botanical paradise is designed as a series of separate areas; like the house, each area has its own distinct character. Most enchanting is the Walled Garden, enclosed by handsome brick and combining many elements of formal landscape design. Another highlight is the rose garden, featuring at least 250 varieties, including the Bing Crosby, named after the guy who used to live down the road.

Filoli is a huge operation, run by the National Trust for Historic Preservation. Tours include a walk through the house and gardens. Afterwards you may spend as much time as you'd like having afternoon tea or browsing in the garden and a gift shop featuring plants, gardening books, cookbooks, and potpourri made from the plants grown on the grounds. However, you must have reservations, even if you plan only to visit the gift shop. Saturdays during the summer are particularly busy times, so be sure to call two weeks to a month in advance of your visit.

A tip: It is easiest to get a reservation at the beginning of the season, mid-February through March. The gardens will not be as showy as in the summer and early fall, but there ought to be plenty of magnolias, camellias, and daffodils in bloom.

FILOLI, *Cañada Road, Woodside. (415) 364-2880. Open mid-February through mid-November. Admission: $6 per person; children under 12 not admitted.*

HOW TO GET TO FILOLI: *From San Francisco, take Highway 101 South to Route 280. Exit at Edgewood Road (the exit right after Highway 92); go right (west) on Edgewood a short distance until the road ends. Make a right turn and you will be on Cañada Road. Less than a quarter mile later you will see a sign for Filoli; the gate will be on your left.*

ALLIED ARTS GUILD

The suburbs of the South Bay are dotted with symbols of the old and new California. As you drive through communities like Palo Alto, Los Altos, and San Mateo, you see the old Spanish architecture (white adobe homes with red tile roofs) and the new all-American-type shopping mall. At the Allied Arts Guild in Menlo Park, the two influences are combined. Once a part of the Spanish land grant known as the Rancho de las Pulgas ("Ranch of the Fleas"), the Arts Guild might have been the first shopping center in the state. It certainly is a lovely place to visit and shop. Located in the middle of an attractive tree-lined neighborhood, the Guild is a series of small shops and artists' work spaces. Stone and brick pathways lead you through a beautiful garden and courtyard; murals, statues, and tiles decorate the walkways. It resembles the great crafts guilds of Europe and was built in the 1930s, before grand projects like this became economically prohibitive.

The Guild is operated by volunteer groups to benefit the nearby Children's Hospital at Stanford. The Palo Alto Auxiliary runs a charming tearoom; the Woodside-Atherton Auxiliary runs the Traditional Shop, the largest store in the complex, featuring fine china, silver, antiques, and gifts for the home. In case you're not familiar with the communities of Atherton and Woodside, they are among the wealthiest suburbs in the nation, and the merchandise in this shop reflects a lifestyle of elegant entertaining. The rest of the shops offer a variety of items for a variety of tastes and budgets. At last check, there was an art gallery, a kitchen shop, a candle shop, a children's store, and shops for weaving and sewing supplies. In barns at the end of the pathway are large crafts operations: glassblower, carpenter, furniture restorer. These are private businesses that rent space from the auxiliaries, so a portion of the proceeds from any sale goes to the hospital, which serves children from all over the world.

There's even a backroad of sorts at the Allied Arts Guild. All the way behind the complex is a 100-year-old barn believed to be one of the few original buildings left from the land grant days when this was the Rancho de las Pulgas. Here's where you'll find Al Kieninger. If you called central casting and requested a friendly, wise master carpenter type, they'd send somebody much like Al. He's been making custom furniture and repairing antiques for more than 50 years in The Barn Wood Shop. He's a large man with grey hair, suspenders, glasses, and a soothing deep voice. So many visitors have told him that he belongs on the *Backroads* program that when we did call to arrange for an interview, he said he was expecting us.

As you enter Al's barn, you'll see his showroom of custom chairs, tables, and cabinets. Then you can wander into the large workshop area where Al and his apprentice (who is also his son) are busy fixing and making things. Some of the tools they use are 200 years old, powered only by hands and arm muscles. Their only "power" equipment is a century-old planer and a 90-year-old band saw.

I visited with Al while he was caning a 100-year-old rocker. He says he feels like he's fixed every chair in the area. Most amusing was the rush job he had finished recently. It seems a local man had a party while his wife was out of town. Somehow a bowl of hot chili managed to burn its way through an antique table, and three chairs were broken. Everything had to be fixed within two weeks. Apparently Al rose to the occasion, and everybody lived happily ever after.

Al's Barn is the kind of place people mourn when they say "They don't make things like they used to." Kieninger takes the time to make things like they used to, meeting his own high standards. Al runs the kind of place that inspired the European craft guilds in the first place.

ALLIED ARTS GUILD, *Arbor Road at Creek Drive, Menlo Park. (415) 324-2588. Shops open 10 A.M. to 5 P.M. Monday through Saturday; closed Sunday. Tearoom seatings are at noon, 12:30 P.M. and 1 P.M. Monday through Friday; a buffet lunch is served on Saturday. Reservations are a good idea. Al Kieninger can be reached at The Barn at (415) 322-2295.*

HOW TO GET TO ALLIED ARTS: *From San Francisco, take Highway 101 South to* *the University Avenue exit in Palo Alto. Turn right and follow University through the center of town to El Camino Real. Turn right on El Camino and continue to Cambridge Street. Turn left on Cambridge and follow it to the end, which will be Arbor Road and the center.*

There have been many attempts to describe the California lifestyle. Those who do not live here often characterize it as trendy, kooky, and glitzy. And though those adjectives all have a grain of truth in them, if you want to see how Californians see themselves, then pick up a copy of *Sunset* magazine. Better yet, you can visit the magazine's headquarters, gardens, and test kitchens in Menlo Park, just a few minutes away from the Allied Arts Guild.

In case you're not familiar with the publication, *Sunset* magazine is an extremely successful monthly publication that focuses on four aspects of life on the West Coast: food, travel, gardening, and home improvement. It began publication in 1898 as the house organ for the Southern Pacific Railroad, enticing passengers riding the Sunset Limited from New Orleans to Los Angeles to move out West. Later *Sunset* became a literary magazine, featuring the likes of Jack London, Mark Twain, and Bret Harte. Later still it was sold to the Lane family, which continues to operate the company and has made the magazine a coffee-table staple in California.

A tour of the magazine's spacious facilities begins in the sprawling lobby of the magazine's main building, which is designed to look like the ultimate California ranch house. (In the lobby, make sure you look closely at the receptionist's desk; it dates back to the 1600s.) Your guide will take you through three major areas of the building: the editorial offices; the entertainment center, which is a large conference-type room where the magazine holds some of its major social functions and which features the ultimate appliance of the West, a large barbecue grill; and the test kitchen for the recipes that appear in each issue. Unfortunately, tasting is not usually a part of the tour but watching the folks at work certainly is interesting. The experiments you see on your tour could be the West's next culinary trend.

But the highlight for most people is seeing the spectacular *Sunset* garden. This part of the operation can be seen with or without the tour. The garden features nearly 300 species of plants and is arranged to show off the plants native to the Pacific states, from Northwest rhododendrons to desert cacti. The plants surround a 1-acre lawn with flat, easy-to-walk paths around the perimeters. As you stroll, keep in mind that until the magazine moved here in the 1950s, this was a barren field. Everything, including the redwood trees, was brought in by gardening experts. I was told by one of the gardeners here that the soil is now so rich and loamy, you can sink your entire arm down in each of the beds. The stroll through the garden can be enhanced by picking up a pamphlet that identifies each plant on the path; these are available at the reception desk in the lobby. The best times to visit are spring and fall, but something will be blooming all year-round.

SUNSET MAGAZINE LABORATORY OF WESTERN LIVING, *80 Willow Road, Menlo Park. Phone: (415) 321-3600. Tours of the building are offered at 10:30 A.M., 11:30 A.M., 1 P.M., 2 P.M., and 3 P.M. Monday through Friday; closed Saturday, Sunday, and holidays. The gardens are open 9 A.M. to 4:30 P.M., Monday through Friday. Admission: Free. Wheelchair accessible.*

HOW TO GET TO SUNSET MAGAZINE: *From San Francisco, take Highway 101 South to the Willow Road exit in Menlo Park. Follow Willow Road west to the intersection of Middlefield Road. Sunset's visitor's center is on the southwest corner.*

SANCHEZ ADOBE ⑦

If you tell someone to meet you at the Ramada in the town of Pacifica, chances are you'll end up in the back yard of the Sanchez Adobe. Ramada is Spanish for "arbor," and the grounds of the Sanchez estate feature an impressive shelter of trees.

The adobe itself is a noteworthy architectural achievement. Built in 1846 when the Mexicans still ruled California, the whitewashed adobe was the home of Francisco Sanchez, a recipient of one of the large Spanish land grants that carved up Alta California. Unlike many of his peers, this landlord assimilated into American society and even became one of the first supervisors for the city of San Francisco. Sanchez's home was a showplace for the community, the setting for many festivals and celebrations.

The county historical society keeps the tradition alive by staging fiestas and cultural events at the adobe. Inside, the house is set up with a furnished parlor, bedrooms, and kitchen to show what life was like for the Peninsula's upper crust in the late nineteenth century.

The 5-acre estate is also the site of an archaeological dig. Long before the Spanish arrived, the South Bay coast was the home of Ohlone Indians. The Spanish called them "Costonians" ("people of the coast"). What you see on the property now, in a field about 100 yards from the adobe, is the ramada, which includes an arbor and an Indian roundhouse.

When I visited, my guide was Shirley Dyre, a trained archaeologist who works at a local savings and loan but spends her spare time at the adobe. She recently published her research about the place in a pamphlet about the adobe and its place in history. She says her motivation was to show how cultured and industrious the early inhabitants of the area were and to fix the land and the adobe in history. The pamphlet is available on the premises.

The Sanchez Adobe is not the kind of place you would drive a long way to see, but if you're in the area it's a worthwhile diversion.

SANCHEZ ADOBE HISTORICAL SITE, *1000 Linda Mar Boulevard, Pacifica. Phone: (415) 359-1462. Open 10 A.M. to 4 P.M. Tuesday and Thursday, 1 to 5 P.M. Saturday and Sunday. You can visit the site anytime between 8 A.M. and 5 P.M. to see the Ohlone remains and to look through the windows at the downstairs rooms; but if you'd prefer to go inside, visit during open hours or call ahead and arrangements will be made for a guide to take you through the home. Admission: Free.*

HOW TO GET TO THE SANCHEZ ADOBE: *From San Francisco, take Highway 101 South to Highway 280 South to Highway 1 South to the Linda Mar Boulevard exit. Turn left (east) and go about a mile.*

MOSS BEACH

Just 20 minutes south of the Sanchez Adobe is a small, uncrowded county park that features some of the best tidepooling you'll find anywhere. The James V. Fitzgerald Marine Reserve is in the town of Moss Beach, right off the main road.

In the parking lot there's a small visitor's center with descriptive information, displays about the various kinds of marine life to be found at the reserve, and current information about tides. The best time to visit is at low tide, and you can call ahead to check when that will be. Bob Breen is the chief naturalist at the reserve, and he is a storehouse of information. He's also a delightful guide; jokes about "clamming up" and "mussel beach" are not beneath his dignity.

It's a very short walk to the beach itself. There you'll find a series of unusual reef formations that make perfect subdivisions for crabs, sponges, sea anemone, mollusk, starfish, rockfish, abalone, eel, and a seemingly endless variety of seaweed. It is a veritable marine laboratory. In fact, in the 75 years that scientists have been studying the reserve, at least 25 new species of marine life have been discovered here. You can wander around on your own or tag along on a group hike led by one of the naturalists on duty. I suggest the latter because the guides invariably point out things that are dismissed by the untrained eye. Speaking of eyes, Bob suggests you keep one of them on the ocean at all times when tidepooling because a wave can sneak up on you suddenly; his tip for the day: never turn your back on the ocean.

Even though this is a quiet, small, low-key park, there is much to see. You might find yourself spending several hours here without realizing the time has gone by. Plan ahead and pack a lunch—a picnic area is provided.

JAMES V. FITZGERALD MARINE RESERVE, *Moss Beach. Phone: (415) 728-3584. Open sunrise to sunset daily, but the best time to visit is at low tide. Call ahead for information. Admission: Free.*

HOW TO GET TO THE MARINE RESERVE: *From San Francisco, take Highway 101*

South to Highway 280 to Route 1. The Marine Reserve is right off Route 1 in the town of Moss Beach. Just look for the sign on the right side of the road as you head south from Pacifica. Turn right and follow the driveway to the parking lot and visitor's center.

LIGHTHOUSE HOSTELS

Within an hour of San Francisco you can have oceanfront accommodations in an historic setting for just a few dollars a night. All you have to do is pitch in a bit and suspend desire for room service and privacy.

I'm talking about staying in places run by the American Youth Hostel Service. Don't let the name put you off; people of all ages are welcome. The goal of AYH is to make hostelling as popular in this country as it is in Europe.

Along the South Bay coast, the AYH accommodations are the Montara Lighthouse Hostel, about 25 miles south of San Francisco, and the Pigeon Point Lighthouse Hostel, about 50 miles south of the City. Both establishments are clean, friendly places. If you're not familiar with the hostel setup, these are cooperative overnight accommodations. The hostel provides shelter, a bed, and kitchen facilities; the visitors provide their own food and pick up after themselves. These lighthouse hostels offer wonderful settings for the experience.

Montara Lighthouse is set in a restored 1875 lighthouse and fog signal station. The seven-bedroom duplex can accommodate 35 guests, with two fully equipped dining rooms, a common living room, and a laundry. There's also a volleyball court, a private beach, and an outdoor hot tub. Not bad for roughing it. You can rent a bicycle and head to the Fitzgerald Marine Reserve at Moss Beach, just a few miles away.

At Pigeon Point, the setting is a former Coast Guard residence—three bungalows, each with its own kitchen, accommodating a total of 50 persons. The lighthouse there is a beauty, one of the tallest in the United States. It's open for tours and a 150-step climb to the top on Sundays. The former fog signal building has been converted into a communal recreational lounge. Pigeon Point is only a few miles from Año Nuevo Beach (see item 11).

Space at either facility costs $5 or $6 a person and is available on a first-come, first-served basis. Reservations can be made sending the first night's fee in advance. Remember, these are minimal accommodations, an experience that is not enjoyed by everyone.

For information and reservations for either facility, call the American Youth Hostel office in San Francisco: (415) 771-4646. You can also call the Montara Lighthouse at (415) 728-7177 and the Pigeon Point Lighthouse at (415) 879-0633.

HOW TO GET TO THE MONTARA LIGHTHOUSE: *From San Francisco, take High-*

way 101 South to Highway 280 to the Route 1 exit and follow it south on the coast. The hostel is in the town of Montara right off Highway 1 at Sixteenth Street.

HOW TO GET TO PIGEON POINT LIGHTHOUSE: *From San Francisco, follow the directions to Montara and continue down Route 1 past Half Moon Bay. After the town of Pescadero, look on the right for the lighthouse.*

The town of Half Moon Bay is famous for one thing: pumpkins. This is the pumpkin capital of the state, maybe even of the world, and it is a destination for thousands of families each year around Halloween. In fact, the annual Pumpkin Festival each October draws so many tourists that the usual one-hour drive from San Francisco takes three hours.

Other annual events bring people to town. The Portuguese community celebrates its heritage with the Chamarita Festival each May, and in July the Coastside Country Fair celebrates the summer fruit harvest. However, many visitors never make it past the farms on Route 92, the main backroad that takes you to the coast. That's a shame because the town itself is a wonderful destination all year-round.

It was originally called Spanishtown by the Mexican settlers, a name that lasted into the twentieth century even after other residents referred to the place as San Benito. The area all around became an abundant farming region, attracting immigrants from Portugal and Italy. The town's proximity to San Francisco and its secure, half moon-shaped harbor made it a popular rum- and whisky-running site during Prohibition. Eventually everybody started calling the place Half Moon Bay.

A walk down Main Street will give you an idea of what Carmel and Mendocino used to be like before they became major tourist attractions. The town is not only picturesque, compact, and easy to walk around, but it also feels more like a warm community than a commercial tourist attraction.

The local historical society has recently prepared a map for a self-guided walking tour. In just a few blocks you can see interesting buildings, nice shops for browsing, and several good inns and restaurants. The tour begins by crossing the white concrete bridge that leads you onto Main Street. At 326 Main you will see the town's oldest building, the Zaballa House. Built in 1859, it is currently used for offices. It is next door to one of the South Bay's best places to eat a light lunch or a fancy dinner, The San Benito House (at 356 Main). The upstairs of this historic hotel has been restored for lodging, and is a good place to stay if your needs and/or budget are modest. If your comfort requirements are greater, you can stay down the street at a charming bed-and-breakfast place called The

Old Thyme Inn (at 779 Main Street), a small Victorian House with each room named for an herb; or if you're in the mood to splurge, the Mill Rose Inn is just a block or so off Main Street (at 615 Mill Street).

Other points of culinary and historic interest on Main Street are the Half Moon Bay Bakery (at 514 Main), which still uses a brick oven from the nineteenth century; Pasta Moon (315 Main Street) for an excellent Italian lunch or dinner; and McCoffee (522 Main), the best place in town for an espresso drink and local gossip, run by a nice lady named McCaughey.

On your way in or out of town on Highway 1, you might notice an abundance of flower fields. That's because this is one of the largest flower-growing centers in the nation. In fact, flower sales here outgross vegetable income. As one flower farmer poetically said to me, "Flowers are food for the soul." Unfortunately, due in part to insurance problems, most flower farms are not set up for public tours. But many of the greenhouse operations along Route 92 do welcome visitors and sell their plants retail. During the summer, the city holds several Saturday flower market days, during which time all local growers display their wares in the center of town.

HALF MOON BAY, *Route 92 at Route 1. You can pick up a copy of the Historic Half Moon Bay Walking Tour Map at almost any shop along Main Street or at the Chamber of Commerce (415) 726-5202, located in a red railroad caboose at the Shoreline Station Shopping Center.*

HOW TO GET TO HALF MOON BAY: *From San Francisco, take Highway 101 South to Highway 280. Continue on Route 280 South to Route 92 to Half Moon Bay. Main Street is the last street before you hit Route 1 and the coast. Turn left at the stoplight onto Main to get to the shopping and restaurant district.*

HOME OF THE ELEPHANT SEALS ⑪

One of the Bay Area's most popular shows featuring sex, violence, and larger-than-life characters is to be found at Año Nuevo State Beach. It is under the auspices of the state park service, and tickets are so much in demand you must make reservations weeks, if not months, in advance.

The stars of the show are the elephant seals that have adopted this beautiful stretch of land as their winter home. Some loll around here all year, but the prime time to see them is mating season, from December to April. Perhaps the idea of watching elephant seals mate isn't your idea of a good time, but I've never heard of anyone regretting the trip, even those who have been caught in one of the area's frequent rainstorms during showtime.

The audience checks in at the visitor's center. Then the group walks about a mile and a half to the ocean. Just about the time you begin to wonder if you really want to be doing this, you catch a sight of the first elephant seal, a 6000-pound blob with a prehistoric-looking face. He'll probably be asleep, but he'll wake up every 20 minutes. You see, elephant seals don't breathe while sleeping; when it's time for some air, they'll awaken, take a whiff, then catch some more zzz's until it's time to breathe again.

Soon you will reach a point where everywhere you look there are elephant seals. Though it may look like nothing but a random assortment of bodies, there is a definite order to the living arrangements. The dominant males, led by one king bull, live in one area; they brawl occasionally to establish the power structure. Another section has been nicknamed the "Bachelors' Pad"; this is where the males who do not get to mate this year must hang out. They too will occasionally start a brawl, in the hope of proving themselves worthy of membership in the dominant club next year.

Actually, the "bachelors" were the first residents of this beach. Elephant seals have always bred off the same shore. The frustrated losers would inhabit this beach while a mating party went on on a nearby island. Then for reasons no one has yet figured out, females started showing up in 1975. The dominant bulls followed, and Año Nuevo became the only mainland breeding colony for elephant seals north of the equator.

Though you will see a lot of bodies lying around on the beach, these elephant seals are not being lazy. The males don't want to go in the water because they might lose a chance to mate. The females don't want to leave their babies. So they stay on shore and fast for the several months of this particular part of the life cycle.

This once endangered species is protected by laws, to the point that their rights come before tourists'. Today visitors must remain at least 20 feet away from the seals, and if one comes your way, it's your obligation to move. Anyway, the rule makes sense; who wants to argue with a 6000-pound animal? Elephant seals have no desire to attack humans but can inadvertently trample one when angry. And they are much faster than they look, so be careful.

In the last two years, a surprising new development has made Año Nuevo a year-round attraction. The seals now hang out on the beach in the summer as well as in winter. Though there is less action than during the mating season, you can wander out to see these marvels of nature. What's more, like most tourist places, there are fewer humans in the off season so you won't need an advance ticket.

AÑO NUEVO BEACH. *Winter tickets are sold through Ticketron; to find the location of the most convenient outlet, call (415) 392-7469 or (408) 247-7469. Tickets cost $4.*

Since parking space is at a premium, public transportation is available on winter weekends. The San Mateo County Transit District picks up passengers in San Mateo and Half Moon Bay. The cost is $8 per person and includes the round-

trip ride and the tour. For reservations and information, phone (415) 348-SEAL. During nonmating season, from April through November, visitors are free to roam around on their own, though groups of 15 or more must make reservations.

HOW TO GET TO AÑO NUEVO: *From San Francisco, follow the directions to Half Moon Bay and continue on Route 1 until you come to Año Nuevo, which is well marked, on your right.*

CHAPTER **5** Santa Clara County

AREA OVERVIEW

Santa Clara County is the center of Silicon Valley. This is where you'll find computer terminals in coffeeshops and floppy discs next to the pantyhose in supermarkets. Stanford University is here, the former site of a farm. Now, there's a strong movement to preserve what remains of the area's fruit-farming past. The surprise for many people is that Santa Clara goes way south from San Jose. That's where you will find more wide open spaces and a still active agricultural center. There's a booming wine industry in the south near Gilroy, which is also known as the Garlic Capital of the World. Again, Routes 101 and the more scenic, less crowded, 280 take you south to the major population center, San Jose. Plan on an hour to reach some of the northernmost destinations.

ELECTRONICS MUSEUM
①

Here in the heart of Silicon Valley is a museum dedicated to the electronic wonders before the computer. Perhaps you're old enough to remember big console radios, the kind you were never supposed to touch because the dials were set for Grandpa. Well, this type of radio is on display at the Electronics Museum, on the campus of Foothill College in Los Altos. It takes a little work to find the place, but if you are fascinated by anything to do with radio, television, and telephones, it's well worth the effort.

The Electronics Museum is the object of affection for a group of former broadcast and telephone company engineers. Together they managed to collect and build a wonderful exhibit of artifacts from the earliest ham operations to the dawn of the tiny portable. No boom boxes here. You'll see all sizes and shapes of tube radios, most of them still working, and you'll see the smallest transistor jobs. You'll see early television sets, including the first portable (which, by the way, Arnold Schwarzenegger would have a difficult time lugging around). There are telephones of all vintages, sizes, and shapes, and microphones used by

Palo Alto

880

680

82

280

5

San Jose

6

8 9

7 Saratoga

11

101

10

Santa Clara

152 Gilroy

12

Groucho Marx and Bob Hope, and, for real connoisseurs, an artful display of telephone cable insulator covers—very colorful!

Other displays trace the history of communications and show the technical process by which sound is transmitted. The hero of the place seems to be Lee DeForest, who made radio possible by developing the first electronic tube that would amplify sound. Another treat is meeting the people who run the museum. All are volunteers, and they are here because they truly love equipment and communications and showing people around. They'll operate a ham radio for you or deliver a brief lecture on the comparative contributions of David Sarnoff and Thomas Edison, if requested. The guides are especially turned on when they get to show kids the glories of radio.

FOOTHILL COLLEGE ELECTRONICS MUSEUM, *12345 South El Monte Road, Los Altos Hills. Phone: (415) 960-4383. Open 9:30 A.M. to 4:30 P.M. Monday through Friday, 1 A.M. to 4:30 P.M. Sunday, closed Saturday. Admission: Adults, $2; children, 50 cents.*

HOW TO GET TO FOOTHILL COLLEGE: *From San Francisco, take Route 101 South to Route 280 and take the Foothill exit. You will see the college on the right. That's the easy part. Now enter the campus and ask directions for the museum. If no one can help, wind up the main road as it climbs a hill to the right and look for a building on top of the hill with a radio tower outside. It's not really all that difficult; it's just that at last report, there was no sign in front of the building indicating the museum.*

PALO ALTO BAYLANDS
②

There are several places in the Bay Area that birdwatchers love. Baylands Nature Preserve near Palo Alto is near the top of the list. More than 100 species of birds have been seen on this marsh, including a variety of ducks, hawks, herons, and owls. And even if you are not a bird fan, you can get a sense of what the Bay was like years ago, before development.

Situated at the end of Embarcadero Road, this 120-acre salt marsh is alive with birds and plants. Though it's just a short drive from Route 101, it feels far removed from the noise and pollution of the freeway; possibly due to the influence of plant life and the Bay, the air feels better out here.

The activities are low-key and simple. At the attractive interpretive center you can see what to look for once you go out on the trails. The trails are a system of boardwalks and levees that take you at water level into the marsh. You can roam on your own with your binoculars or hook up with one of the trained naturalists for a guided walk.

BAYLANDS NATURE PRESERVE, *2775 Embarcadero Road, Palo Alto. Phone: (415) 329-2506. The boardwalks are usually open during daylight hours, but the guided tours and the interpretive center are subject to changing schedules; it's best to call ahead. The most recent schedule for the interpretive center was 2 to 5 P.M. Wednesday through Friday, and 1 to 5 P.M. Saturday and Sunday. Admission: Free.*

HOW TO GET TO BAYLANDS: *From San Francisco, take Highway 101 South toward San Jose. Exit onto Embarcadero Road in Palo Alto and go east, which is to the left, until you come to the end of the road. You will be at Baylands.*

BARBIE DOLL HALL OF FAME

From the outside of the Doll Studio in Palo Alto you would think that this is just another store that sells dolls. But no. Inside, you will find the world's largest collection of Barbies. Owner Evelyn Burkhalter says her collection is more complete than that of the manufacturer, Mattel Toys. She has collected 14,000 Barbies and Kens, including the first black Barbie, a hippie Barbie, Barbie as the first woman astronaut, and Barbie as the ultimate yuppie, complete with an Oscar de la Renta suit. Evelyn has collected examples of every single outfit ever designed for Barbie, and there's only one version of the doll that she does not yet have.

When I visited, Evelyn and her husband were making plans to expand the display, but in the meantime it will remain in the back of the Doll Studio. Even in these cramped quarters you get a history of modern America as evidenced by the changes in Barbie's clothes, accessories, and hairstyles. The fact that Evelyn bears a striking resemblance to America's doll sweetheart will not escape you. She says she likes Barbie because they symbolize that women are survivors, capable of anything.

BARBIE DOLL HALL OF FAME, *460 Waverly St., Palo Alto. Phone: (415) 326-5841. Open 1:30 to 4:30 P.M. Tuesday through Friday, 10 A.M. to 12 noon, 1:30 to 4 P.M. Saturday; closed Sunday and Monday. Admission: Adults, $2, children $1.*

HOW TO GET TO THE BARBIE DOLL HALL OF FAME: *From San Francisco, take Highway 101 South to the University Avenue exit. Turn west toward downtown Palo Alto. In downtown Palo Alto, turn right on Waverly Street. The Barbie Doll Hall of Fame will be in the middle of the first block.*

NASA

It comes as a surprise to many people to learn NASA has a major facility in the San Francisco area. While Houston is the center of activities in outer space, the giant NASA–Ames research facility at Moffett Field near Mountain View is a center for studying such issues as commercial aviation flight safety and aircraft design.

The center is open for public tours. They begin in an auditorium with a film that outlines the kind of work done at this facility, followed by a question-and-answer period. It's important to get a lot of the talking out of the way here because the rest of the tour is quite noisy; the human voice is often drowned out by the roar of engines and the hum of wind tunnels. In fact, the largest wind tunnel in the world is here at Ames, with an interior test space of 80 feet in height and 120 feet in width. The wind is too strong to permit visitors to go inside, but you can look through windows. All in all, there are 20 wind tunnels on the property.

Until recently, hangars and wind tunnels were the main tools used to test aircraft. But now the computer has been introduced for testing aircraft safety—not surprisingly, considering the facility's location in Silicon Valley, one of the major computer development centers in the world. The world's largest computer is used at Ames to simulate aeronautical conditions and is expected to be the most valuable device yet for preventive safety.

The tour makes selected stops throughout the facility, depending on the nature of the work being done at the moment. You might see a flight simulation laboratory, and you will certainly be taken into one of the immense hangars that house experimental aircraft.

There is no charge for the tour, but you will probably not be able to resist the small gift shop back in the visitor's center, which offers space memorabilia and even sells the space snack astronauts use. The freeze-dried ice cream is really something.

NASA–AMES RESEARCH CENTER, *Moffett Field, Mountain View. For information about visiting, call (415) 966-5976. Wheelchair accessible.*

HOW TO GET TO THE RESEARCH CENTER: *From San Francisco, take Highway 101 South. After the Palo Alto exits and just before Mountain View, you will see the huge hangars from the road. Look for the NASA–Ames exit and follow the signs.*

SAN JOSE HISTORICAL PARK ⑤

Here's some trivia you can use to dazzle your friends. Long before Dionne Warwick sang "Do You Know the Way to San Jose?" a famous Frenchman asked the same question. Who was he?

Answer: Alexander Eiffel, of tower fame. Monsieur Eiffel came to this small California town back in the 1880s to get some ideas for the tower he was to build in Paris. He wanted to see the famous San Jose Tower of Light.

The story of the light goes like this: Two years after Edison perfected the light bulb, electric light was introduced to the town of San Jose. The town fathers had the bright idea to save on the cost of individual street lights by erecting one giant tower to illuminate the entire community. A magnificent tower was built. Unfortunately, it lit the sky more than the streets. It was so intense that nearby farm animals became confused and couldn't sleep. Roosters crowed at the wrong times; cows didn't know when to give milk. The tower stood for several years until it fell over in a storm. Once the beacon hit the dirt, it was decided to leave well enough alone and relegate the memory of the tower to a historical park.

Today, a half-size replica of the infamous tower of light is the centerpiece of a park that commemorates the early days of San Jose. It stands in the midst of a re-created Main Street. Here you can wander inside a full-scale version of the Pacific Hotel, where you could get room and board for $1 a night in 1881. There's the original Banca d'Italia, started by A. P. Giannini, who later built the Bank of America. You can get a soda in O'Brien's Candy Factory, the place that first served ice-cream sodas west of Detroit, and you can visit a firehouse and many other buildings that give you a taste of the olden days. It's done on a small, easily manageable scale, so you are not overwhelmed by induced nostalgia.

Several new exhibits have opened since my last visit. The most impressive is the Stevens Ranch Fruit Barn, located opposite the Tower of Light. The barn was originally located twelve miles away, in the path of what became an extension of Highway 101. Thankfully, some foresighted folks saved the historic structure and moved it to its current site. Now it houses a wonderful display about Santa Clara farm life of yesteryear. On display is antique farm machinery (considered high-tech in Grandma and Grandpa's day) and photographs taken by such well-known photographers as Dorothea Lange and Ansel Adams.

The historical park is inside a larger community park of 150 acres of picnic grounds, a miniature train, a children's petting zoo, and room to roam. Kelley Park also includes a very different sort of attraction, the Japanese Friendship Garden. As you might expect, this is a serene, well-manicured, formal Japanese garden, complete with bridges, paths, waterfalls and streams filled with colorful Japanese goldfish called Koi. Here you can wander at your own pace or ask one of the guides to explain the various symbols in the garden.

SAN JOSE HISTORICAL MUSEUM, *in Kelley Park, 635 Phelan Avenue, San Jose. Phone: (408) 287-2291 or (408) 287-2290. Open 10 A.M. to 4:30 P.M. Monday through Friday; noon to 4:30 P.M. Saturday and Sunday. Admission: Seniors, $1.50; kids, $1; all others, $2.00.*

THE WAY TO SAN JOSE AND THE HISTORICAL PARK: *From San Francisco, take Route 101 South to Route 280 South to San Jose. Exit at Tenth Street and go to Keyes Street. Turn left and continue to Senter Road. The entrance to the park is at Senter and Phelan Avenue.*

LICK OBSERVATORY

One of the most powerful telescopes in the world is located atop Mount Hamilton, above the metropolis of San Jose. Astronomers from all around the globe come here to use the 120-inch reflector telescope. The operation is run by the University of California, Santa Cruz, and tours are available.

The story behind the observatory is almost as fascinating as the place itself.

Its benefactor, James Lick, was one of the more eccentric Gold Rush million-aires. He became obsessed with Egyptian culture and had a plan to build a pyramid in the center of San Francisco. The city fathers talked him out of it (though many years later, the Transamerica Corporation built its office building in the shape of a pyramid, and now it is a city landmark).

Lick also became obsessed with astronomy. He was convinced that there was some form of life on the moon. So he decided to build the largest telescope and observatory possible, again in the center of San Francisco. And again the city fathers talked him out of it. Undaunted, Lick found a remote mountaintop for his project. The task of building the observatory was monumental. To begin with, there was no road, so one had to be built to accommodate all the heavy machinery and supplies for the construction of the place. As a matter of fact, Lick turned out to be a shrewd negotiator. He agreed to provide the $700,000 necessary to build the complex only if the county would build a road to the top. The road was finished in 1876, the same year Lick died. His dream observatory wasn't completed until 12 years later. His remains are buried at the base of the telescope.

Early visitors had to take a five-hour horse-drawn stage ride to the top. No doubt the scientists and tourists found it worth the trip. After all, it was the first attempt at a mountaintop observatory, and at the same time, it was the largest telescope in the world.

Today a small community resides atop the mountain to study at the observa-tory and maintain the property. The road is paved, but the drive up the 4200-foot mountain takes at least an hour. It is not recommended for anyone who tends to get carsick on winding roads. The scenery, however, is spectacular, and the even longer road down the back side takes you into the least developed sections of Santa Clara and Alameda counties.

Atop the mountain, several buildings house telescopes. Visitors have many things to see, determined by the time of year and the various projects in progress. Always there is the visitor's gallery, where you can browse through a large institutional-type building and see photographs of the skies as seen by the tele-scopes. There is also a gift shop and of course the featured attraction, the giant telescope, which has the power to see stars 10 billion light-years away. If you want to imagine how big this instrument is, imagine a telescope the height of a six-story building. A huge domed ceiling opens to allow the telescope its view of the sky.

On Friday nights from April to October, special programs are conducted at the observatory, such as a lecture by an astronomer and a nighttime peek at the heavens through the big lens.

LICK OBSERVATORY, *Mount Hamilton. Phone: (408) 274-5061. Open to the public daily except Thanksgiving, Christmas, and New Year's Day from 10 A.M. to 5 P.M. Programs change often, so it is best to call ahead.*

HOW TO GET TO THE OBSERVATORY: *From San Francisco, take Highway 101 to San Jose. Exit at Route 130-Alum Rock Road and continue up the hill until you reach the top. You will see signs marking the way; at some points the road will be called Mount Hamilton Road.*

VILLA MONTALVO

The town of Saratoga reminds me of Carmel-by-the-Sea without crowds, the beach, or Clint Eastwood. The main street is filled with expensive shops and restaurants, serving for the most part the wealthy residents of this lovely community. In fact, Saratoga had its beginnings as a private community with a toll road, to keep the riff-raff in San Jose. Today, there are some less opulent touches, too, such as the bank that was a bar and the bar that used to be a bank.

Saratoga has its share of spacious country estates, but none is more impressive than Villa Montalvo. It was one of the last great estates built in California in the days before income taxes made such dream palaces impossible. It was built for James Phelan, a three-term mayor of San Francisco and a U.S. senator. Phelan befriended artists and writers, and using the fortune he made in banking, he built his estate to fulfill a lifelong dream of being a patron of the arts. He used the Italian Renaissance-style villa to entertain lavishly, and he bequeathed the estate to be used as a special place for musicians, writers, and painters to work. He named it after a Spanish writer, Ordonez de Montalvo, who, in the sixteenth century, used the word California in a fantasy novel to describe a place of great beauty and fertile soil.

Villa Montalvo is now a park and cultural center, where artists are given room and board in beautiful surroundings, with nothing to worry about but their work. From the front of the villa, you can look out on a vast expanse of green lawn bordered by rows of trees. Behind the home you will find terraces, courtyards, and a small area for evening concerts. Though picnicking is not allowed, it is lovely to wander around. In addition, immediately behind the house is a 170-acre arboretum and bird sanctuary maintained by the local county parks department, perfect for a stroll on nature trails for a look at a wide variety of plant life.

Inside Villa Montalvo, the first floor has been transformed into an art gallery to display the works of the artists-in-residence. The villa is an active arts center, offering many types of cultural programs. The carriage house has been converted into a theater.

Unfortunately, some portions of the historic and beautiful cultural center suffered during the earthquake of October 1989. When you visit you are likely to see some evidence of the quake, notably some damage to the columns in the Spanish courtyard. But because the damage was mostly cosmetic, activities at the villa have continued unhindered.

VILLA MONTALVO, *15400 Montalvo Road, Saratoga. Phone: (408) 741-3421. Arboretum open 8 A.M. to 5 P.M. Monday through Friday; 9 A.M. to 5 P.M. Saturday and Sunday. Admission: Free. The villa, including the art gallery, bookstore, and gift shop, is open 1 to 4 P.M. Thursday and Friday, 11 A.M. to 4 P.M. Saturday and Sunday. Admission: $1.00. Wheelchair accessible.*

HOW TO GET TO VILLA MONTALVO: *From San Francisco, take Highway 101 South toward San Jose. Take the exit for Highway 17 South to Santa Cruz. After passing San Jose, exit at Route 9/Saratoga Avenue. Follow Saratoga Avenue west, past Los Gatos. About half a mile before entering the village of Saratoga, look for Montalvo Road on the left. Follow Montalvo Road to the entrance of the villa.*

HAKONE GARDENS
(8)

Rare and unusual gardens seem to thrive in the town of Saratoga. Just a few minutes away from the Sasos' world-class herb garden (see following entry) is a world of peace and tranquility, the Hakone Gardens. This is a city park, just a few blocks from the downtown area. Once inside, you would swear you are in Japan.

Hakone Gardens was built in the second decade of this century by Isabel Stine, a wealthy San Franciscan. Having once lived in Japan, she wanted to create the unique quality of a Japanese garden on her estate in Saratoga, which was used by her family as a summer retreat. At first the garden was used only by the family, their children swimming in the pond with neighbors such as the young sisters who came to be known as Joan Fontaine and Olivia de Havilland.

In 1932 the garden was sold to Charles Tilden of Berkeley's Tilden Park fame, and in 1966 it was made a city park to preserve the place for future generations. The 16-acre park is said to be the finest hill and water garden outside Japan. Named after the national park at the foot of Mount Fuji, Hakone is a living example of a seventeenth-century Zen garden. The hillside creates several levels, with streams and bridges. Typical of traditional Japanese gardens, it is elegantly simple and basically monochromatic; the belief is that too much color calls attention to itself, a dissonant chord in the overall harmony of the place.

The park is not only lovely, but the components have symbolic meanings. The footbridges are arched, and the paths and walkways are curved. This geometry suggests purity; straight lines are avoided due to the belief that evil spirits travel only in straight lines.

A Japanese house built on the property shows how a samurai might have lived 200 years ago. It's apparent that the traditional Japanese home hasn't changed much. You will learn that Japanese homes are measured not in square feet but by the number of tatami mats a room can accommodate. You will also see how Japanese design makes a tiny space function on many levels. All furniture is kept behind screens. When it's time to eat, the proper table is brought out; when it's time to sleep, the futons are brought out; and when guests arrive, the correct number of tatami are put into place. Most of the time, however, the room is bare, save for a few tatami and a floral arrangement.

A visit here requires that you have no expectation other than wanting to tune out the busy world and relax. It is quiet, the only sound being the pleasant rush of streams over rocks. This is a place to do nothing. The busiest activity is the serving of green tea on weekends in the teahouse.

HAKONE JAPANESE GARDENS, *21000 Big Basin Way, Saratoga. Phone: (408) 867-3438. Open 10 A.M. to 5 P.M. Monday through Friday; 11 A.M. to 5 P.M. Saturday and Sunday; closed legal holidays. Admission: 25-cent donation.*

HOW TO GET TO HAKONE GARDENS: *From San Francisco, follow the directions to Saratoga (under "Villa Montalvo"). Once in the center of Saratoga, at the stoplight at the intersection of Routes 9 and 85, take Big Basin Way, which is the main street of town, up the hill until you come to the entrance to Hakone Gardens.*

SASO HERB GARDENS

On a quiet street not far from Saratoga City Hall is a place that attracts visitors from all over the world. Still, many people in the Bay Area have never heard of it, unless they happen to love herbs. But for those who know, the Saso Herb Gardens are truly first-class.

On the acre of land that surrounds their modest home, Louis and Virginia Saso have devoted a quarter of a century to growing herbs and spreading the word about what they can do for us. Their garden, which Louis says he's sure is the most extensive herb collection in the country, is well worth a visit.

First of all, the place is beautiful; 1000 plants are arranged in display areas you can stroll through at your leisure. This is also an educational experience because as you wander around, you can read about the various kinds of herbs. Did you know that basil symbolizes love? There's a medicinal section, with herbs that resemble organs of the body; the herbs are supposedly good for the part they look like, like lungwort for the lungs. Though Louis is quick to point out that he is not practicing medicine, he will tell you about the latest research. He told me about a healing herb called feverfew that is supposed to be good for headaches, but I haven't gotten around to trying it yet. Another area of the garden shows home gardeners how to rid themselves of pests without resorting to chemicals. One of the Sasos' favorite devices is to plant garlic chives as a protective ring around plants. This is supposed to be particularly good for discouraging aphids.

There's an astrological garden watched over by a statue of St. Phac, the patron saint of herb gardens. In a circle, the herbs that refer to each sign of the zodiac are neatly arranged.

Organized tours are available, and twice a year, in April and August, the Sasos hold a giant open house. Otherwise, the visitor is pretty much left to wander independently, since Louis and Virginia are busy taking care of the garden. Virginia also makes dried flower arrangements, available for sale in the small gift shop.

SASO HERB GARDENS, *14625 Fruitvale Avenue, Saratoga. Phone: (408) 867-0307. Open 9 A.M. to 2:30 P.M. Monday through Saturday; closed Sunday. Admission: Free. Call about guided tours.*

HOW TO GET TO SASO HERB GARDENS: *From San Francisco, follow the previous directions to Saratoga (under "Villa Montalvo"). After you pass Los Gatos and the village of Monte Sereno, look for Fruitvale Avenue on the right. Turn right onto Fruitvale Avenue. The Saso's place is .7 mile on the left, on the corner of Farwell. There is a sign at the driveway.*

FORTINO WINERY

As you head west on Route 152, also called Hecker Pass Road, you pass through the outskirts of the town of Gilroy. Most times of the year, Gilroy is a quiet farming community. But one weekend every autumn it is jammed with people from all over who adore garlic. Gilroy is the garlic capital of the world; the annual garlic festival celebrates the fact that most of the nation's garlic used to be grown here. Recently, most of the "stinking rose" farms have moved south, but most of the processing continues to be headquartered in Gilroy.

As you leave Gilroy and head for the Monterey Peninsula, you are soon in rolling hillside country. And just about anywhere in the Bay Area that you see beautiful countryside, you can be sure wineries can't be far.

Indeed, the wineries of the South Santa Clara Valley are not nearly as well known as their neighbors to the north, but that means that these small, family run wineries fall more into the category of special finds. A good example is the Fortino Winery, run by Ernest Fortino, who is also likely to be your tour guide. Ernest is a charming middle-aged man who speaks with the accent of his homeland. He and his family run the place like a family farm. This "little old" winemaker learned his trade from generations of winemakers in Italy. He operates by instinct as he walks through his vineyard, picking a grape here and there to see if it is yet ready to be made into wine. He does not use fancy wine-tasting vocabulary words like *bouquet* or *nose* to describe his product; either it tastes good or it doesn't.

According to Ernest, whom you'll be calling "Ernie" soon, wine to the Italians is like milk to Americans—an important part of family life that everybody can enjoy. The setting is in keeping with the Fortino philosophy. A visit here is like dropping in on a small winery in Italy. This is a working farm, with just enough buildings on the property to get the job done. There are no fancy tasting rooms or special visitors' centers. The tasting often takes place at one of the picnic tables that border the vineyard.

Ernest is also a driving force in the community of winemakers in the Santa Clara Valley. They often get together and stage public events, such as the annual harvest celebration in the fall. At this function, you're invited to take off your shoes and participate in an old-fashioned barefoot grape crush. This is only for fun, though; state health codes forbid making wine the really old-fashioned way.

FORTINO WINERY, *4525 Hecker Pass Road, Gilroy. Phone: (408) 842-3305. Open 9 A.M. to 6 P.M. daily.*

HOW TO GET TO FORTINO WINERY: *From San Francisco, take Route 101 South to Gilroy and then Route 152. Turn right, which is west, and stay on Route 152. You will pass several small wineries on the way. Fortino's is well marked, right on Route 152, which is also called the Hecker Pass Road.*

It seems to me that one of the benefits of traveling the backroads is that it offers one a chance to renew one's perspective. Those of us who spend time in cities can get very jaded. An unusual character becomes just another face in the crowd; a unique building is easily overlooked as you pass through a neighborhood filled with places that can dazzle the eye.

And yet, if you took Irv Perch and his Flying Lady complex and put them in the center of Manhattan, this guy and this place would manage to attract attention. It just so happens they're in the middle of nowhere, on the outskirts of Morgan Hill, which really makes them stand out.

First, Irv. For most of his life he ran a trailer manufacturing company, then made a fortune by selling out to a conglomerate. One day his wife decided she wanted to learn to fly. So Irv built her an airport. Then she wanted a place to play golf. So Irv built her a golf course next to the airport. He's always been a collector, obsessed with buying mementos of the past. Instead of buying one of a kind, he bought entire collections of things and became a one-man Smithsonian. So he decided to open a museum in the airport hangars, and what the heck, he might as well open a restaurant, too.

All this can be found in the Flying Lady complex, about 2 miles off Highway 101. What do you like? Cars? Irv's got a zillion of them: antique cars, buses, and trucks. Planes? There are several, from the Ford trimotor job that Steven Spielberg borrowed for the movie *Raiders of the Lost Ark* to small craft from all over the world. How about license plates? One of Irv's prize possessions is his complete set of the license plates of Canada.

FLYING LADY COLLECTION OF NEARLY EVERYTHING

But that's not all. Up the hill from the hangars, the Flying Lady restaurant features—you guessed it—more collections. First of all, the place is big enough to accommodate 1200 diners simultaneously. Irv's large-scale model airplanes fly above the tables on motorized tracks. The restaurant also houses a collection of jukeboxes and telephones. The Wild West Saloon in the basement displays cowboy memorabilia. The only thing I can't rave about here is the food. But who comes for the food? This is a place to *see*.

THE FLYING LADY, *15060 Foothill Avenue, Morgan Hill. Phone: (408) 779-4136. Museum open 8 A.M. to 5 P.M. Wednesday through Friday; 9 A.M. to 5 P.M. Saturday and Sunday; closed Monday and Tuesday. Admission: Free. Restaurant open Wednesday through Sunday, serving lunch and dinner. Wheelchair accessible.*

HOW TO GET TO THE FLYING LADY: *From San Francisco, take Route 101 South past San Jose to Morgan Hill. Exit onto Tennant Avenue, and take Tennant to the left, which is east. Stay on Tennant until you come to Foothill Avenue. Turn right, which is south, on Foothill to the entrance to the Flying Lady.*

CASA DE FRUTA
⑫

Remember the old Burma Shave billboards, the ones that used to dot the byways back in the days before interstate highways? Well, you might think you're back in the good old days when you're tooling down Highway 101 south of San Jose and you start seeing signs for Casa de Fruta. One by one, they promise you just about everything you could want or need, if you'll just get off the main road and head over the pass to the intersection of Routes 152 and 156.

I should point out that Routes 152 and 156 are not quiet country roads. These are rather big truck routes leading to and from the Sierras. Because of that built-in traffic flow, many years ago, the Zanger family decided to add to the income of their cherry farm by putting a little fruit stand out by the road. It did pretty well, but then the mother of the family had an idea that would turn the place into a major roadside attraction: bathrooms. "People on the road need a good, clean rest room," Mama told her sons. "Put one in and our business will double." Mama Zanger was right. Pretty soon the fruit stand and comfort station, known as Casa de Fruta, turned into one of the strangest empires you'll ever hope to see. People on the road want a cup of coffee, so the Zangers added a little coffeeshop and called it Casa de Coffee. People on the road want a snack; voila: Casa de Burger.

Today Casa de Fruta includes 100 acres of attractions, including a trailer park, a miniature zoo, gardens, a train ride, and a Casa de Gifts. The Zangers have never forgotten that it was the cherries that got them started. Every June, when the cherries are in full bloom, there is a giant Cherry Festival, including a pit-spitting contest. All year there is a 24-hour coffeeshop, and you can picnic on the grounds overlooking a duck pond labeled Casa de Cold Duck. The Zangers have a sense of humor as well as a sense of good business.

CASA DE FRUTA ORCHARD RESORT, *6680 Pacheco Pass Highway, Hollister. Phone: (408) 637-0051. Open 9 A.M. to 6 P.M. daily. Admission: Free to the grounds; use fee for trailer park.*

HOW TO GET TO CASA DE FRUTA: *From San Francisco, follow Route 101 South to the Route 152 turnoff. Head east to the intersection of Route 156. Be careful —this is a heavy truck route, and accidents are frequent.*

CHAPTER **6** Santa Cruz County

AREA OVERVIEW

Santa Cruz County begins where San Mateo and Santa Clara counties end, stretching from the inland mountains to the Pacific Coast. The severe earthquake of October 1989 was centered here, about ten miles north of the town of Santa Cruz. Though the city's downtown commercial center, called the Pacific Garden Mall, was the scene of much damage, most of the community came through okay. So in spite of what all the pictures on the TV news might have suggested, most landmarks came through unscathed. This includes such landmarks as the old wooden roller coaster on the Boardwalk and the other destinations in this chapter.

Once a beach playground for residents of Northern and Central California, Santa Cruz is now a financial and commercial center with a major university and a growing high-tech industry. At the same time the town and the namesake county feature fun beaches, rugged coastline, beautiful beautiful forests, thriving farms, and funky remnants of the 1960s. The county has bounced back from the devastating emotional and physical toll of the earthquake and offers much for the visitor.

Route 17 south of San Jose is the main route from San Francisco, taking you over the Santa Cruz mountains on a winding, at times treacherous, road. An alternative way is to take Route 1; it is slower but does take you along the scenic coast.

Of all the stories that have appeared on the *Bay Area Backroads* television program, none has received as many inquiries for directions as the Corralitos Market and Sausage Company. I don't know what to make of this. Maybe people in the Bay Area are addicted to sausage; perhaps they're simply fascinated by the

CORRALITOS SMOKEHOUSE

idea of a small town where the main attraction is a combination grocery store and smokehouse.

The Corralitos Market is tucked away in a small town called Corralitos in the Santa Cruz Mountains. It is a family-run business, an all-purpose community store with bread and milk in front and a terrific smokehouse in back. The owner, Joe Cutler, wiped his hands on his white apron and took a break to show me around. I saw the slabs of curing bacon and sausages smoking slowly over applewood from Joe's own orchard. In another room were chickens being prepared for the smokehouse. Not an artificial ingredient or shortcut in the process, just the sweet smell of burning applewood mingling with smoking meats.

After a tour of the place, we stepped outside and talked about the rest of the town, which seems to be slowly dissolving into an extension of nearby Watsonville. Pointing in all directions, Joe talked about the many farms that used to surround the few buildings of downtown Corralitos and observed that the apple trees are being replaced by TV antennas. All this seems to make Joe even more determined to hold out. He says there will be no TV antennas atop the Corralitos Market in his lifetime.

CORRALITOS MARKET AND SAUSAGE COMPANY, *569 Corralitos Road, Corralitos. Phone: (408) 722-2633. Open 9 A.M. to 6 P.M. Monday through Friday, 9 A.M. to 5 P.M. Saturday and Sunday.*

HOW TO GET TO THE CORRALITOS MARKET: *From San Francisco, Route 101 South toward San Jose. Exit at Route 17. Follow Route 17 South to Route 1 at Santa Cruz and continue south to the Freedom Boulevard exit. You will cross over the freeway and continue down Freedom for about 5 miles to Corralitos Road. Turn left and continue to the end of the road (about 2 miles); you will see the market on your left. Corralitos is about a 30-minute drive inland from Santa Cruz.*

PICK-YOUR-OWN-FRUIT
②

Your image of Santa Cruz may well be that of the boardwalk, surfers, and beach boys, but if you go just a few miles in almost any direction you will soon see that this is farm country. On just about every hillside you see something growing for the dinner table. There are more artichokes in this region than anywhere else in the country. The combination of sunny days and cool, foggy nights is also perfect for Brussels sprouts, lettuce, kiwis, and pumpkins. And if you travel inland to the area around Watsonville, there are many farms specializing in fruits.

If you'd like to visit a working farm and enjoy its bounty, Gizdich Farms is a worthwhile destination. If you choose, you can pick your own apples off a tree or berries off a bush. The people who run the place will send you off on your own with a bucket, after making sure you know how to pick fruit without destroying the rest of the plant. Picking fruit may sound simple, but even a guy like me who

Santa Cruz

Santa Cruz

Watsonville

grew up in Indiana was surprised to find that there's a right way and a wrong way to pick an apple. You don't yank; it takes the finesse of an upward flick of the wrist.

Even those not inclined to pick fruit enjoy visiting with Nita Gizdich. She runs the place and her sons are her top hands. Nita is a charming hostess who loves to show people around her very attractive farm. In addition to orchards, there are barns with the latest equipment. Nita showed me her coring machine, which can core 58 apples in a minute. The apples are not cored in vain; they get turned into some of the best apple cider and apple pie you've ever tasted.

Gizdich Farms also offer special events to celebrate each crop. Fall is the apple time; springtime is for berries—strawberries, olallies, and raspberries. Again, you can pick them yourself or buy already picked fruits or jellies. And if you visit when the farm is not too busy, there are carriage rides for the kids.

GIZDICH FARMS, *55 Peckham Road, Watsonville. Phone: (408) 722-1056. Open for the spring berry harvest from 8 A.M. to 5 P.M. every day, May through June; open for the fall apple harvest from 9 A.M. to 5 P.M. every day from September through January. Closed Christmas afternoon and from February through April. The seasonal schedule may vary by a week or so, depending on when the crop is ready, so it is a good idea to call ahead.*

HOW TO GET TO GIZDICH FARMS: *From San Francisco, take Highway 101 South to Gilroy. Take the Route 152 West exit and go over the Hecker Pass toward Watsonville. This is well past Fortino's and the other wineries of the South Santa Clara Valley. Continue to Carlton Road and turn left. Soon you will see signs directing you to Gizdich Farms (the entrance you use depends on which crop is in season).*

CAPITOLA
(3)

Just 3 miles south of Santa Cruz is a sweet little beach town. Capitola was built as a resort community in the late 1800s. Whereas almost every nineteenth-century California community had a major fire or flood, Capitola escaped such a fate. As a result, there was never any need for urban renewal. Today you will see the town dotted with the original summer cottages and Victorian homes and, most significant for tourists, very narrow streets, which were built for horse-drawn wagon traffic. Thus, on a warm day, especially during the summer, there are immense traffic jams.

I was taken around town by Sandy Lydon, a historian who teaches at nearby Cabrillo College. As he teaches in his local history lectures, Capitola was originally a haven for people from the steaming inland cities of Fresno, Modesto, and Madera who came to the beach to escape the sun. Trains would bring folks in from the valleys to sit on the foggy beach and cool off. Even when the sun would burn through the coastline fog, visitors would sit on the beach fully clothed. That's because in those days pale skin was a sign of luxury; tan skin meant you were a humble farmworker.

After Coco Chanel and Douglas Fairbanks popularized the suntan as a symbol of prosperity and health, bathing suits appeared on the beach. Nowadays during foggy times visitors to the area hang out in one of the many restaurants or boutiques in town, most of which are right on the beach.

Sandy took me upon one of the many hills above Capitola for what he considers the best way to see the town. From above you can see the little town that once had grand plans. Somebody thought the place would be the ideal location for the state capital, hence the name. You can see the remains of the original municipal wharf, much of which was washed away (a section has been restored and is a magnet for fishermen); the original railroad trestle, below which is a small historical museum; and the Esplanade, the elegant name for the walkway along the beach. You can also see what Sandy calls "the first condos in California": a string of Venetian-style court apartments built in 1924; these connecting housing units have been individualized by colorful paint jobs.

In the mid-1980s the yuppies discovered Capitola. According to Sandy, the measure of yuppiedom is the number of espresso machines within a given radius. He claims there are more espresso machines in Capitola than in any village in the South Bay. If his definition is right, I admit that I'm a yuppie after all. Spring and fall are the best times to visit, but no matter when you come, park in the first space you find when you get close to town. Parking is difficult all year-round. Capitola is small, and it is easy to walk to the beach and commercial area.

CAPITOLA, *right off Route 1, a short drive south of Santa Cruz.*

HOW TO GET TO CAPITOLA: *From San Francisco, follow the directions to Santa Cruz and continue on Route 1 South until you come to the Capitola exit, about 10 minutes from Santa Cruz.*

MYSTERY SPOT

I'm a sucker for hokey places, and there is nothing hokier in Northern California than the Santa Cruz Mystery Spot. It's a tourist attraction that should be approached with a sense of humor and a sense of affection for the times when we were more easily entertained. This pre-high-tech amusement (it opened in the 1940s) is designed to give you your money's worth.

The tour starts at a painted white line marking the spot where the mystery begins. Stand on one side of the line and you are shorter than your guide; stand on the other side and you are taller. Intrigued?

Next you start the long hike up a paved path to the mystery house. As you turn a corner, it suddenly gets harder and harder to walk, as if something is pushing you back down the hill. It's just "the Force," your guide will tell you knowingly.

At the top of the hill you come to a little cabinlike house that looks like it is about to slide down the hill—just held up by the Force, the guide will explain. Inside, everything is on a slant, and it is difficult to walk upright and keep your balance. Like a carnival fun house, the place is designed to make your perceptions go haywire. Hold a purse by its shoulder strap and it appears to rise; roll a golf ball down a slanted board and it will stop and, seeming to defy gravity, roll back up.

Personally, I have a weak stomach and found it hard to keep my lunch inside the place, so I waited outside while the others in my group frolicked inside. A busload of Japanese tourists were having the time of their lives. They couldn't figure it out any more than I could, but so what? I don't want to know how it works. Mysteries are more fun when they stay mysteries.

SANTA CRUZ MYSTERY SPOT, *4 miles north of Santa Cruz, on Branciforte Road. Phone: (408) 423-8897 or 426-1282. Open 9:30 A.M. to 5 P.M. daily; last tour at 4:30 P.M. Admission: Adults, $3.00; children 5 to 11, $1.50; under 5, free.*

HOW TO GET TO THE MYSTERY SPOT: *From San Francisco, take Highway 101 South to Highway 280, then Route 17 South toward Santa Cruz. Before entering Santa Cruz, at Scotts Valley, exit onto Glen Canyon Road and head east, to the left of the freeway. Follow Glen Canyon Road to Branciforte Drive and turn left. Then watch for signs for the Mystery Spot.*

CALIFORNIA'S CONEY ISLAND ⑤

There are beaches, and there are beaches. Some beaches are warm and timeless expanses of sand, like you'll find in the Caribbean. Others are rugged, down-jacket-in-the-summer affairs, surrounded by craggy cliffs, the kind of beach you'll find at Big Sur, further north near Mendocino, and on the Oregon coast.

Then there are the "nostalgia beaches," the kind that are caught in a time warp of the early- and mid-twentieth century, with rides and hotdogs and the smell of Coppertone. This is the kind of beach you'll find at the Boardwalk in Santa Cruz.

Santa Cruz became a beach resort before the turn of the century when the rail barons in San Francisco set the town up as a day trip destination. Then some entrepreneurial type set up some tents on the beach and charged the surf bathers 2 cents for changing their clothes in privacy. Not far behind were the developers who built a classy amusement strip, complete with a beautiful carousel, a heart-stopping roller coaster, and the opulent Coconut Grove, a dance hall where the great big bands came to play and ladies in evening gowns came to dance.

Today the city hosts a major university, beautiful homes, and scads of motels and restaurants. There is no grand hotel here, perhaps due to the town's original design as a day-trip destination.

Several years ago, a great deal of money and effort were spent to spiff up the Boardwalk. Now it's one of the last old-fashioned amusement parks left on the West Coast, and if you like this sort of thing, it's a pleasure to visit. The historic carousel, complete with brass rings (if you grab one while riding the carousel and successfully toss it through a hole, you get a free ride) has been restored; each carousel animal is a museum piece, and the original Wurlitzer still plays. The Big Dipper, a world-famous roller coaster, is still in action, and the Coconut Grove is open for dancing in the dark.

As you walk down the Boardwalk itself, past the corn dog stands, bikini emporiums, and souvenir shops, you might notice the name Marini. Joe Marini has sold saltwater taffy here since the 1920s, so successfully that he and his sons have opened several kinds of businesses bearing the family name on the Boardwalk. In front of the Marini saltwater taffy shop is one of the attractions of the Boardwalk: the automatic taffy-pulling machine. People watch this contraption for hours. The stretchy candy batter drops off one blade and—ooops—gets caught just in time by another blade, endlessly, or until the candy is ready to be packaged into bite-sized pieces. By the way, Joe assures me there is no saltwater in the taffy. The name came from Coney Island, where a taffy stand caught fire and water had to be pumped from the Atlantic to put out the blaze. The clever entrepreneur put up a sign advertising "saltwater taffy," and the name stuck.

There's no admission charge to the Boardwalk. You can spend what you dare on miniature golf, bumper cars, and sno-cones. If you visit on a weekday in winter, most of the rides and fast-food stands will be closed. That, too, makes for an interesting visit. You can stroll along the beach and just imagine all the laughing children and the roar of the Big Dipper as the cars speed along the roller coaster. The Boardwalk beach is adjacent to the Municipal Wharf, where you will find souvenir shops, informal diners, and nice restaurants, and probably some seals waiting for generous tourists and fishermen and women to feed them.

SANTA CRUZ BOARDWALK, *at the main beach, Santa Cruz. Phone: (408) 426-7433. Open daily to 10 P.M. during the summer; on weekends and holidays the rest of the year, including Easter Week. Admission: Free.*

HOW TO GET TO THE BOARDWALK: *From San Francisco, take Highway 101 South to Highway 280. Follow Route 280 to Route 17 South to Santa Cruz. Exit for the municipal center and the beaches. You will be on Ocean Avenue. Follow Ocean to the end; then turn right. At the first stoplight, turn left on Riverside. At the first stop sign, turn right. Then at the next stop sign, turn left again (there is a series of one-way streets to deal with). You will now be heading directly toward the Coconut Grove. Turn left on Beach Street and park in the lot on the left.*

UCSC ARBORETUM

The University of California at Santa Cruz has one of the most beautiful campuses I have ever seen. With its various buildings hidden from the road by redwood trees and surrounded by hillside meadows, it's like going to school in a national park. Tours are offered all year-round, but if you only have enough time to see one thing, make it the arboretum, which takes up 150 acres on the west side of campus.

Even if you don't have a green thumb, this is a beautiful place to enjoy nature, a getaway from the bustle down the hill at the beach and in downtown Santa Cruz. The climate here is perfect for growing the nation's largest collection of plants native to the Mediterranean, South Africa, New Zealand, and Australia. This arboretum is blessed with an incredible range of soil conditions and temperatures, some areas filled with warm sun, other valley sections dipping to temperatures as low as 18 degrees in winter. As a university project, the main function of the arboretum is to experiment with new kinds of plants for this region and to pass this newfound knowledge on to those who make a living in the plant and flower industry. The arboretum staff has introduced more than 200 new plants to the United States.

The protea garden alone is worth the trip. These spectacular plants, which sell for as much as $20 apiece in some flower shops, grow in an unimaginable variety of sizes, shapes, and colors. The arboretum's output of proteas is outranked only by South Africa's.

The Australian gardens have the feeling of the Outback, with a thick growth of exotic plants, bushes, and trees that you will find nowhere else but "down under" and at UCSC. This includes some 70 species of eucalyptus trees.

The staff—a few paid employees and many volunteers—consists mostly of folks who either are associated with the university or are local residents who want to spend their spare time in the gardens. My guide was a gentleman with the wonderful name Linton von Beroldingen, who turned out to be the retired editor of the *San Francisco Examiner*. He told me that the daily grind of newspaper life can't hold a candle to the excitement he has found learning about life in the arboretum.

If you do have any questions about gardening or want to learn how to introduce new life into your garden, Linton or any other member of the staff will be glad to help you. Staff members are also available for tours and advice on Saturday, Sunday, and Wednesday afternoons.

UCSC ARBORETUM, *on the campus of the University of California, Santa Cruz. Phone: (408) 427-1305 or (408) 426-8750. Open to the public 2 to 4 P.M. Wednes-*

day, Saturday, and Sunday. Admission: Free. The university admissions office conducts two-hour tours of the entire campus twice each weekday throughout the year; for a reservation, call (408) 429-4008.

HOW TO GET TO THE ARBORETUM: *From San Francisco, take Highway 101 South to Route 280 to Route 17 to Santa Cruz. Exit on Route 1 North, which is Mission Street. Follow Mission to Bay Street and turn right. Take Bay to the main campus gate. Turn left on High Street, which changes its name to Empire Grade Road. It's a short ride to the arboretum, which will be on your right.*

LONG MARINE LAB

One of the great tourist attractions in the South Bay is the Monterey Bay Aquarium in Monterey. What most people don't know, however, is that there's another marine wonderland at the north end of the same bay, in Santa Cruz. Though it's on a smaller scale than its counterpart to the south, the Joseph M. Long Marine Laboratory is rarely, if ever, crowded, needs no reservations, and is free.

Situated right on the beach on a 40-acre site of land, wetlands, and marine terraces, this facility is run by the Center for Marine Studies at the University of California, Santa Cruz. This is a study center for marine ecology and marine mammal behavior. Trainers and scientists work with dolphins and sea lions daily, learning more and more about such things as communication and survival. It is a highly sophisticated research center; it's also one of the few marine labs on the West Coast that allows visitors to watch undergraduate and postgraduate trainers and researchers in action. Visitors can get very close to this free show.

The tour is led by one of more than 80 docent volunteers. It begins in a small indoor aquarium that highlights the marine creatures that live in Monterey Bay. First stop is an open touching tank. Adults usually shudder and squirm, while kids immediately plunge their arms in to pick up a crab or a starfish. The tour continues past 20 or so other tanks filled with interesting critters. Magnifying glasses are available for close-up views.

After the aquarium section comes a visit to the outdoor tanks. The day I was there I was able to watch the sea lions go through the paces of a communications experiment with their trainer. Next door was a tank of rare Alaskan fur seals, about to be sent back home to the Pribiloff Islands after the completion of a round of experiments. The stars of the show, the dolphins, were viewed from a platform overlooking their tanks.

The tour ends in a small museum featuring whale and shark bones and teeth, plus a gift shop. Visitors are encouraged to come to the lab. This is a comparatively new facility, only about 10 years old and still growing. Plans call for a large visitor's center with even more exhibits and an auditorium for lectures and movies. Tours last about an hour.

The lab is located next to Natural Bridges State Park, a place I also recommend, especially at wintertime, when this becomes a favorite spot for monarch butterflies. On a cool day they will be everywhere.

JOSEPH M. LONG MARINE LABORATORY, *100 Shaffer Road, Santa Cruz. Phone: (408) 429-4308. Open for tours 1 to 4 P.M. Tuesday through Saturday; closed holidays. Appointments necessary only for groups of 10 or more. Admission: Free.*

HOW TO GET TO THE MARINE LABORATORY: *From San Francisco, take Route 101 South to Route 280, then Route 17 South to Santa Cruz. Exit onto Route 1, heading north toward Half Moon Bay. This is also called Mission Boulevard. Turn left at Swift Street to Delaware Avenue. Turn right on Delaware and continue to the entrance of the lab.*

An alternate route is to take Route 1 from San Francisco all the way down the coast into Santa Cruz. At Swift, turn right and follow to Delaware. Turn right on Delaware.

SURFING MUSEUM
(8)

Thirty years before the Beach Boys were even born, a group of die-hard surfing enthusiasts caught the waves on the beach of Santa Cruz. Today they are among the volunteers at what is probably the only museum in the continental United States devoted to the sport of surfing.

In this brick lighthouse high on a bluff above a surfing beach below, you're likely to meet Dave "Buster" Stewart, Harry Mayo, and Bill Grace. They're all pushing 70 now and are full of stories about the days on the beach before fiberglass and wetsuits. In the 1930s, with the music of Glenn Miller in their heads, they lugged 100-pound boards around; to keep warm, they wore old-fashioned wool-knit bathing suits they found at the Goodwill. There's a picture of their club on the wall, taken about 1941, not long before they all went to fight in World War II. Some of the boys in the picture didn't come back.

Harry, the museum's unofficial historian, says the parents thought their sons were crazy and were certain these pioneer beach boys wouldn't amount to anything in life. Bill's father expressed his opinion of his son's surfing buddies when he said, "When you sleep with dogs, you get fleas."

Well, today the gang is less muscled, less hairy, and more bi-focaled than they were in the photograph, but at least they can laugh and say they all turned out OK. One's a retired fireman; the other two were businessmen. They still talk with a gleam in their eyes about the joy only catching a wave can bring, even though most gave up surfing years ago. When I asked if they ever wish they could get back on their boards just once more, sweet sad smiles of longing accompanied their affirmative answers.

You'll bump into surfers of all ages at the museum. But if you want to get the story from the real pioneers, just look for the old-timers with the wistful looks. The museum itself is small, but chock full of photographs, newspaper and magazine clippings, surfboards of every age and size, all housed in a lighthouse on the ocean. And when the weather is right, the new breed will be surfing right below the museum.

THE SURF MUSEUM, *Lighthouse Point, Santa Cruz. Phone: (408) 429-3429. Open hours are iffy since staffing is solely by volunteers and sometimes someone has to miss a shift, but general hours are noon to 5 P.M. daily. Admission: Free.*

HOW TO GET TO THE SURF MUSEUM: *From San Francisco, take Highway 101 South to Route 280, then head south on Route 17 to Santa Cruz. Take the downtown Santa Cruz exit onto Ocean Street. Follow Ocean to Water Street and turn right. Take Water to Front Street and turn left toward the ocean; keep to the right for the ramp up to West Cliff Road. This is where the large Dream Inn Hotel is. Take West Cliff to the right until you arrive at the lighthouse.*

"THE LAST SUPPER" IN WAX

Santa Cruz is probably the last place in the world you would expect to find a tribute to the work of Leonardo da Vinci, yet here it is, as big as life. This version of "The Last Supper" is in the gallery of the Art League of Santa Cruz, an organization run by very nice elderly ladies. These ladies would look totally out of place on the boardwalk or nearby beaches, but they have a tourist destination of their own to occupy their time: a life-size wax replica of the Leonardo masterpiece.

All of the figures from the famous meal are there, seated around a table loaded with wax food. Jesus awaits betrayal, Judas with his moneybags looks the other way, just like in the original in Milan. The figures are very lifelike, down to details like the hair, reportedly put into place strand by strand.

When "The Last Supper" was unveiled in Santa Cruz in 1951, it was national news; more than a million pilgrims from around the world have come to see it. Though the idea may sound a bit bizarre, it is presented quite tastefully. A friend who went to the University of California at Santa Cruz says he always wanted to sneak in one day and put a bottle of ketchup on the table, but so far the waxwork has escaped vandalism and pranks.

THE LAST SUPPER, *in Santa Cruz Art League Galleries, 526 Broadway, Santa Cruz. Phone: (408) 426-5787. Open 11 A.M. to 4 P.M. Tuesday through Sunday; closed Monday. Admission: Free, but donations are requested.*

HOW TO GET TO THE LAST SUPPER: *Follow the directions to Santa Cruz, but take the exit to the municipal center and beaches (not Highway 1 North). You will be on Ocean Avenue. Continue on Ocean to Broadway and turn left. There will be a sign pointing to The Last Supper.*

ROARING CAMP AND BIG TREES RAILWAY

The most scenic route in these parts is to be seen by rail, and a very old-fashioned railroad at that. Lumberjacks rode these narrow-gauge rails in the 1880s on their way to and from work; so did Teddy Roosevelt, on a whistlestop campaign tour. Until 1941, families on an outing could pack a picnic lunch, ride these rails on the "Suntan Special" to the beach at Santa Cruz, and return home by nightfall. Then passenger service stopped; for years this scenic railway service simply traveled a 5-mile loop past the Big Trees, the first grove of redwoods to be preserved as a tourist attraction.

But in 1986 the necessary negotiations and paperwork were completed, and the Santa Cruz, Big Trees, and Pacific Railway Company was again in the business of taking visitors all the way to the beach at Santa Cruz and back. The trip begins at Roaring Camp, a re-created 1880s Western village just outside the town of Felton. You enter by walking across the oldest covered bridge in California; then you'll find a snack bar, the obligatory souvenir shop, a general store, and a lovely picnic area with lots of lawn, tables, and a duck pond.

But the real reason to come here is to see and ride the steam trains, all of them built around the turn of the century. The main ride, up 6 ½ miles of narrow-gauge track, takes about an hour and 15 minutes, round trip, and offers a chance to stop and picnic in the woods. The round trip to Santa Cruz takes two hours, if you stay on board and head right back. You can also disembark for a day at the beach and return to Roaring Camp and your car later. Both rides take you through a virgin forest of coastal redwoods, and you'll see the generations-old tourist attraction of the Big Trees, purchased in 1867 by a San Francisco businessman who wanted to be sure these natural monuments would not fall prey to the lumber industry. As the train chugs up the steepest narrow-gauge railroad grade in North America, you can sit inside the railroad cars or, if the weather is pleasant, head out to one of the open flatbed cars to breathe some of the freshest air in this part of the world. Tour guides will fill you in on the history of the place and identify the passing trees and plant life.

ROARING CAMP AND BIG TREES NARROW-GAUGE RAILROAD, *Felton. Phone: (408) 335-4400. Trains run every day of the year except Christmas. Round-trip fare: Adults, $10.50; children 5 to 17, $7.50; under 5, free. Daily schedule varies according to the time of the year, so call ahead.*

HOW TO GET TO THE ROARING CAMP RAILROAD: *From San Francisco, take Highway 101 South to Highway 280 to Highway 17 toward Santa Cruz. Exit at Mount Hermon Road and follow it into Felton. Turn south (left) on Graham Hill Road to the entrance, which will be on your right.*

Ever heard of Flying Cigar Wine? How about Clos de Gilroy? These are the creations of one of the more unusual and entertaining wine producers in California. He's Randall Grahm, and he's headquartered, appropriately, in the attractive and eccentric Santa Cruz hills in the town of Bonny Doon.

You will find the place by driving about five minutes inland from the ocean until you come to a sign that says "Welcome to Bonny Doon." Then, after you pass the winery tasting room across the street, you will see another sign that says, "You are leaving Bonny Doon." That will give you some idea of the nature of the place.

The tasting room used to be the Lost Weekend Saloon, a notorious hangout for the bikers who zoom around these hills. Randall says that every so often a big, burly guy on a Harley will stagger into the place, look around bewildered, and then roar away. Once in a while, though, the biggest, meanest biker will wander in, sample a glass of white wine, and carry on a connoisseur's discussion about the relative merits of the vintage.

Most of the visitors, however, are your average backroads adventurers out to explore the countryside. The winery itself is on a hill above the tasting room, where you will probably encounter Randall and his very small staff. Someone will make time to give you a tour that is so folksy that you might imagine yourself opening your own little winery. A tour of the grounds, where you will see some old barrels, some storage equipment, and a basketball court, is rounded out by the sight and sound of the neighbor's turkey ranch. In other words, this is not your typical boutique wine operation.

You'll probably want to end up back in the tasting room or at one of the picnic tables in this lovely and remote wooded area. If the opportunity presents itself, engage Randall in a conversation. He's an original: a long-haired, disarming former Los Angeleno who once considered becoming an alchemist but instead has won a national reputation for his Bordeaux-style claret, his burgundy-style chardonnay, and Le Sophiste–Cuvée Philosophique, his own white table wine.

Though he makes serious and not inexpensive wine (he is one of the few American winemakers who closely follows the traditional bordeaux way of growing grapes and making wine), he likes to give them funny names. He has been known to barge into fancy New York restaurants with bottles in a milk delivery basket, offering tastes to owners and chefs. His top salesperson is his mother, whom he calls "the terror of the L.A. wine market."

BONNY DOON WINERY, *10 Pine Flat Road, Bonny Doon. Phone: (408) 425-3625. Tasting room open May 1 through October 1, Wednesday through Monday noon to 5:30 P.M.; closed Tuesday. Winter hours: Friday through Sunday, noon to 5:30 P.M. Tours by appointment only.*

HOW TO GET TO BONNY DOON WINERY: *From San Francisco, follow the directions to Año Nuevo Beach and continue down Route 1 past the town of Davenport to Bonny Doon Road. Turn left and the winery is 3.7 miles away on the right-hand side of the road.*

Two major bridges connect San Francisco to the rest of the Bay Area. We have already used the Golden Gate Bridge as our link to Marin, Napa, and Sonoma; now we will use the larger, more heavily traveled Bay Bridge to take us to the broad area called the East Bay. For our purposes this will include Alameda County with the major cities of Oakland and Berkeley; Contra Costa County, farther east, featuring a vast suburban sprawl reminiscent of the San Fernando Valley; the counties of Solano and Yolo, whose promotional agencies have banded together as "Yolano" to offer tourists a Farm Trails guide of places to visit; and last but not least, the Sacramento Delta.

Much of this area is practically ignored by most visitors. People from Chicago or Rome usually don't make it out to Hayward or Walnut Creek or the Delta. But they are missing out on a scenic and cultural diversity that is truly wonderful. Here you will find touches of the Old West, the Deep South, and the American heartland. The spaces are wider open than anywhere else near San Francisco. And in this setting the attractions are surprising. The closest East Bay destinations are in Alameda County, just over the Bay Bridge. If you avoid the rush hour from 4 to 6 P.M. weekdays, the trip will take you about a half hour from the city to the rolling hills of Tilden Park above Berkeley. Most of Contra Costa

County is reached by driving through the Caldecott Tunnel north beyond Berkeley and, again in ideal traffic conditions, can be reached within an hour. Keep in mind that once you travel through the tunnel, you will be in another climatic zone; the weather will usually be 10 to 20 degrees warmer than in San Francisco. Hayward and Fremont are also about an hour from San Francisco, to the south of Berkeley. They are also much warmer than San Francisco. Solano County destinations such as Vallejo and Fairfield can be reached in an hour or so from San Francisco, whereas such Yolo County destinations as Woodland will add another 30 minutes to the trip. The Delta begins about 90 minutes from San Francisco.

Once you cross the Bay Bridge, the major highways will be Route 80 to the north, Route 580 to the east, and Routes 880 and 680 to the south.

CHAPTER **7** Alameda County

AREA OVERVIEW

Alameda offers the most contrasts of any county in the Bay Area. There are the major cities of Oakland and Berkeley to the north, Hayward and Fremont to the south, and the booming suburbs of Dublin and Pleasanton with their gleaming new industrial parks and roadside hotels. In between all these population centers, there are miles of untouched land, thousands of acres of protected parks, even some hidden lakes.

As you'd expect, the major action is near the main roads, Route 80 up to Berkeley, Routes 880 and 580 through Oakland and Hayward, Routes 580 and 680 through Pleasanton and Livermore. But away from these busy highways, you'll find one of the earliest wine countries in Northern California, the state's first major film community, the highest concentration of Ph.D.'s in the world, a Hindu shrine, and many more surprises.

TREASURE ISLAND
①

To tell the truth, Treasure Island is technically in San Francisco County. But when you leave San Francisco heading toward Alameda County via the Bay Bridge, it is your first possible stop, and it feels like you're in the next county. Amazingly, hundreds of thousands of motorists whiz by the Treasure Island exit and have never made the turnoff to visit. They are missing something wonderful.

Most of the island is now a naval base, but at one time it was a world-famous attraction. Treasure Island is one of the largest artificial islands in the world, created from tons of silt from San Francisco Bay and the Sacramento Delta to be

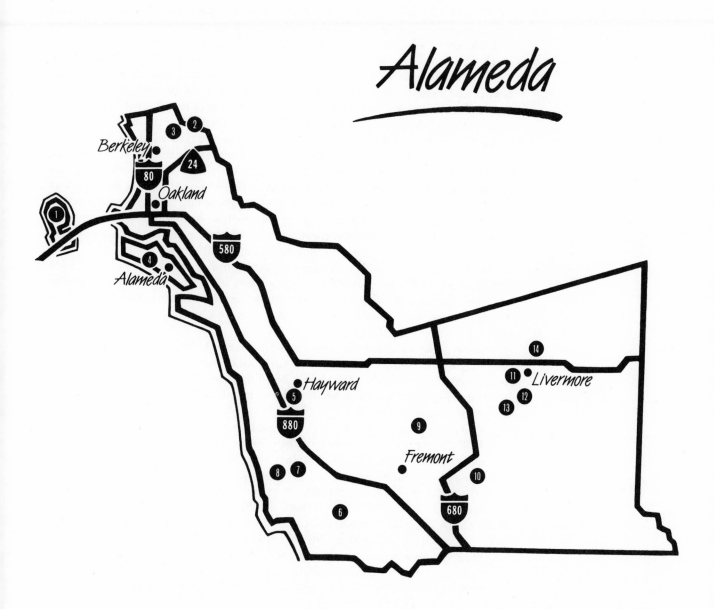

Alameda

the site of the 1939 World's Fair, or Golden Gate Exposition, as it was also called. There was competition from the New York World's Fair of 1939, but in 12 months some 10 million people descended on the island.

Let's set the scene a bit more. In 1939 the country was coming out of the Great Depression; two new bridges had just been constructed (the Bay Bridge and the Golden Gate), connecting the city of San Francisco with land to the east and north; and there were hopes of a new alliance with the nations of the Pacific. The Golden Gate Exposition was to herald a new era of Pan-Pacific partnership. Only two years later, the attack on Pearl Harbor would alter those plans.

In the meantime, optimism hung in the air like the colored lights all over the new island. The fair had everything: rides, fireworks, gardens, industrial exhibits, and entertainment extravaganzas like Billy Rose's Aquacade and Sally Rand's Nude Dude Ranch. In 1989, many of those memories were rekindled as the area celebrated the 50th anniversary of the great fair. This renewed interest led to the renovation of about 20 giant statues that had been stored away in a warehouse. As of this writing, there are plans to move these sculptures, called the People of the Pacific, outside Building One for all to see.

After the fair, the island was supposed to become an airport. The famed China Clipper had landed here, delivering passengers to the fair from the Orient. But the site was soon discovered to be too windy and too close to the Bay Bridge to be safe for regular commercial air traffic, so the city leased the island to the Navy. Now it is federal land.

Almost all of the glitzy, futuristic buildings from the fair have been torn down, and only three original structures remain. Two of them are hangars, which were to be used for the airport. The other is Building One, the original fair administration building, which was to be the airport terminal building. Now it houses a museum open to the public.

The Treasure Island Museum is well worth a visit, if for nothing else than the unparalleled view of San Francisco from its parking lot. But even better, inside the museum are real treasures. Displays show the building of the island (named for Robert Louis Stevenson's book because dirt from the Sacramento Delta was thought to have gold in it), the history of sea services in the Pacific, and, most interesting to me, memorabilia from the fair. I could spend hours combing through the old ads, buttons, postcards, and photos from the ambitious exposition. I am happy to say that this World's Fair exhibit, which had once been temporary, is now a permanent part of the museum.

TREASURE ISLAND MUSEUM, *on Treasure Island. Phone: (415) 765-6182. Open seven days a week from 10 A.M. to 3:30 P.M.; closed on federal holidays. Admission: Free. Wheelchair accessible.*

HOW TO GET TO TREASURE ISLAND: *From San Francisco, get on the Bay Bridge;*

stay in the left-hand lane and midway across look for the Treasure Island exit (it is a left-side exit). Follow the road signs to Building One. If you are stopped by a guard at the gatehouse, simply say you're going to the museum.

Two thousand-acre Tilden Park is the closest thing to a wilderness area you can find in the center of the Bay Area. Unlike Golden Gate Park, with its manicured lawns and distinctly urban atmosphere, Tilden offers expanses of wooded hillsides, grassy meadows, and a variety of trails where you can be virtually alone in the hills of Berkeley and Oakland.

If you are not looking for solitude, Tilden Park also features an antique carousel, Anza Lake for swimming and sunbathing, the aptly named Inspiration Point (located on a very popular jogging trail), a golf course, and tennis courts.

There are three additional attractions in Tilden Park that I'd like to highlight. Each one alone is worth a trip over to the East Bay.

✔ **Miniature Train Rides.** The first of these additional attractions is tucked away in the south section of the huge park. Here you'll find two—count 'em—two separate collections of old-fashioned steam trains. The first is the Redwood Valley Railway. It has been in operation for nearly 40 years, taking children and their parents on a 15-minute ride through the trees of Tilden Park. You ride in open cars while the steam engine chugs its way through the woods. The engineers and train operators are dressed in authentic railroad uniforms (just like in the movies), and when they yell "All aboard!" it's a thrill to see the excitement on the faces of the passengers.

Eric Thompson owns and runs the railroad and has been working on this rail long enough to have seen generations of Bay Area kids take their first train ride at Tilden. His daughter is now one of the conductors. Eric charges only $1 for the ride, but he says even that embarrasses him because he can remember when the ride cost only a nickel. If you thought video games, space travel, and television were the only things kids are interested in these days, you're in for a pleasant surprise. Business is brisk enough that Eric would like to add more trains.

Downhill, just below the platform of the Redwood Valley Line is where you'll find the Golden Gate Steamers. This is a club of train lovers who build their own miniatures—scale models of actual trains that once traveled in the Wild West. Club members bring their creations from home to tinker and then run them on the club's 1½-mile track.

This attraction is quite different from the professional operation up the hill. Though the Steamers do offer free rides on the one train set strong enough to carry a passenger load, you're never quite sure when a train might be running. Here the attraction is the fun of watching these guys work on their hobby and to see the beautiful miniature trains they have created. Every member is a combination of engine builder, engineer, maintenance person, and conductor. It's wonderful to watch these club members—retirees, history buffs, amateur mechanics—working away on their creations and using toy-sized shovels to put tiny pieces of coal into their engines. The trains vary in size, but most cars are 2- to 10-feet long and only a few feet off the ground. They are short enough to make the men running them look like adults on kids' bikes; it's not uncommon to see two elderly gents in greasy overalls riding the rails with their knees up against their chest.

Although the rides given to the public are free, donations are gratefully accepted; the money goes to keep the facility, which involves quite a lot of track plus an intricate series of connecting portable tracks that can be rolled around the inside of the main track to act as work stations. I should mention that the intricate engines are perfect in detail, the result of exacting, painstaking, and time-consuming work. The members have every reason to be proud of their trains.

✓ **Native California Plant Garden.** The next stop, by car, will be the Botanical Gardens, about 10 minutes away from the train area. Here you'll find 6½ acres of land on which you can see the entire state of California, horticulturally speaking. The garden represents every plant that grows naturally in the state.

Pick up a brochure at the visitor's center and it's easy to give yourself a tour. One path takes you to the desert area, where you'll find a variety of cacti and succulents. Then maybe you'll want to visit the redwoods, the Shasta Cascades, or the sea bluff regions. Remember, you'll find the plants native to the regions, not all those trees and shrubs brought into California by people who moved here from back East.

The Botanical Gardens also serve an important function of preserving endangered plants. For example, there is more of the once prominent manzanita in the garden than remains elsewhere in the entire state. The garden paths are easy to walk, and each plant is clearly labeled.

It takes four visits to really see the garden, one visit each season. In fact, the Tilden Botanical Gardens is one of the few places in the Bay Area where you can see a dramatic change from season to season. All year-round there is something to see: a solid wall of flowers at the sea bluff in spring, coastal plants in bloom all summer, and colors in fall. Steve Edwards, the director of the gardens, says his favorite time is in winter right after a rainstorm; the creek suddenly becomes 6 to 8 feet deep, and an area that is dry and warm in the summer is suddenly filled with the rushing sound of high water.

✔ **The Little Farm.** The third stop within Tilden Park is in the north end of the park. Everyone who lives in the Bay Area has heard the commercial for a local milk company that ends with a slogan, "Farms, in Berkeley?" Well, even though the farms that used to dot the university town are long gone, there is one very lovely working farm within Berkeley's city limits. Luckily for us, this farm is set up for visitors, complete with park rangers and naturalist who work with the animals and give tours for people.

The Little Farm is a good name. The place is, well, little, and quite manageable. It is also spotlessly clean and reasonably devoid of the odors that can discourage city slickers from breathing deeply. The place was built in the 1950s by a Berkeley High School woodshop class, constructed to half scale so the barns aren't as cavernous (and therefore hard to manage) as the ones you'll find out in the country. It's like Old MacDonald's place had come to life, with chick-chicks here and quack-quacks there, running freely. Don't be alarmed if they charge up to you; they just think you might have something to feed them. In addition you'll find cows, goats, sheep, rabbits, and a donkey who's called the Boss. It has nothing to do with Bruce Springsteen; it's simply that the donkey has been there longer than most of the other animals and knows how to get its own way. My favorite Little Farm animals are two pigs named Broccoli and Tofu. They were named by a visiting schoolboy who thought those names would ensure that the pigs would never be eaten.

The best time to visit is in the morning, between 7 and 10 A.M., when the animals are frisky and eager to be fed. You'll probably also want to stop in next door at the interpretive center. Along with many farm and wilderness exhibits, you'll find a 10-foot stuffed lizard called a Komodo dragon; it's a very popular display.

TILDEN PARK, *Berkeley. General information number: (415) 531-9300.*

TILDEN PARK REDWOOD VALLEY RAILWAY, *Phone: (415) 548-6100. Runs from 11 A.M. to dusk on weekends and holidays all year and from 1 to 6 P.M. on weekdays during Easter week and all summer. A ride costs $1 per person. The Golden Gate Steamers set up their own tracks every Sunday, from about noon to 3 P.M., weather permitting. Phone: (415) 540-9264.*

HOW TO GET TO THE TRAINS OF TILDEN: *From San Francisco, take the Bay Bridge to Highway 24, following the signs to Walnut Creek. Take the Claremont Avenue exit. At the stoplight at the bottom of the exit ramp, turn left. Follow Claremont all the way to the major intersection of Claremont and Ashby. The Claremont Hotel will be on the hill on your right. Go straight, ignoring most of the traffic which will veer to the left, and continue alongside the back of the hotel all the way to the top of the hill until you come to Grizzly Peak Boulevard.*

Turn left and after a few minutes or so look for the sign on the right for the Tilden Park steam trains.

TILDEN BOTANICAL GARDENS, *Wildcat Canyon Road near South Park Drive. Phone: (415) 841-8732. Open daily 10 A.M. to 5 P.M. In June through August, free tours start at the visitor's center after lunch (usually 1:30 P.M.); garden tours for groups are available by appointment. Admission: Free.*

HOW TO GET TO THE BOTANICAL GARDENS: *From the steam trains, take the South Park Drive and you will end up at the gardens. There is a small parking lot across the road from the entrance. From San Francisco, follow the directions to the steam trains, but instead of turning off at the train entrance continue on Grizzly Peak Boulevard until you come to the Shasta Road entrance to the park. Turn right and follow the signs to the gardens.*

TILDEN LITTLE FARM, *(415) 525-2233. Open from dawn to 10 P.M. every day; the interpretive center is open from 10 A.M. to 5 P.M. Tuesday through Sunday. Admission: Free.*

HOW TO GET TO THE LITTLE FARM: *From the Botanical Gardens, go back to Grizzly Peak Boulevard and follow all the way to the intersection of Spruce. Turn right and then immediately bear left at a 45-degree angle and follow Canyon Road until you enter the Tilden Nature Area. Technically, this is separate from Tilden Park, but there is no practical difference for the visitor. Park your car at the first lot and walk up to the farm and interpretive center.*

LAWRENCE HALL OF SCIENCE

③

One of the best sunset-viewing spots in the Bay Area is from the parking lot of the Lawrence Hall of Science. Facing west, you have a hilltop view of the Bay, Alcatraz Island, Marin County, San Francisco, and both the Bay and Golden Gate Bridges, all backlit by the setting sun.

But it's worth arriving early to take advantage of the inside of the building serviced by the parking lot. From the outside, the Lawrence Hall of Science looks like a concrete airline bunker. But once you're through the door you'll be in an inviting, open wonderland for the kid in all of us.

The Lawrence Hall of Science is a hands-on science museum. Most of the exhibits are designed for touch and interaction. Computer games illustrate everything from your reaction time to what is in the food you ate for lunch. Two telescopes are open to the public for viewing the heavens, and there's a prehistoric animal exhibit featuring moving, bellowing dinosaurs. In addition, the Hall of Science offers special seasonal programs on a variety of topics. Certainly the most popular of these is the dinosaur exhibit which gets more elaborate and more fun each year. With the help of a Japanese company that makes lifelike computer operated dinosaurs, the great halls are filled with moving animals that are likely to thrill youngsters and scare adults. This usually begins around the

Christmas holidays and continues for a few months. The latest addition is live theater, in which actors dressed as dinosaurs perform a musical play that delights and teaches at the same time.

For me, the most remarkable exhibit came about by chance. It is a life-size replica of the Challenger space shuttle. It sits just outside the main building, poised as if ready to take off any second.

This shuttle model began as a class project at UC Berkeley. A teacher and former NASA scientist, Larry Kuznetz, was so moved by the shuttle tragedy of 1986 that he wanted to create a tribute to the Challenger crew. So as a class project his "Life in Space" students designed and built a shuttle replica. At first the plan was simply to build a papier-mâché and cardboard model on the grass outside the museum. But then the project took on a life of its own. A contractor heard about it and offered to donate some concrete, establishing a solid and permanent foundation. Then a tilemaker came by with some gleaming black-and-white tiles to decorate the exterior. Suddenly the temporary structure became a permanent structure. This caused a conflict with the museum folks, who had not planned or budgeted for a space shuttle on the premises, but there it was. And the craftsmanship was so good that it only made sense to make it part of the Hall of Science.

The most impressive work was done inside. Every button, every switch, every detail of the Challenger has been re-created. There's even a computer program that simulates the navigational function of the craft. You can get an idea of what space pioneers must endure. Clearly, space travel is not for the claustrophobic. First stop on the visit is a chamber where space walkers must stand for several hours until the nitrogen in their bodies is removed before venturing into space. The next door takes you into the main living quarters, a room about the size of a large closet containing sleeping compartments that resemble built-in dresser drawers. When the replica was first built, Larry Kuznetz had to sleep in one of the bunks to protect the shuttle project from nighttime vandals. Upstairs is the cockpit, with seats for a pilot and copilot and room for one or two standing crew members. Again the most remarkable thing is the detail. Looking from the pilot's seat out the front windows, there is the effect of soaring above the Bay Area, especially at night. Tours are available on weekends.

LAWRENCE HALL OF SCIENCE, *University of California, Berkeley. For information about exhibits, phone (415) 642-5133; for booking reservations, call (415) 642-5134. Open Monday through Friday, 10 A.M. to 4:30 P.M.; Saturday 10 A.M. to 5 P.M.; Sunday noon to 5 P.M. Admission: Adults, $3.50; students and seniors, $2.50; under 6, free. Special rates are available for groups of 12 or more; reservations must be made at least four weeks in advance. Wheelchair accessible.*

HOW TO GET TO THE LAWRENCE HALL OF SCIENCE: *From San Francisco, take the Bay Bridge and continue on Route 80 to the University Avenue exit. Follow University several miles until it ends at the edge of the UC Berkeley campus. Turn left, go one block, then turn right on Hearst. Follow Hearst up the hill to Gayley Road and turn right. At the Strawberry Canyon left turn you will see a sign to the Lawrence Hall of Science. Follow the signs up the hill.*

CRAB COVE

Though most people in the Bay Area know there is a county called Alameda, surprisingly few know the town with the same name. This old city, which can be reached only by tunnel or bridge, remains a bit of a mystery. Alameda is an interesting amalgam of old-time sea resort, naval air station, and new condo developments. It also happens to have a fine beach—a narrow, 2-mile strip where you can sun, swim, toss a frisbee, and picnic. And at the western end of the beach you'll find one of the Bay Area's hidden treasures, a small shoreline park officially named Robert Crown Park but more commonly known as Crab Cove.

Run by the East Bay Regional Park District, Crab Cove is the site of what was once a huge amusement park. At the turn of the century this was Neptune Beach, sort of a West Coast Coney Island, a place to ride a carousel, have a clambake, take a romantic promenade. But time was not kind to Neptune Beach, and after the Depression the place was torn down. After years of abuse, the park district took over the land and established the first marine reserve in the state.

The visitor's center is a good place to start a visit to Crab Cove. Here you'll find a large saltwater aquarium so you can see what lives out there in the Bay without having to don scuba equipment. You'll also find exhibits about the marine environment and the history of Alameda, including pictures of long-gone Neptune Beach. Once you are acquainted with the region, park rangers will take you out to the mud flats to show you firsthand what you saw in the exhibits. On the rocky shore, the crabs are the main attraction. Turn over almost any rock and you will find one of the little creatures. As I learned during my visit, the crab is a fine example of one of nature's wonders. If it loses a leg, it will grow another, a phenomenon scientists are trying to understand in the hope that it will lead to eventual human limb regeneration.

Out in the mud flats, boots are a necessity (bring your own; they don't have any to loan you). While sloshing around out there it is difficult to imagine that any kind of life resides at the water's edge. But as the exhibits inside illustrate, this area contains the highest concentration of life of any habitat. Marine algae abound, as do many forms of sea lettuce. You can look at the marine life but not take souvenirs; this is an environmentally protected area, and everything must stay where it is.

This is not the sort of place I would recommend to adults who are traveling on a tight schedule. But it is a wonderful destination for a family outing.

CRAB COVE MARINE RESERVE AND VISITOR CENTER, *Crown Memorial State Beach, 1252 McKay, Alameda. Phone: (415) 521-6887. Visitor's center open 10 A.M. to 4:30 P.M. Wednesday through Sunday; closed Monday and Tuesday. Robert Crown Park and Memorial Beach have showers, a snack bar, picnic tables, and a 10 P.M. curfew. Admission: Free.*

HOW TO GET TO CRAB COVE: *From San Francisco, take the Bay Bridge to Route 880 South toward San Jose. Exit at Broadway-Alameda and proceed on the service road parallel to the freeway. Watch for a 45-degree turn left to Alameda. Go through the tunnel. You will be on Webster Street. Take it to the end where it intersects with Central. Turn right on Central and go half a block to McKay; turn left and follow the Crab Cove signs.*

VICTORIAN FARMHOUSE

There are wonderful Victorian houses throughout the Bay Area, but I didn't expect to find any in Hayward, a city synonymous with suburban housing. But right on busy Hesperian Boulevard, across from a McDonald's, is the McConaghy estate, a 12-room farmhouse furnished in the style of 1886 and open to the public. This was the home of the town's original "Big Mac," John McConaghy, who lived in it from age 15 to his death at 101 in the late 1970s. Concerned citizens with an interest in preserving the community's history convinced the city to buy the house.

Today volunteers dress in clothing of the period to set the proper mood for leading tours. Every room has been restored and furnished with pieces from the period, even down to the hairbrushes and nail files that sit on dresser tops. In the children's room you'll find antique dolls and other toys; in papa's office you'll find a deer-head rifle rack, a footstool made of antlers, and a roll-top desk stuffed with bills yet to be paid. Downstairs you'll see such up-to-the-minute conveniences as a working icebox and an original washing machine, the tub with a hand crank. Also on display is some wonderful vintage clothing, including Victorian gentlemen's underwear and ladies' bustles. (I had always wondered how women could sit down while wearing one of those things. I learned at the McConaghy house that it was easy: the bustle was wooden and collapsed like a fan.)

The McConaghy House is different from the Victorians open to the public in San Francisco. The Hass-Lillienthal House and the Spreckels Mansion in the big city are examples of homes of the very rich; the McConaghy House is set up to show how a middle-class farm family lived. It will strike you as pretty opulent anyway, certainly compared to the typical modern middle-class home in the rest of town.

Special events are staged throughout the year, including a Victorian Christmas during the month of December when the entire house is decorated for the holiday with a Christmas tree in every room. There are also special displays at Easter, the Fourth of July, and, in late July, an outdoor antique sale with dealers throughout the East Bay offering their wares.

In back of the home is a carriage house with wagons and buggies. You will also find a boutique on the second floor of the main house selling country-style gifts, books, and items for children.

MCCONAGHY ESTATE, *18701 Hesperian Boulevard, Hayward. Phone: (415) 581-0223. Open 1 to 4 P.M. Thursday through Sunday. Donation: Adults, $2.00; seniors, $1.50; children, 50 cents. Special rates for senior and youth groups.*

HOW TO GET TO THE MCCONAGHY ESTATE: *From San Francisco, take the Bay Bridge to Route 880 South to the Hacienda exit in Hayward. Go right on Hacienda to Hesperian Boulevard and turn left. The house is well marked and will be on your right. Hayward is about 45 minutes from San Francisco, 30 minutes from Oakland and Berkeley.*

A GHOST TOWN CALLED DRAWBRIDGE ⑥

Our next stop in this area involves a ghost story of sorts. Let me set the scene. Back in 1876 two characters named Hog Davis and Slippery Jim Farr decided to build a train from Santa Cruz to Fremont. To do this they needed to provide a drawbridge for the wetlands around the community of Newark. This drawbridge needed an operator, so Hog and Slippery built a shack for the bridge keeper. As the legend goes, they noticed that the area was full of ducks, birds, and fish, and told a few friends. Before long the area around the drawbridge became a hunter's paradise; more shacks were built, and a duck club was established. Soon there was a community called Drawbridge. One could get there only by boat or train. There was no police department, no government; everybody simply agreed on proper rules of behavior and got along just fine.

Today Drawbridge is a ghost town. It was a victim of the development of the wetlands. Office complexes, housing developments, and industry crept in from all sides. In addition, airports were built, and it wasn't long before the ducks and other wildlife that had attracted people to Drawbridge were gone from the area. Where there were once two hotels and lots of vacation cabins there are abandoned shacks sinking in the mud flats on both sides of the railroad track, now an active Amtrak line.

I was shown around by a docent for the San Francisco Wildlife Refuge Center, an amateur historian named Monty Dewey. Monty thinks Drawbridge is a symbol for the Bay Area. As we stood out in the mud flats he observed that once the entire area, as far as we could see, was bay. Now only one-eighth of the wetlands remain. The rest has been lost to so-called progress. He says Drawbridge is a vivid reminder of what can happen when land and wildlife are not protected. This is not to say that a visit to Drawbridge is grim. There are still birds to see and the nearby salt ponds, in addition to the curious appeal of strolling through a ghost town.

To see Drawbridge and understand its role in our present life, you must first check into the San Francisco Wildlife Refuge Center, and a guide will escort you. As long as you're here, by all means take a look around the Refuge Center. It is filled with interesting displays about the Bay and its environment as well as photographs of the original town. Also, many well-marked nature trails lead from the center through protected marshland abuzz with wildlife.

SAN FRANCISCO BAY WILDLIFE REFUGE CENTER, *Newark. Phone: (415) 792-0222. Open all year, except on major holidays. Tours begin at 10 A.M. and end around 1:30 P.M. Saturday and Sunday, May to September. Admission: Free. Reservations are a must.*

HOW TO GET TO THE REFUGE CENTER: *From San Francisco, take Highway 101 South to the Dumbarton Bridge (Highway 84); once across, look for signs to the San Francisco Wildlife Refuge Center on your right. It is located very near the junction of Highway 84 and Thornton Road.*

ARDENWOOD

Just across from the huge auto plant that marked the first cooperative venture between General Motors and Toyota, tucked away in a clump of eucalyptus trees, past Ardenwood Industrial Park, you can find a real park that offers not only a place to rest and enjoy nature but also the chance to see what life was like around here 150 years ago.

This is Ardenwood Historical Farm, a faithful re-creation of life on the farm in the old days. This is the original home of a golddigger and sharecropper named George Patterson. His small farm stayed active until the last of the family died out. Then the house was simply abandoned and hidden from view by the eucalyptus grove.

A few years ago an East Bay Regional Parks District employee named David Luden noticed the old house as he was taking a backroad to work. He notified the city of Fremont that the abandoned mansion, which sits on city property, was going to waste. The city then asked Luden and his wife to move in as caretakers; they could live there free in return for fixing up the place. David had been waiting for a chance like this all his years as a parks naturalist.

Luden enlisted the help of volunteers, and before long the Victorian farmhouse sparkled and the farm was back in operation. Farmers from around the state donated antique farm equipment left by their parents; others donated cows, pigs, sheep, goats, rabbits, and chickens. Eventually the East Bay Parks District took over, and Luden and his wife moved on to restore another crumbling mansion elsewhere in the East Bay.

So today visitors can enjoy the fruits of the labors of the Ludens and their hundreds of volunteers. Ardenwood is a living history center. Grains are grown on the grounds of the 205-acre preserve and processed like the Pattersons did for generations. You can churn butter, or watch somebody else do it, and visit a working blacksmith shop on the premises. On weekends you can go on a tour of the house and ride a hay wagon and horse-drawn railcar. School groups book for months in advance for this firsthand hands-on experience of nineteenth-century farm life.

ARDENWOOD HISTORICAL FARM, *Fremont. Phone: (415) 796-0663. Open between the first weekend in April though mid-November, 10 A.M. to 4 P.M. Thursday through Sunday. The first weekend in December is an annual Christmas program. Admission: Adults, $5.00; seniors, $3; children 4-18, $3; under age 4, free. Wheelchair accessible.*

HOW TO GET TO ARDENWOOD: *From San Francisco, take the Bay Bridge to Highway 880 South toward San Jose. After you pass the Hayward exits, look for State Highway 84 to the Dumbarton Bridge. Exit to the right toward Newark until you come to Newark Boulevard. Turn right and watch for the sign on the right for Ardenwood Historical Farm. Don't be confused by all the signs to the Ardenwood Industrial Park. The sign to the farm is clearly visible shortly after you turn onto Newark Boulevard.*

HOME OF THE OHLONE BRAVES (8)

You may have noticed that most historic places I've recommended so far attempt to re-create California life of the Gold Rush days or the Victorian era. Well, here's a place that looks back even further, to the original inhabitants of this area, the Ohlone Indians.

The Ohlones were a remarkable people, a tribe that lived here in complete harmony with their environment. These people lived on this land for 5000 years; Ohlones were born, lived, and died on the same land as their parents and grandparents, century after century. They lived in a supportive environment that provided a kind of stability that allowed them to remain in a place that offered abundance and variety. If the acorns failed one year, there were buckeyes; if salmon didn't run one year, there were shellfish or deer. Their myths assured them that they lived at the center of the universe and that the gods meant well.

The Ohlones may have been perfectly integrated with their environment, but tragically for them, their lives changed when the Spanish arrived. By the 1790s the Spanish had cleared the East Bay of Indians, moving them to Mission Dolores in San Francisco. There many Indians died from the epidemics of the time: smallpox, measles, and cholera. The survivors eventually drifted south. Some married into the Mexican-American population around Monterey, and others moved back to the East Bay and assimilated into the white man's culture.

You can visit the remains of an Ohlone village in Coyote Hills Park near the sprawling suburb of Fremont. This was one of several Ohlone villages in the area, each with a community of about 100 people. When I visited I couldn't help but wonder about the arrogance of the present inhabitants of this state. We've made more changes around here in the past five years than the Ohlones made in 5000.

A trip to the Ohlone shell mounds begins at the visitor's center. There you will find a guide to escort you (you must have a guide to enter the re-created village). First you will see three or four structures, a home, a sweat house, and a dance hall. Then you will notice several shell mounds, the Ohlone version of a dump. All this may not seem like much at first until your guide starts telling you stories about the Ohlone way of life. You learn that such mounds hold the key to the day-to-day life of the people. The Indians created layers and layers of clam, oyster, and mussel shells, plus other discarded organic material. When a mound reached a certain height, they would simply move a little farther away and start over. The homes were built to last only a season or two anyway, so it was easy to keep moving. There used to be over 400 such archaeological treasures in the Bay Area; most have been destroyed by development.

The ingenuity of the Ohlone Indians is demonstrated further inside the visitor's center. Naturalists will show you how fires were started (the old rubbing-two-sticks-together method), acorns were ground, and boats and baskets were made. On special occasions a surprisingly seaworthy longboat made of tule strands is taken out into the Bay. And there are numerous exhibits and photos.

The rest of the park is also of interest, 1200 acres of wildlife sanctuary set up for environmental education and recreation. You'll find grassy hills, freshwater marshes, and willow runs. In winter and during migrations thousands of birds can be seen in the park. Trails will take you through all major habitat areas, with a convenient boardwalk crossing the marsh. Serious hikers may want to take advantage of the 11-mile Alameda Creek Trail, leading to the mouth of Niles Canyon. Picnic areas with tables and brazier for grilling are provided, as are bicycle trails, day-camping sites, and nature study programs.

COYOTE HILLS REGIONAL PARK, *8000 Patterson Ranch Road, Fremont. Phone: (415) 795-9385. Park open 8 A.M. to sunset daily; visitor's center open 9 A.M. to 4:30 P.M. daily; special programs on Sundays, 2 to 4 P.M. Ohlone Village and shell mound is open only at certain times with a guided tour, so call ahead. Admission: $2.00 parking fee, plus $1.00 per dog. Visitor's center is wheelchair accessible.*

HOW TO GET TO COYOTE HILLS: *From San Francisco, take the Bay Bridge and follow Route 880 South to the Route 84-Dumbarton Bridge exit. Go west on Route 84 to Newark Boulevard; turn right and continue to Patterson Ranch Road. There will be signs directing you to the park entrance. It's just a few minutes down the road from the Ardenwood Farm. Again, don't be misled by the huge industrial park; there is a "real" park in there.*

THE ORIGINAL HOLLYWOOD ⑨

Once upon a time, before Hollywood became established as the American movie capital, the little town of Niles was one of the major centers for moviemaking. Niles was the West Coast headquarters of the Chicago-based movie company Essanay Studios. Between 1911 and 1916 over 450 Essanay one-reelers were filmed and edited in Niles, including the hit westerns that featured Bronco Billy Anderson. Such stars as Ben Turpin, Wallace Beery, Zazu Pitts, and Marie Dressler worked in Niles. And at the end of the silent classic *The Tramp,* when Charlie Chaplin waddles down a country lane to a brighter tomorrow, he's walking on a tree-shaded avenue somewhere in Niles. Chaplin made several films here, commuting from San Francisco, until Mack Sennett offered him a fortune to come to Hollywood.

In its day, Essanay was one of the most modern and complete film studios on the West Coast. The main section of the studio was a sprawling two-story facility, mostly devoted to a large stage for shooting interior scenes; other areas were taken up by costume storage, editing suites, and props. Nearby weather-perfect Niles Canyon became the setting for Bronco Billy's adventures. And Niles itself, with its quaint hotels, storefronts, and saloons, was a perfect set for town scenes.

Niles still looks like a perfect set for small-town scenes. It is a quiet little community that is remarkably untouched by its moviemaking past; the citizenry was unimpressed with the movie crowd back then and it still is. Old-timers love to tell stories of how the cowboy extras would get drunk every night and do things much wilder than anything that ever made it onto film. There's very little left of the original studio, and the town offers no organized tours of the hotels, saloons, or other locations used in the movies. The one concession to the past is the town merchant's association's small collection of films made in Niles; once a year they'll dust off a couple and hold a little festival.

But anyone remotely interested in silent movies might get a kick out of visiting the site of a once lively moviemaking center. The main part of the studio stretched out between Niles Boulevard and Second Street between G and F. Today the spot is marked by the presence of a gas station. The only part of the original studio left standing is a row of cottages on Second Street between G and F. These were inhabited by the stars when they came to town to work on a picture. Around the row at 153–155 G Street are the cottages used by Bronco

Billy as his office and dressing room (in addition to starring in over 200 films, Bronco Billy Anderson also ran the studio). On I Street you will see the former train depot that made its way into a forgotten film or two. It now functions as the office of the Chamber of Commerce and is a good place to stop for directions.

The other reminder of the days when Niles was California's first movie capital is the town's version of the Hollywood sign. High on a hill overlooking the rail depot you can see the giant letter NILES. Folks around town seem very pleased that the movie affair never went further than it did.

HOW TO GET TO NILES: *From San Francisco, take the Bay Bridge to the Nimitz Freeway (Route 880). Follow the Alvarado-Niles off-ramp east. It becomes Niles Boulevard as it approaches the railroad tracks. Continue to F Street; turn right and you will see the remaining cottages left from Essanay's heyday.*

MISSION SAN JOSE

As every student in a California public school is taught, Catholic missionaries established a well-designed system of missions in the state, 21 in all, each within a day's walk of the next. Some of the missions, like the Mission Dolores in San Francisco, wound up in heavily populated areas; others, like the Mission San Jose de Guadalupe in Fremont, are more removed from major centers. Perhaps that's what makes this mission stand out. The city of Fremont is a sprawling suburb, with housing developments, industries, and shopping centers built around the major highway, Route 880. Far to the east of the main town is an area called the Mission District, and that's where you'll find this gleaming white adobe structure, an unexpected sight out in the suburbs.

Mission San Jose is the most recently restored of California's 21 missions. Originally built in 1797, the mission had fallen victim to traditional enemies of California buildings, earthquakes and fires. The major restoration was completed in 1986. Now Mission San Jose is considered to be a jewel.

From the outside the mission, the grounds, and adjoining museum are very inviting. Every effort was made to maintain the look of the original adobe, down to the adobe refuse cans. Inside, the 295-seat chapel shows the painstaking six years of work by art restorers and architects. Every wall is adorned with beautiful paintings; elaborate chandeliers hang from the high, wood-beamed cathedral ceiling. The centerpiece of the project, the altar, was reconstructed from 180 ornate pieces highlighted with gold leaf and evoking the spirit of high mass.

Father Michael Norkett can tell you about each piece, such as the candelabras fashioned as exact replicas of the ones in the original mission. Father Michael is a sight as unexpected as the mission itself. During the summer months, when the temperature often hovers in the 90s, it is not unusual to see this hip, young fellow roaming around the mission in a polo shirt and shorts. That's Father Michael, who came to the Fremont mission after spending years in the rougher sections of San Francisco. Since Mission San Jose is the working church of his parish, he is a key figure in the neighborhood. He's also great fun and brings a good sense of humor to his role. He says his mother once asked him if he even owns a clerical collar and cassock (he does, but prefers to avoid wearing black when the temperature pushes 100 degrees).

MISSION SAN JOSE DE GUADALUPE, *corner of Mission and Washington Boulevards, Fremont. Phone: (415) 657-1797. Open 10 A.M. to 5 P.M. daily.*

HOW TO GET TO MISSION SAN JOSE: *From San Francisco, take the Bay Bridge to Route 880 South to Fremont. Exit at Route 84 and follow the road east toward the Niles junction. At Mission Boulevard, turn right (south) and continue to the mission.*

HINDU TEMPLE
(11)

Like most towns and cities in the Bay Area, Livermore is growing by leaps and bounds. Suburban tract developments sprout up at nearly every turn, pushing small ranches out in favor of houses and endless rows of cul-de-sacs. Near the area of town called Springtown, not too far from a new housing tract called California Cabernet, is the most unusual new development in the entire East Bay. It's the Shiva-Vishnu Temple, an authentic place of worship for Hindus.

As you might expect, Livermore is not exactly the Hindu hotbed of the West Coast. First the sect tried to build a temple in nearby Pleasanton (which seems just as unusual), but the town turned it down; apparently there were fears that a new Jonestown might be created. The good townspeople of Livermore either didn't mind or didn't pay attention, for a permit was granted without much ado. Now, in the shadow of split-levels, is an ornate temple hand-crafted by artisans from India.

Visitors are welcome, though there is no formal, organized tour. Instead you may roam peacefully on your own, speak to any priest who knows English, and simply marvel at the architecture. You will see shrines to Vishnu, Shiva, Krishna, Rama, and other deities. You are asked to remove your shoes before entering the temple area.

So far, only phase I of the project is complete. Eventually there will be a large study center, a tower, and other buildings designed to bring together various Hindu communities of Northern California. Chances are you will be visiting during some phase of construction since the building plans will take years to complete.

SHIVA-VISHNU TEMPLE, *Arrowhead Avenue, Livermore. For information or an appointment, call (415) 449-6255.*

HOW TO GET TO THE TEMPLE: *From San Francisco, cross the Bay Bridge and take Route 580 East from Oakland toward Stockton. At Livermore, look for the Springtown Boulevard exit; then cross the bridge back over the freeway. At the first light, turn right onto Bluebell Drive. After you see a church, turn right onto Wisteria Way, then left on Arrowhead Avenue. Suddenly you are there.*

In the late 1930s Robert Lawrence, one of the founding fathers of nuclear science, assembled a distinguished coterie of scientists (including Robert Oppenheimer and Edward Teller) at the University of California, Berkeley. Much privacy was needed for research and development of sophisticated nuclear weapons, so two remote sites were chosen. One was Los Alamos in New Mexico. The other was the little town of Livermore, about 30 miles from Berkeley.

Today Livermore has grown to a busy town with more than 50,000 residents, and the Lawrence Livermore Laboratory has expanded to employ 8500 people, who work in more than 700 buildings squeezed into 1 square acre of land. Although run by the university and funded by the U.S. Department of Energy, the primary purpose of Livermore Labs is the nation's defense. No weapons are built here. This is a center for research, design, and development for various projects ranging from creation of new fusion devices to "Star Wars" weaponry. Not surprisingly, Lawrence Livermore Laboratory is often the scene of anti-nuclear demonstrations. And perhaps since that's the kind of coverage the labs usually get in the media, the persons in charge have decided to try to drum up some positive PR by encouraging visitors to come and see what their research is all about.

At the east gate, off Greenville Road, there is a visitor's center open seven days a week featuring interesting exhibits, including many of the "touchy-feely" variety that let you play while you learn. The public can also take a tour of some of the other inside facilities, by advance appointment. The only rules for tours of inside facilities are that tourists must be at least 18 years old and that groups have a minimum of 15 and a maximum of 30 people.

In the visitor's center you can begin your tour with an 11-minute multimedia slide show telling the story of the place. It's very well done. As for the exhibits, I must confess that I barely passed high school chemistry (didn't even attempt physics), so a lot of it was beyond me. But there is a wonderful globelike sculpture with a colorful light shooting out from the center; the energy of your hand moves the light toward you. Other popular attractions include computers that talk, a hologram of Robert Lawrence, and a model train that travels through a model of the laboratory and teaches . . . well, I'm not quite sure what it teaches, but it's a nifty train.

If you go beyond the visitor's center, you are bound for some really heavy science. In the laser room I was told about how they are creating tiny stars by combining deuterium and tritium nuclei to form a helium nucleus and neutron, the point of which is to illustrate that Lawrence Livermore scientists are hoping to create a safe, renewable source of energy.

As you might expect, the most frequently asked question is how the people who work here feel about working on the design and development of weapons that can destroy the world. The most frequent answer is that they feel just fine, proud in fact, for they believe they are helping prevent destruction of the planet by developing deterrents. Whatever you believe, it's worth the trip, even if for no other reason than to see your tax dollars at work.

LAWRENCE LIVERMORE NATIONAL LABORATORY, *Livermore. Phone: (415) 422-9797. Visitor's center open 9 A.M. to 5:30 P.M. Monday through Friday; noon to 5 P.M. Saturday and Sunday; closed holidays. Admission: Free (your tax dollars at work). Tours of some of the other areas of the laboratory are offered to groups of 15 or more and must be arranged at least two weeks in advance. Wheelchair accessible.*

HOW TO GET TO LAWRENCE LIVERMORE LABS: *From San Francisco, take the Bay Bridge to Route 580 toward Stockton. Stay on Route 580 until you come to the Livermore area. Exit on Greenville Road to the right and drive 2 miles to the south until you come to the entrance to the center. It's clearly marked.*

WENTE BROTHERS SPARKLING WINE CELLARS ⑬

As I mentioned before, the Livermore Valley has a rich history as a wine-producing region. Nowhere is that history more in evidence than at the Wente Brothers Cellars. The Wentes have been operating as a family business since 1883, and the site for their sparkling wine operation is a state historical landmark that once housed the old Cresta Blanca Winery. If you're old enough, you might remember Cresta Blanca as the first wine to advertise on the radio. (I can still hear the jingle, "C-R-E-S-T-A B-L-A-N-C-A, Cresta Blanca.")

Back to the Wentes. They run what they say is the oldest continuously operating family-owned winery in California (and thus, presumably, the United States). Since this statement was printed in our first edition, it has been challenged by Sherry Mirassou of the South Bay winery family. We'll leave that for them to settle. Anyway, back once again to the Wentes. Founder C. H. Wente chose the gravelly soils of the Livermore Valley well before anyone ever knew the chic places would be well to the north in Sonoma and Napa. In the 1930s Wente Brothers became the first American winery to use varietal labels rather than generic names. In other words, they produced "sauvignon blanc" rather than "white wine," a practice that most certainly paved the way for today's boutique wineries and their specialty wines. The Wentes' sauvignon blanc won the Grand Prix in Paris in 1937, the first international recognition of an American wine.

For years the Wentes ran their winery in Livermore while Sonoma and Napa became tourist attractions. Finally, in 1986 they began competing as a destination when they finished building new sparkling wine cellars. To do this, they bought the old Cresta Blanca Winery, about 8 miles from their main operation. They spent five years restoring the place and adding new buildings. They have also built a conference center and a beautiful restaurant. The result is one of the most attractive winery complexes you'll find anywhere. The buildings are old California style, done in white stucco with red tile roofs, set on more than 100 acres of vineyards, gardens, and lawns. It could be the setting of a luxury resort.

Tours are given hourly. You will be taken through the *methode champenoise* process, from the vineyards to the winery, and will end up back in the visitor's center for a tasting. The highlight for me was the original sandstone caves built into the hillside by Cresta Blanca. Even though the temperature can reach the 100-degree mark in Livermore Valley in the summer, the caves keep the wines cool, between 50 and 55 degrees, all year round. Even if you visit on a warm day, you might want to have a sweater with you for the walk through the caves.

A word or two about the contemporary Wente Brothers operation. The name may soon have to be changed since one of the three key executives is a Wente sister—Carolyn Wente. She heads up marketing and public relations. She and her co-executives, her brothers Eric and Philip, continue to operate Wente as a family business and take pains to make visitors feel at home. The Wentes grew up in the valley, and despite their success, they try to maintain a homey quality that is sometimes missing in the large operations in Sonoma and Napa. In other words, don't look for a glamorous spread on the Wentes in *Vanity Fair* or *GQ*. Carolyn says she is still a "Livermoron," a term only locals are advised to use.

WENTE BROTHERS SPARKLING WINE CELLARS, *5050 Arroyo Road, Livermore. Phone: (415) 447-3023. Open 11 A.M. to 6:30 P.M. daily. Admission: Free. Wheelchair accessible.*

HOW TO GET TO WENTE BROTHERS: *From San Francisco, take the Bay Bridge to Route 580 East to Livermore, about a 45-minute drive from the City. Exit at Portola Avenue. Turn right (south) and follow Portola to North L Street. Turn right and L will eventually become Arroyo Road. If you get lost and have to ask directions, be sure you specify that you want to go to the Sparkling Wine Cellars and not the original Wente operation.*

From Livermore Labs, take East Avenue, heading west, to the center of town. At Fourth Street turn left and then left again on South L, which will eventually become Arroyo Road. Follow it all the way to the Sparkling Wine Cellars.

ALTAMONT WINDMILLS

When driving on Route 580 near the Altamont Pass, most people are stunned by the presence of hundreds of windmills on the hillside. It is a remarkable sight, one that often prompts the question, "What in the world are they doing here?"

As it turns out, this is California's premiere wind farm. These windmills generate power that is sold to PG&E, which in turn sells the power to its customers. In fact, power is the first crop anybody has been able to raise on this land.

For years farmers tried everything, but nothing would grow because of the ceaseless winds. Finally, the family at the Jess Ranch decided to use the land for cattle grazing. They applied to PG&E to install electricity in their ranch house, but the cost of bringing power to the place was astronomical. So the family decided to put up some windmills and generate their own power. It worked, and by law the electric company had to buy it. The Jess family sends a bill to PG&E, rather than the other way around.

Although no organized tours are offered, Connie Jess told me that people are always stopping by just to gawk or to listen to the metallic whirl of the windmills. Sometimes she'll look off her front porch and see 10 to 15 photographers clicking away; the major "photo opportunity" is the unusual sight of cows grazing next to a field of windmills.

In case you've never seen one of these modern, high-tech windmills, they look like an airplane propeller in a giant Erector Set stand. On a clear day the effect is dazzling. They appear to dance together in different patterns with one set of windmills on one hill moving clockwise, the next set on the next hill moving counterclockwise, and still another set on another hill moving in another pattern.

ALTAMONT WINDMILLS, *on both sides of Highway 580 between Livermore and Tracy. It's at least an hour from San Francisco. You can't miss them.*

HOW TO FIND THE WINDMILLS: *From San Francisco, take the Bay Bridge to Route 580 East and follow it all the way past Livermore until you see the windmills on both sides of the highway.*

CHAPTER **8** Contra Costa County

AREA OVERVIEW I hope the good residents of Contra Costa County will take it as no insult when I describe it as the Bay Area's version of Southern California. First of all, the weather is definitely warmer than in San Francisco or Oakland. Beyond that, there is a San Fernando Valley look and feel to the area that tells you this may be the look of the future. Wide boulevards connect more shopping malls than main streets, girls and boys are blonder, cars are everywhere, and driving long distances to get somewhere is routine. Contra Costa is the newest of the area's boom communities, and it's still growing with astonishing speed. Yet, this is

Contra Costa

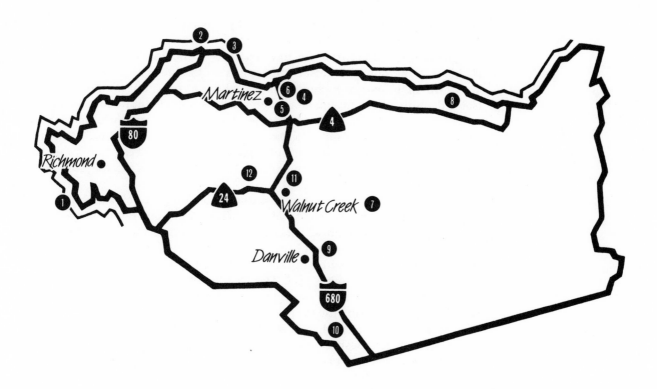

where John Muir settled down and did much of his writing, and this is where you can still find a remote island to spend the weekend.

Walnut Creek and Concord are the major cities, connected to the rest of the Bay Area by Routes 24, 4, and 680. The eastern part of the county is much less populated, which makes for interesting backroads destinations. For the citizens, though, it makes for a feeling of being ignored, to the point that there is always a movement afoot to secede and form a separate county.

POINT RICHMOND

As I travel around I am endlessly amazed by the hidden towns and villages that offer charm and history just a few minutes from a crowded freeway or heavily industrialized zone. Point Richmond is a case in point. Just down the road from a huge Chevron plant, often hidden from view by huge tractor-trailers and road construction crews, and reached via a really ugly road, Point Richmond is a little oasis, as quaint as a New England village.

Point Richmond is part of the industrial city of Richmond. During World War II this was the home of Kaiser shipyards and Richmond was a 24-hour town. Today the main part of Richmond is an industrial zone, but the Point remains isolated, a throwback to a quieter, more gracious time. Point Richmond has only a few streets to roam, each with some nicely restored buildings and inviting restaurants, plus there's an old hotel, an old theater still used for live performances, and a restored jail that now houses lawyers' offices (there must be a message there somewhere). The best way to see the town is to park your car and stroll.

All roads seem to lead to the most unique building in Point Richmond, the Natatorium. From the outside it looks like a huge museum, but inside you'll find a busy community swimming pool that also functions as the town's community center. The beautiful façade of the Natatorium is a bit misleading. Instead of finding an art deco treasure inside, you might think you have gone back to your high school or Y swimming pool. The first memory flashback for me was the smell of heated chlorine. At the entrance there is a small gray industrial lobby with posters advertising the swimming schedule and other local events. Behind the doors is the huge pool with its high glass ceiling. The pool itself is well designed, with a horseshoe-shaped balcony for viewing.

Visitors are welcome to drop by and see the Natatorium, learn more about its history from an exhibit near the entrance, and swim or watch. (The infants' swimming lessons are a great show.)

This large facility might strike you as out of proportion to a community this small, but it is for the entire city of Richmond. It ended up here because of a quirk of fate. What happened was that the land was originally owned by a family who thought there was oil underneath. After drilling, all they came up with was water. So in the 1920s the family gave the land to the city with one stipulation: that it build a community swimming pool. As long as the pool remains, the city owns it. If the pool is removed, the land goes back to the heirs of the original owners.

The pool remains and offers an elaborate schedule of classes, social events, and lap-swimming times. You don't have to be a town resident to swim there. If you ever meet anyone who grew up in Richmond, chances are he or she learned to swim in the Richmond Natatorium, nicknamed "The Plunge."

Immediately behind the Natatorium, a drive through a tunnel takes you to a lovely town park and a beach on the Bay, a nice place for a picnic or simply to get some peace, quiet, and sunshine.

POINT RICHMOND NATATORIUM, *1 East Richmond Boulevard (at Gerrard), Point Richmond. Phone: (415) 620-6820. Open Monday, Wednesday and Friday 7 A.M. to 8:30 P.M.; Tuesday and Thursday 7 A.M. to 10 P.M.; Saturday 7 A.M. to 4:30 P.M. Admission to the building is free. To swim: Adults, $1.75; youngsters aged 7 to 17, $1.25; children 6 and under, $1. Richmond residents get a 25-cent discount.*

HOW TO GET TO POINT RICHMOND: *From San Francisco, take the Bay Bridge to Route 80 North toward Sacramento. After the Berkeley exits, look for the exit on the left to Route 580 and the San Rafael Bridge. After you make a left turn onto Hoffman Boulevard, which is still Route 580, get to the left side of the road and watch for the left turn into Point Richmond. Do not follow the traffic turning right to the San Rafael Bridge. The Natatorium is behind the business section of town, within easy walking distance of the cafes and restaurants.*

As you drive north to the wine country on Route 80, you cross the first bridge built to span the bay, the Carquinez Bridge. If you look to the right and see the giant C & H sugar manufacturing plant, you know you've reached the town of Crockett. This is a touch of small-town America that is often lost so close to our major freeways.

CROCKETT

The town of Crockett is a middle-class hillside community, on the shores of the Carquinez Strait. The unofficial community center is Pedrotti's hardware store, located at the corner of Pomona and Second streets, also the site of the town's only stoplight. Here's where you can find out what's going on in town. If you're there in the morning, you will probably see a bunch of local men huddled around a stove, drinking coffee and exchanging gossip. Maybe this is the major appeal of Crockett. It's an old-fashioned small town, the kind of community you don't see much anymore, where everyone knows everyone by name. You can just stand in the store and be amazed by the familiarity people have with every person from town who walks through the door.

If there is an attraction specifically geared for tourists, it is the row of antique stores along Pomona Street. Each store appears to have its own specialty, whether it's furniture, knickknacks, or, as in the case of Another Time Antiques, neon. This place is run by "Pink" Floyd Wyrick, who keeps his personal collection of antique neon all over this shop—incredible old signs advertising everything from cleaners to dentists. It's like a very funky museum of neon; in fact, most of the items are not for sale, just for show.

If you are a movie buff, you might like to know that Crockett gave the screen world Aldo Ray. In fact, the world headquarters of the Aldo Ray Fan Club is in town. The muscular, raspy-throated character actor (who appeared in such classics as *The Naked and the Dead, Pat and Mike,* and *God's Little Acre)* is a hometown boy. His mom still lives here and so does Aldo, when he's not out on location. There is even a small Aldo Ray exhibit at the town museum. This is a volunteer-run place that is well worth a visit. Set up in a former train station, right across the street from the C & H sugar plant, the town's history is set out in a very informal fashion. Three wonderful characters, Tony, Joe and Skipper, all retired employees of C & H, take care of the museum and give history as Damon Runyon might have written it.

Crockett used to be a company town; C & H provided the housing, parks, and other services for years, until the plant was unionized—then the workers and the town's government were on their own. Today most of the town is still employed by C & H.

What makes the museum so special is the personal feel to the place. It's like browsing in an entire community's attic. Along with the expected historical artifacts and sugar company memorabilia, there are objects from people's homes: a giant stuffed sturgeon (the largest caught in the area), a poster from the movie *Yes, Giorgio* (Tony's cousin Dave played accordion in the movie). Items are piled up in every corner and plastered on the walls and ceilings.

One thing Crockett is proud of is the fact that it was the last town in California to give up the old manual telephone switchboard on which an operator would personally connect callers. That last switchboard and the chair operator Myrt sat in are on display inside the museum.

This is a town filled with characters, and the reason may be that the Wild West has always been alive and kicking here. That's because there's no police force. Law enforcement has always been left up to the highway patrol and the county sheriff's department. The town was once characterized by fierce feuding between the Italians on one side of town and the Portuguese on the other. Ethnic peace was finally reached in the 1950s, but soon there was a new element in town—the hippies, who knew they could grow and smoke whatever they liked here; "rooms for rent" ads placed by Crockett landlords in the *Berkeley Barb* used to advertise "cheap rent, no cops." By the 1980s the yuppies had started to move in, finding Crockett to be an affordable suburb. Today all factions seem to get along well enough to make Crockett an inviting place for visitors.

CROCKETT HISTORICAL MUSEUM, *at Ralph and Loring Streets, in the old railroad station across from the C & H plant. Phone: (415) 787-2178 or (415) 787-1229. Open Wednesday and Saturday or by appointment.*

HOW TO GET TO CROCKETT AND THE TOWN MUSEUM: *From San Francisco, take the Bay Bridge to Route 80 toward Sacramento. At the Carquinez Bridge, exit at the Crockett sign before the toll booths. The exit will lead you onto Pomona Avenue. Continue to a 3-way stop at Pomona and Ralph Streets. Turn left on Ralph and continue to the corner of Ralph and Loring.*

MURIEL'S DOLLHOUSE

Port Costa is a rarity in a county filled with town after town of unrelieved suburbia. Enclosed by farmland and forest, this waterfront town is situated at the end of a country lane, which makes getting here half the fun. Port Costa's weathered storefronts and warehouses (left over from the days when the town was a bustling grain-shipping port) have been turned into artist's studios, antique shops, and restaurants. The town has a lot of charm and character.

Port Costa also has a lot of charming characters. Perhaps the best known of them is a sweet little old lady named Muriel Whitmore. She is the curator, owner, and sole employee of an amazing museum of dolls. Even if you're a guy like me who has never had the slightest interest in dolls, Muriel makes the place worth a visit. As you enter the door of the little house she has converted into the museum, you know you're in for something different. On my last visit, Muriel, who stands about 4 feet 10 inches tall, was wearing a babushka around her hair, a checked shirt, bobby sox, a rock 'n' roll T-shirt, and a cardigan sweater. I would guess her to be in her seventies, and she is a bundle of energy, sharp as a tack.

Several years ago Muriel moved to Port Costa with her lifelong collection of dolls and decided to open a museum. Crammed into three rooms are hundreds of dolls, all of them antiques. Her dolls are made of china, wood, wax, apple, tin, and papier-mâché and are arranged in thematic displays. This setup allows Muriel to tell you stories about her brood. She claims to know each one personally and has given them all names and life stories. In the schoolroom display, for example, she will point out that the little girl with her hand in the air and tears in her eyes has been trying to get permission to go to the bathroom for 15 years. She can't be excused because the room is quarantined due to a case of mumps in another doll. And Muriel will point out that the teacher is pregnant, which was scandalous in the old days. As you can see, Muriel does not lack for humor or imagination.

There are other items of interest. One is an elaborate dollhouse with each room completely outfitted. This is a model of the Ohio farmhouse where Muriel grew up and where she began her lifelong love of dolls. She also has a reproduction of "The Last Supper" on the head of a pin. I know that sounds impossible, but Muriel has a good magnifying glass handy, and you can make out a crude copy of Leonardo's masterpiece. It was painted by a 75-year-old Ecuadorian who, according to Muriel, uses a hair from his arm as a brush and paints rhythmically between his heartbeats. (If you're not yet impressed, Muriel will add that he doesn't wear glasses.)

Muriel takes her congregation seriously. She makes a distinction between being a doll collector and running a museum. She says that if she were merely a collector, she would only choose her favorites, which are French dolls. But as a museum operator she has searched for variety, and many of her dolls are one-of-a-kind, just like their mistress.

MURIEL'S DOLLHOUSE MUSEUM, *33 Canyon Lake Drive, Port Costa. Phone: (415) 787-2820. Open 10 A.M. to 5 P.M. Tuesday through Sunday; open Monday by appointment. Admission: Adults, $1.00; children 12 and under 25 cents.*

HOW TO GET TO MURIEL'S DOLLHOUSE: *From San Francisco, take the Bay Bridge and continue on Route 80 toward Sacramento. Exit at the Crockett-Port Costa exit. Continue past Crockett for 3 twisty miles until you come to the main street of Port Costa, which is Canyon Lake Drive. Muriel's is on the right-hand side on the corner of Canyon Lake Drive and Erskine.*

ADOPT-A-PIONEER
(4)

You can learn a lot about any town by visiting its cemeteries, but the one in Martinez is truly special. In the 1970s the historic Alhambra Cemetery was a mess. Vandals had desecrated the grave sites, weeds had taken over, and the growing community of newcomers had very little connection to the history buried on the hill. Then a group of concerned citizens started the Adopt-a-Pioneer Gravesite program. Volunteers came two days a week to care for a selected gravesite—pulling weeds, planting flowers, sweeping. They also researched the occupant of each plot and uncovered a treasure trove of history.

Today volunteers still help maintain the place. Many have family ties; for example, the chairman's grandfather was county sheriff in 1888; others care for the sites of their grandmothers and great-aunts. Even though this is a lovely spot on its own, overlooking the Bay, the best time to visit is when the volunteers are in action. They are an extremely lively and likable group that will change your preconceptions about cemeteries. They will also entertain you with stories about their families and their love for their community. As one of the volunteers said to me, "We are all so transient. I'm taking care of someone's grave in the hope that someone will come along years from now and take care of mine."

ALHAMBRA CEMETERY, *on Carquinez Scenic Drive, Martinez. Open Sunday; other days you must get a key from the police station in the heart of town, at 525 Henrietta Street. For more information, you can call Charlene Perry, (415) 228-2364.*

HOW TO GET TO ALHAMBRA CEMETERY: *From San Francisco, take the Bay Bridge and follow the signs to Route 24 toward Walnut Creek. Continue on 24 to Pleasant Hill Road. Turn left on Pleasant Hill Road and continue until you reach Alhambra Avenue. Turn right onto Alhambra. The police station where you can pick up a key for the cemetery is at the corner of Alhambra and Henrietta. One does not need a key on Sundays. Key in hand, continue on Alhambra Avenue north to Escobar Street, turn left to Talbart Street, and follow Talbart to Carquinez Scenic Drive. The cemetery is about a fourth of a mile up the hill on the right.*

VIANO WINE AND GOOSE EGGS

There is no shortage of wineries in the Bay Area. Go to just about any rural road, look for a beautiful setting, and chances are you'll find one.

However, it is unusual to find a winery in a densely populated suburban environment, which makes the Viano Winery a special treat. Just a few minutes from a busy intersection in Martinez you will see a hand-written sign advertising wine, goose eggs, and lemons. Follow the sign.

Three generations of Vianos live and work here. It looks like the average working farm with a couple of barns, several other small buildings, and lots of equipment scattered about. There is no attempt to put on a show for visitors. The tasting room is in the basement of Papa Viano's house, where you will be served in good solid drinking glasses, like water glasses—not chic goblets. Instead of fancy talk about the wine's bouquet, the Vianos are more likely to show you pictures of the family or talk about how their area used to be filled with farmers growing apricots, walnuts, and grapes. They are the lone holdouts against the developers now, and the Vianos say they are determined not to join the trend.

You can purchase not only the Vianos' homemade wines but also eggs, walnuts, lemons, and whatever else happens to be on hand. The wine is very good, but the best part of the experience is a visit with the Vianos to catch their enthusiasm and determination.

VIANO WINERY, *150 Morello Avenue, Martinez. Phone: (415) 228-6465. Open 9 A.M. to noon and 1 to 5 P.M. seven days a week.*

HOW TO GET TO VIANO WINERY: *From San Francisco, take the Bay Bridge and stay on Highway 80 toward Sacramento. Go past Pinole and Rodeo to Highway 4. Take Highway 4 East and wind through the canyon about 10 miles. One mile past Martinez, exit at Morello Avenue and turn left at the bottom of the ramp. The Vianos' place will be about another mile down the road on the right.*

JOHN MUIR HOUSE

After native son Joe DiMaggio, John Muir was the most famous citizen of the town of Martinez. It was here that the famous naturalist and conservationist lived the final 25 years of his life, in a house built by his in-laws.

There is irony here. In Muir's day, around the turn of the century, Martinez was a quiet little town, a community in harmony with the principles Muir stood for. But today Martinez is a booming suburban community. Though many citizens are trying to preserve what's left of the town's past, Muir the environmentalist would shudder at today's view from the hillside house—a confluence of highways below, an occasional helicopter above. The irony is that such recent developments as the John Muir Motel, the John Muir Shopping Center, and the John Muir Parkway have been named for the environmentalist. Certainly Muir Woods and Muir Beach in Marin are more fitting honors for the father of the conservation movement! More about Muir's life when we get to "Yosemite" (in "Beyond the Bay").

His home is certainly worth a visit. Although this is not the largest or best known national park, it is one of the most significant since it was here that Muir wrote the numerous letters and magazine articles that would establish the National Park Service and give birth to the Sierra Club. Upstairs in the modest but spacious Victorian house is Muir's study, on display in creative disarray, with papers spread about, correspondence to be answered, and bill receipts. You can stroll the grounds, which are lovely and restful—8 acres of orchard trees and grapevines, with a creek running by. And at the end of the path you will come to another historic home, the Martinez adobe.

Don Ygnacio Martinez was the former Commandante of the Presidio in San Francisco. In 1837, he became the city's third mayor. When he retired from service he was offered his choice of two gifts: a case of cigars or 17,700 acres of land in Contra Costa County. Even though the cigars were probably worth more at the time, Martinez had many children so he took the land. The adobe on the property was built by his son on his portion of the family inheritance. This two-story ranch house is typical of life in the mid-1800s in California. It's sparsely furnished, but you still get the feeling of what life was like. You can wander through the house, which includes one cutaway section of wall showing the thickness that kept the homes cool in the summer and warm in the winter. Some of the walls are 30 inches thick. There are also pictures of the family along with some pieces of furniture and farm equipment. The Park Service hopes that a visit to the adobe, like a visit to the Muir home, will provoke us to pause and reflect on the influence of those who came here before us, and how what we do will affect the lives of future generations.

JOHN MUIR NATIONAL HISTORICAL SITE, *4202 Alhambra Avenue, Martinez. Phone: (415) 228-8860. Open 10 A.M. to 4:30 P.M. seven days a week; closed* *major holidays. A pamphlet is provided at the visitor's center and then tours are self-guided, with rangers available to answer questions. Admission: Adults, $1; seniors and children 11 and under, free.*

HOW TO GET TO JOHN MUIR'S HOUSE: *From San Francisco, take the Bay Bridge and take Route 80 North toward Sacramento. Exit onto Route 4 and continue to Martinez. Exit onto Alhambra Avenue. Exit to the right on Alhambra; then go back under the highway and head north on Alhambra. The Muir House is directly north of Route 4. Turn left into the driveway and park.*

MOUNT DIABLO

As mountains go, Mount Diablo is a real shrimp, only 3849 feet high. But its claim to fame is that you can usually see more from its peak than from any other place in the United States. So even if you think Mount Diablo doesn't have the *best* view, it at least offers the *most* view. It is, however, a spectacular view. From the observation deck at the mountain's peak, directly north you look out on the rich farmland of Yolo and Solano counties; if the skies are crystal clear you can see Mount Lassen, some 163 miles away. To the northeast the Delta unfolds and leads to Sacramento. To the east and a bit to the south you may see Yosemite Valley and Half Dome, and directly to the south you see San Jose and Mount Hamilton and its Lick Observatory. The Sonoma and Napa Valleys are to the northwest, and directly west are Mount Tamalpais, San Francisco, and the Bay.

But there's more to the mountain than the view. There are trails to hike, many rare species of flora and fauna to explore (as Euell Gibbons could probably have told you, this is one of the few places in the world you can find digger pine trees, with their huge cones and delicious pine nuts), and special areas to visit. One of my favorites is Rock City, a unique formation of huge stones arranged by nature to form lookouts, caves, and tunnels. This area is said to have been a spiritual place for the Indians who lived on this mountain. On hunting trips the stone tunnels and caves were used for shelter, contemplation, and observation of prey.

The best way to get the most out of Mount Diablo is to pick up a map at the ranger station (you have to stop there anyway to pay your $2 day-use fee). Then pick out one or two areas to explore, making sure you save time for the drive to the peak for the view. Don't forget the binoculars.

As for the name, there are many stories about why this mountain was named after the devil. I have yet to hear the definitive legend, but there are many people who believe that spirits roam the mountain. Apparently sober people have told me about hearing strange sounds and seeing strange lights at night on the mountain. All I can say is that if I were looking for a movie location to stage a UFO landing, Mount Diablo would be perfect.

MOUNT DIABLO STATE PARK. *Phone: (415) 837-2525. Open 8 A.M. to dusk every day. Day-use fee: $2 per car.*

HOW TO GET TO MOUNT DIABLO: *From San Francisco, take the Bay Bridge to Route 24 toward Walnut Creek. Exit at Ygnacio Valley Road to the right. Follow Ygnacio Valley Road to Walnut Avenue. Turn right; Walnut runs into North Gate Road, which leads into the north gate of the park.*

BLACK DIAMOND MINES

Gold was not the only treasure in "them thar hills" in the 1850s. Coal was discovered in the shadow of Mount Diablo, and people came from all over the world to work in the mines. This became the largest coal-producing region in the state. Three boomtowns for the miners and their families were created: Nortonville, Stewartsville, and Somersville. Most of their residents came from Wales and Ireland. They came to California hoping to find the American dream; instead, they discovered a very difficult existence, in an area riddled with epidemics of smallpox and scarlet fever. By the turn of the century much of the population had been wiped out and the mines closed.

Today the area around the mines and the now extinct towns has become the Black Diamond Mines State Preserve. It's a lovely park with a sad history. The main attraction is an underground mine that is open as a museum. With advance reservations, guides will take you through the huge tunnels. This was a sandstone mine; inside you will see the enormous excavations and even a few signs of mishaps. The park provides a hard hat and a flashlight, though you may bring your own if you wish. Outside you can walk through the hills where the towns once existed. Rose Hill Cemetery tells the story of the hard lives of the immigrants. Reading the epitaphs on the gravestones, it is easy to imagine their dreams of what life would be like in the New World.

If you happen to be in the area during the last week of April, you may want to attend Black Diamond Days, the annual gathering of descendants of former residents of Nortonville, Stewartsville, and Somersville. It is a celebration at the mines, with music, dance, an oral history forum, and food.

In addition, the park offers 20 miles of hiking trails; one 12-mile trail leads to Mount Diablo.

BLACK DIAMOND MINES REGIONAL PRESERVE, *Antioch. Phone: (415) 757-2620. Park open 8 A.M. to dusk seven days a week; mines open Saturday and Sunday only, by reservation. Mine tours at 10 A.M., 11 A.M., 1:30 P.M., and 2:30 P.M. Admission: Adult, $2; children 7 to 11 and seniors, $1; children under age 7 are not permitted in the mines.*

HOW TO GET TO THE MINES: *From San Francisco, take the Bay Bridge to Highway 24 toward Walnut Creek. Stay on Route 24 to Route 4 toward Pittsburg and Antioch. Turn right onto Route 4 and follow it to the Somersville Road. Turn right and go straight to the entrance.*

When America's greatest playwright, Eugene O'Neill, and his wife Carlotta were looking for "a final home and harbor," they decided to live in Northern California. They looked in Marin, the South Bay, everywhere, in fact, until the day O'Neill saw this special parcel of 158 acres in Contra Costa County overlooking the Las Trampas wilderness and said, "This is it."

Using funds from the Nobel Prize O'Neill won in 1936, he and Carlotta built a beautiful home with gardens, a swimming pool, and plenty of peace and quiet so that O'Neill could write. They named their home Tao House, from the Chinese, meaning "the right way of life"—a simple, unencumbered existence. Recently, the National Parks Service opened Tao House to the public.

Situated on a hill high above the town of Danville, this is a must stop for anyone interested in the American theater. O'Neill wrote some of his major works in this house, including *The Iceman Cometh, A Moon for the Misbegotten,* and the autobiographical *Long Day's Journey into Night* (for which he would, posthumously, win his fourth Pulitzer Prize).

The home has been restored to look and feel as it did in the 1940s when Eugene, Carlotta, and their beloved dog Blemie lived here. I mention the dog because O'Neill was exceptionally attached to Blemie; you will see a replica of the dalmatian's crib with a silk pillow that was custom-made at Gump's, the fine San Francisco specialty store and, in the pasture south of the house, her tombstone. You will also see Rosie's Room, the playwright's favorite place in the house, the room where he had his morning coffee. Rosie is O'Neill's beloved player piano; neighbors claimed that on warm days, with the windows of Tao House open, they could hear Eugene O'Neill's player piano.

EUGENE O'NEILL NATIONAL HISTORIC SITE, *Danville. Open seven days a week, but by reservation only; closed on major holidays. No private cars are allowed on the site. The National Park Service has van service to get there. Call (415) 838-0249 to make arrangements. Admission: Free at publication time, though there are plans brewing to charge an admission fee.*

EUGENE O'NEILL'S HOUSE

Right in the center of the suburban sprawl, in the community of San Ramon, is an oasis of lush flowers and vegetables. Better yet, it's located behind a very attractive restaurant that prepares the food with the bounty from this garden. The restaurant is a commercial enterprise called Mudd's; the gardens are the project of a nonprofit organization called the Crow Canyon Institute. Its purpose is to develop new ways to grow edible landscapes, to provide classes on gardening and food preparation, and to make nature available to schools and other groups.

Using every inch of a few acres of land, you will see fruits, vegetables, and

EDIBLE LANDSCAPING

edible flowers (yes! primroses, nasturtiums, and marigolds, to name but a few), all flourishing naturally without the aid of chemicals. Abundance is their form of pest control; enough is grown for everybody, including the bugs. Since this is hot, dry territory, the institute's gardeners specialize in drought-resistant plants. For them, trying to grow a lush, English-style garden would be downright irresponsible. If they had their way, the neighboring corporations would develop their own edible landscapes and "pocket orchards" instead of planting thirsty lawns and manicured flower gardens.

In addition to the garden and restaurant, there is a greenhouse and a shop selling seeds and gardening tools. Part of the institute's land includes a serene park in the actual Crow Canyon, which runs along San Ramon Creek. This is a very restful, shady spot for a picnic, hidden away from the rest of the world. It also happens to be a popular spot for weddings.

CROW CANYON INSTITUTE, *10 Boardwalk, San Ramon. Phone: Gardens, (415) 820-3634; restaurant, (415) 837-9387. Gardens and nature park are open sunrise to sunset daily; guided tours by appointment. Admission: Free. Restaurant is open for lunch and dinner every day, plus Sunday brunch.*

HOW TO GET TO THE CROW CANYON INSTITUTE: *From San Francisco, take the Bay Bridge to Route 24 toward Walnut Creek. Turn right onto Route 680 South. Exit at Crow Canyon Road, turning right onto Crow Canyon. Turn left at Park Place and you will see the sign for Mudd's restaurant. The gardens are in back.*

JUNIOR MUSEUM
(11)

Maybe it's just me, but I have a great time whenever I visit a place intended for kids. For example, I was hooked by the Alexander Lindsay Junior Museum, which is in Larkey Park in Walnut Creek. The building used to be an East Bay Utility District pumping station. Now it's an indoor wildlife sanctuary, where you can come nose-to-nose with some of the strangest-looking creatures you've ever imagined. For example, you'll encounter Lord Bradley, a turkey vulture, sitting on a perch. Though he is chained down, he is not in a cage. And when he spreads his giant wings, it is a simply awesome sight. His roommates include a Swenson's hawk, a yellow-billed magpie, a giant owl, and other birds all native to Contra Costa County. Some of the birds that live here were raised from chicks by the volunteer staff; others were psychological or physical misfits, unable to survive in the wild, and were given a new lease on life, uncaged, in the museum.

There's also a reptile room. Thankfully, these guys are behind glass, aquarium-style. Here you'll encounter snakes of every variety. Another room has exhibits intended to teach kids about the wonders of nature. The highlight here is the feely boxes. You're supposed to stick your hand inside, feel what's there, and guess what it is. To find out if you're right, you lift a flap and see what's inside. When I tried it, I felt something small, round, and hard, rather nondescript.

Imagine my "thrill" to discover I was fondling owl pellets. Sandy Fender, the museum's wildlife supervisor, explained to me that when an owl eats, it regurgitates its food and makes these pellets. (I think the experience of the feely box works better for kids.)

A popular spot is the museum's medical center, where baby animals are nursed back to health. Almost every day someone walks in with a wounded bird or a damaged wild animal. You can watch the dedicated volunteers with eyedroppers full of medicine lovingly saving lives.

Finally, the Alexander Lindsay Junior Museum offers an unusual service to locals. It lends rabbits, rats, hamsters, and guinea pigs to families to have the experience of having a pet around. Like lending libraries of books, the family must give the animal back in a week or so, but then they will know if they are suited for a full-time pet.

ALEXANDER LINDSAY JUNIOR MUSEUM, *in Larkey Park at 1901 First Avenue, Walnut Creek. Phone: (415) 935-1978. Open Wednesday through Sunday, 1 to 5 P.M. Admission: Free.*

HOW TO GET TO THE JUNIOR MUSEUM: *From San Francisco, take the Bay Bridge to Route 24 toward Walnut Creek. Route 24 joins Route 680 North. Continue on the freeway to the Geary Road exit. Turn left at the exit and go 1 mile to Buena Vista. Turn left to continue to First Street; Larkey Park is on the right. There is a parking lot in the park, and the museum is well marked.*

MUSEUM OF VINTAGE FASHION

I thought I had gone to the wrong address when I pulled up the hill to Patti McClain's place. It looked more like a typical suburban house—the sort of nice, normal place where Steven Spielberg likes to set his movies—than the home of the country's largest museum of vintage clothing.

Once inside, I was still confused. Where does the museum end and the house begin? Even Patti isn't always sure. In her son's bedroom, for example, next to the photos of friends and sports heroes, is a display of Victorian high-button boots and ladies' hats. In his closet, next to the jeans and sweatshirts, are velvet dresses from the 1800s and lace nightgowns from France. In the master bedroom Patti and her insurance executive husband share the space with mannequins, ancient Chinese ceremonial robes, and Coco Chanel originals. It's a collection that antique clothing dealers would sell their grandmothers for.

Since this is a nonprofit foundation, none of the items is for sale. Patti probably wouldn't part with any of them anyway. As founder and curator of the Museum of Vintage Fashion, she is obsessed by her collection and has dedicated her life to preserving clothes as a history of past generations. She also teaches classes in clothing restoration.

Patti looks forward to the day her son has a closet of his own. She says she has raised the money for a permanent museum space outside her home. Land has been donated, and as you read this, ground-breaking and construction are underway. In the meantime, closet tours in her home continue, by appointment only.

Anyone interested in clothing and accessories from 1720 to 1970 is welcome to see the collection. Many visitors are students of design and fashion; theatrical costume designers travel from all over the country to examine the pieces Patti has in her collection. She prefers to give tours to groups of five or more and can handle busloads at once. Be prepared to spend several hours; your tour guide knows her subject and is a very entertaining storyteller.

MUSEUM OF VINTAGE FASHION, *1712 Chaparral Lane, Lafayette. Phone: (415) 944-1896. Open by appointment. Admission: $5 per person.*

HOW TO GET TO THE MUSEUM: *From San Francisco, take the Bay Bridge to Highway 24. Continue to Pleasant Hill Road; head north, which is to the left on Pleasant Hill until you come to a Y in the road; follow the left fork (Taylor Boulevard), continue to Greenhills Road, and turn left; you will enter the Lafayette Hills subdivision. Turn right on Chaparral Lane and continue up to the top of the hill and 1712 Chaparral.*

CHAPTER **9** "Yolano"

AREA OVERVIEW There is no such place as "Yolano." The name comes from an association of farmers who banded together to entice visitors to visit their farms in Yolo and Solano Counties. These adjoining counties cover a lot of space and border the Central Valley, which produces much of the food for the United States.

Solano County includes the cities of Vallejo, Fairfield, and Benicia. Each has a long military history with the Mare Island Naval Base still in Vallejo, and the Travis Air Base still in Fairfield. Benicia's story follows this brief introduction. Much of Solano is reached by I-80 as it leads to Sacramento and eventually all across the country.

Yolo is much less populated with its major city being Woodland in the northern part of the county. This is a farm country with a national impact because of the importance of the agricultural school at the University of California at Davis.

In these counties, the hills of the Bay area disappear and the terrain flattens out. Driving along some of the farm trails, you might think you are in the plains states of the midwest. For many, this is the real California.

Yolano
(Yolo & Solano)

505

113

Woodland

7
9 8

80

4
5
3
Fairfield
12
12
6

37
Rio Vista

Vallejo
1
2

BENICIA

(1) Once there were big plans for the town of Benicia. It was going to be an international port, a major military outpost, and the California state capital. Luckily for those who like small, charming towns, none of the plans worked out. Now, it's a lovely waterfront community, filled with antique stores on its main street, housing developments on its shores, and a busy arts and crafts community in its old industrial section.

✔ **Camel Barn Museum.** A good place to begin your visit is the Camel Barn, a small museum that is in the original Benicia Arsenal. This building played a role in an unsuccessful and rather humorous experiment by the U.S. Army back in the 1850s. Jefferson Davis, then Secretary of War and soon to become President of the Confederate States, had the bright idea to import a bunch of camels to the United States for military use in the American southwestern deserts. Although the camels did travel easily, carrying heavy loads across the desert, nobody knew how to take care of them, nor were they prepared for the adverse reaction other animals had toward them. The experiment was an expensive failure, and when the Civil War broke out, the camels of the U.S. Camel Corps were driven to the Benicia Arsenal to get them out of the way. They were auctioned off in 1864, but Building 9 of the Benicia Arsenal became known forevermore as the Camel Barn.

It was an interesting building to begin with. Craftsmen from Europe had been hired by the military to design and build a series of buildings that would be used for storage. The Camel Barn, built in 1853, was made of sandstone quarried from nearby hills and featured hand-hewn pine planking on the floors and a series of arched windows. Recently renovated, it is an ideal setting for the community museum that chronicles the unusual history of the town. For example, it was here that I learned why the town is called Benicia. The town fathers— probably the same guys who wanted the place to be a major port, military arsenal, and state capital—wanted to name the town Francisca, after the wife of the ubiquitous General Vallejo, whose land grant extended to this area. But the big power brokers in San Francisco thought that would be confusing and insisted the little town up north choose another name. The town fathers settled for Benicia, the middle name of General Vallejo's wife.

The barn is divided into two large floors. On the ground floor you can see some of the stalls provided for displaced camels, plus huge meeting rooms. Upstairs you'll find the very spacious museum with nicely planned displays. It is in many ways like the historical museums you will find in most small towns, but I find that each town tends to have its own special history.

Not far from the Camel Barn and the old military arsenal is the old industrial section of Benicia, which is now a modern artist's colony. Even before the Emery-ville revival, many of the artists and craftspeople moved up from places like Berkeley because they could get large warehouse spaces at affordable rents. A stroll through the huge old warehouse buildings will take you to studios and workshops of glassblowers, neon makers, potters, and painters. Some of the town's artists, such as Judy Chicago and Victorian wallpaper-maker Bruce Brad-bury, have national reputations. During the week, visiting an artist is a hit-and-miss proposition, but on weekends many of them open their areas to the public for tours and to sell their works, including seconds at a discount rate.

✔ **Old State Capitol.** In the main business section of town, you can get another sense of Benicia's history by visiting the Old State Capitol Building, now a state historic park. Actually, this was California's third capital, from February 1853 to February 1854. (The transfer of the capital to its permanent home in Sacra-mento was considered treasonous by the townspeople, and they never forgave the instigator, Governor John Bigler; perhaps that is why Lake Bigler's name was later changed to Lake Tahoe.) Outside, the former capitol building is very small, about half the size of an average county courthouse these days. Inside you can walk through the old senate chambers, committee rooms, and assembly halls, decorated with such artifacts as newspapers from 1853, the editions prob-ably read by the legislators when they assembled here.

The capitol building is located near the Old Town shopping district, which, of course, features an antique row, plus some very inviting restaurants and an appealing waterfront where you can stroll or just watch the ships go by.

✔ **Mothball Fleet.** One more curiosity you might happen to notice just outside of town is called the Mothball Fleet. Out on Suisun Bay, you will see some 85 warships just sitting there. Actually, the name Mothball Fleet is a misnomer because scores of workers are out there every day, keeping the vessels shipshape for action, in case their country calls. The public is not allowed to go on board, but you can see the ships from the shore.

CAMEL BARN MUSEUM, *2024 Camel Road, Benicia. Phone: (707) 745-5435. Open 1 to 4 P.M. Friday, Saturday, and Sunday in the summer, Saturday and Sunday only the rest of the year; closed on major holidays. Admission: Donations appreciated. Wheelchair accessible.*

BENICIA CAPITOL STATE HISTORIC PARK, *115 West G Street, Benicia. Phone: (707) 745-3385. Open 10 A.M. to 5 P.M. seven days a week. Admission: Adults $1; children, 50 cents. Wheelchair accessible.*

TO GET TO BENICIA: *From San Francisco, take the Bay Bridge to Highway 80 North. After crossing the Carquinez Bridge, take Route 780 into town. Take the Second Street exit and turn right onto Second. Continue several blocks to Military.*

TO GET TO THE CAMEL BARN, *turn left and follow the road until you see the military arsenal and signs to the Camel Barn Museum.*

TO GET TO THE OLD STATE CAPITOL *and the Old Town shopping section, turn right on Military. Go one block to First Street and turn left. The capitol is on the corner of First and G streets; the shops are farther down on First Street.*

TO GET TO THE MOTHBALL FLEET, *take Route 780 East to Route 680 North to the Lake Herman Road exit; there is a vista point next to the highway.*

MARITIME ACADEMY

When driving across the Carquinez Bridge, I would often see a large ship docked on the northern side of the Bay. After passing it enough times I concluded there must be a story there. My conclusion was right. The ship is the *Golden Bear,* and it's a floating classroom for the California Maritime Academy, a training college for the merchant marines. The land campus is tucked away from view in the grove of trees between the Bay and the freeway. It's a lovely campus that could be the setting for any small college. This one just happens to have classrooms filled with computerized simulators and has a merchant marine ship parked outside. The students, 410 men and women, can earn a bachelor of science degree and be prepared for jobs as deck officers or engineers on merchant ships.

The *Golden Bear* is the major attraction for most visitors. Built in 1939 as a first-class passenger ship, this 8500-ton four-decker now carries midshipmen to the Pacific for four months of training each year. Much of the ship has been redesigned to suit this purpose, but there are still some vestiges of the ship's glory days when it made its luxury run from New Orleans to Rio de Janeiro. While walking through the wood-paneled lounge rooms, you can imagine the parties that went on here.

Tourists are very welcome and are usually shown around by senior-year students at the academy. They feel that most people in the Bay Area don't know they exit, so they are glad to show off the place. If your image of the seafaring type runs to *McHale's Navy* and *Mister Roberts,* you might be surprised to see so many women in uniform. My guide was proud to tell me that the first female to be appointed chief engineer of a ship in U.S. history was a graduate of the Maritime Academy.

CALIFORNIA MARITIME ACADEMY, *1 Maritime Drive, Vallejo. Phone: (707) 648-4200. Tours by reservation only. Admission: Free.*

HOW TO GET TO THE MARITIME ACADEMY: *From San Francisco, take the Bay Bridge to Route 80 toward Sacramento. After crossing the Carquinez Bridge, exit onto Sonoma Boulevard and look for signs to the Maritime Academy. From downtown Vallejo and the Mare Island Ferry, take Sonoma Boulevard toward San Francisco. Take the last right turn before entering the bridge and follow the signs.*

Here's an all-weather tour. It's the Herman Goelitz Candy Factory, which played an important role in diplomacy in the 1980s.

This is the home of Jelly Belly, the jelly bean that has for years been the favorite of one Ronald Reagan. His obsession with the candy started years ago, even before he was governor of California. When the future president gave up smoking, he started popping jelly beans whenever he got the urge to light up. Someone introduced him to Jelly Belly, and he was hooked. When he moved into the White House, Reagan brought his jelly beans with him. He served them at cabinet meetings and left commemorative jars for foreign dignitaries when they arrived for state visits (and they probably thought they'd get champagne and a fruit basket!).

All this publicity did wonders for the Goelitz company, which had been in business for 62 years in the industrial section of Oakland. Sales tripled, and the company moved into an industrial park on a backroad in Solano County. With the new plant came a new policy of offering tours to the public. The original founder's great-granddaughter, Becky Joffer, is in charge of the tour operation. Walking you through racks and racks of candy in their football-field-size factory, Becky will proudly show you how her family's beans are cooked, molded, flavored, coated, and packaged. Be prepared for some intense aromas as you pass vats of cinnamon, mint, or peanut butter (yep, peanut butter jelly beans).

You will also see some of their newer products, including those lovable, squishy Gummi Bears, Gummi Worms, and even the new Gummi Rat, which is 9 inches long and is sold complete with pet adoption papers.

By the way, if you're wondering what food business is benefitting from the presidency of George Bush, you might look for a tour of the pork rind company next time you're in Chicago.

HERMAN GOELITZ CANDY FACTORY, *2400 North Watney Way, Fairfield. Phone: (707) 428-2800. Retail shop open 11 A.M. to 5 P.M. weekdays; tours of the factory Monday through Friday by appointment only. Tours are free, with sweet samples at the end. Wheelchair accessible.*

HOW TO GET TO THE JELLY BELLY FACTORY: *From San Francisco, take the Bay Bridge to Highway 80 North toward Sacramento. At Fairfield, exit at Abernathy Road. Then go left on Busch, right on Chadbourne, left on Courage, and left again on Watney Way. The directions may sound involved, but it's really very simple, just a few minutes off the freeway.*

IS MR. WRIGHT RIGHT?

There is a lot more to Fairfield than jelly beans. On a quiet, suburban street a few blocks from the main drag—which for some reason is called Texas Street—you will find the world's only museum of Space Action. It's in the home of Walter Wright, whose major aim in life is to prove that Isaac Newton's theory of gravity was wrong. In Walter's theory, the apple that fell on poor Ike's head wasn't pulled down by gravity; it was pushed.

The museum is scattered over a few rooms in the back of the house, off a back yard that is worth the trip itself. A devoted father, Walter built a series of play areas for his young sons, including a train area and several other interesting designs. It looks like a playground designed by Mr. Wizard and a collection of folk artists.

Walter is a trained electrical engineer and a teacher at heart. His tour lasts for two hours, giving him time to explain many of his theories and answer all your questions. There are over 100 exhibits to see, but the tour doesn't take in every one, unless you are really interested. Basically, each exhibit is another graphic example of the Wright theory of magnetism and how everything is pushed rather than pulled. Some of the displays are more elaborate than others, but all are colorful and fun, whether or not you choose to believe Wright.

So far, the scientific community sticks with Isaac, and Walter is quick to tell you that all he wants is for "them"—meaning the scientific establishment—to just come and look at what he has. He says he may not be right, but so far no one has proved him wrong, so they should take him seriously. For now, he remains the Rodney ("Can't get no respect") Dangerfield of the world of science, but he is sure "they" will catch on someday.

Frankly, I couldn't make heads or tails out of the displays or the theory or even figure out why it makes a difference if gravity is a push or a pull, but I was fascinated by the place and found Walter to be a very sweet, entertaining man. He is very serious and excited about his findings, but also has a sense of humor about them and about life in general. Also, there is something very appealing about a person who takes a stand against all odds and sticks with it, despite the establishment.

WRIGHT MUSEUM OF SPACE ACTION, *732 Ohio Street, Fairfield. Phone: (707) 429-0598. Call for an appointment. Admission: Free.*

HOW TO GET TO WRIGHT MUSEUM: *From San Francisco, take the Bay Bridge to Highway 80 North toward Sacramento. Take the first Fairfield exit, which is West Texas Street. Take West Texas to the courthouse, which is on Union Street. Turn right on Union. Go four blocks to Ohio Street and turn right again. The museum is two blocks down the road.*

The Wright Brothers may have picked North Carolina as the place to fly an airplane for the first time, but California has been an important place for the next steps of aerospace development. That is the theme of the air museum, which is open to the public daily at Travis Air Force Base.

According to Lt. Colonel Lou Tobin, who helped start the museum in 1986 and runs it when he is not flying huge C5 transport planes, there are only a few such museums in the United States. His hopes are for an eventual rival to the main Air Force facility at Wright-Patterson in Dayton, Ohio.

This museum has a definite California slant. One of the prize possessions in the indoor part of the facility is an original Gonzales biplane, built in 1910 by the Gonzales brothers of San Francisco. It was a one-of-a-kind airplane; the brothers would pack it up in boxes, take it on a train to the wide open spaces up north, fly it for a week or so, and then pack it up again and flag down the train for the ride back home. The biplane remained in the family until nephew Bob gave it to the museum with the understanding that it never leave Travis.

There are many other things to see as well, including planes from both world wars, space capsules, training simulators, and a huge transport plane outside that is big enough to drive trucks into. This jumbo is opened on weekends for visitors to climb up and roam around. Another interesting area is the maintenance shop, where the continual process of renovation and repair takes place.

One of my favorite planes at the museum is the old presidential support plane that was used to fly President Roosevelt from his historic meeting in Yalta to a nearby aircraft carrier. This plane really has a checkered past. After the Roosevelt years it was sold to a Brazilian airline for short flights and then was purchased by a private pilot from nearby Rio Vista, who converted it to a restaurant at a small California airport. I'm happy to say that I had lunch once at the Flying Down to Rio Cafe. I'm sorry to say I may have been one of the few because they went out of business and turned the plane over to Travis Air Force Base.

You can spend several hours or just a short time at the museum, but chances are if you have any interest in anything to do with flying or space, you will find something here for you.

TRAVIS AIR FORCE MUSEUM, *Building 80, Travis Air Force Base. Phone: (707) 424-5605. Open 9 A.M. to 4 P.M. Monday through Friday, 9 A.M. to 5 P.M. Saturday and Sunday. Admission: Free. Wheelchair accessible.*

HOW TO GET TO THE AIR FORCE MUSEUM: *From San Francisco, take the Bay Bridge to Highway 80 North toward Sacramento. Exit at the Travis Air Base exit and take Travis Parkway to the entrance. The road ends at the gate. At the visitor's entrance, just tell the guards you are going to the museum, and they'll give you directions.*

ANTIQUE TRAINS AND STREETCARS

Tucked away in the countryside between Fairfield and Rio Vista is a museum devoted to a different America, the one in which the railroad was the key to the future. It's a history rich with romance, style, and technology, when streetcars and trolleys provided mass transit and steam locomotives moved people and goods around the nation. Many rail buffs feel that in this day of automotive gridlock and air pollution, we may once again return to the rail.

At the Western Railway Museum trains and streetcars are kept at the ready. Situated on a 25-acre site, with practically nothing else around, the museum offers a great opportunity to see 85 pieces of operating vintage railcars and to ride on one of them. It might be a wooden electric car from the Midwest or an early California trolley. Trains run every 10 minutes or so on a half-mile track that will carry you past a duck pond, around a good number of scenic curves, and by the barn where cars are being stored and restored.

The price of admission pays for as many rides as you care to take. There are also picnic tables strategically placed with views of the rolling stock. Once you get here you will probably want to stay awhile, so it's a good idea to bring along some food.

Inside the barn almost all the cars are open for visitors to climb aboard and roam around. One prize possession is the 1931 Scenic Limited, which ran from Oakland to Chicago. It was once used by Franklin D. Roosevelt on a whistle-stop campaign tour, and it appeared in the film *Harold and Maude*. It is locked up for protection, but you can see from the outside the still-working radio and Victorola and the kind of luxury afforded by such transportation.

The museum is run entirely by volunteers, who are constantly searching the country for more cars to add to their collection. They've picked up a car for a few dollars, then spent thousands getting it to run again. One treasure had been used as a sewing room for a home in Palo Alto, if you can imagine that. All the restoration work is done faithfully, down to matching the original nails, wood, trim, and glass.

Keep in mind as you roam the grounds that this was nothing but an open field when the organization first bought it in 1960. Every building, every foot of track, even the grass and landscaping, was the result of volunteer efforts.

WESTERN RAILWAY MUSEUM, *5848 Highway 12, at the Rio Vista Junction. Phone: (707) 374-2978. Open 11 A.M. to 5 P.M. Saturday, Sunday, and some holidays; closed Christmas, Thanksgiving, and New Year's. Admission: Adults, $3.00; ages 12 to 17, $2.00; children 3 to 11, $1.00; under 3, free.*

HOW TO GET TO THE RAILWAY MUSEUM: *From San Francisco, take the Bay Bridge to Route 80 North toward Sacramento. At Fairfield, exit on Route 12 East and continue for several miles to the museum, on the right side of the road.*

The town of Woodland, north of Highway 80, is one of the wealthiest agricultural towns of Northern California. Its rich history has been preserved in a beautifully restored opera house and a wonderful museum (more about those later), and, most important, at least for lovers of trucks, the A. W. Hays Antique Truck Museum.

A. W. has amassed what is believed to be the largest collection of antique trucks in the world. He houses them on the same property where he once ran his trucking business. As you pull up to the site, you might think you're in for a disappointment. It certainly doesn't look like an interesting museum as you drive through the gate and park near one of the aluminum storage buildings. But once inside you will see at least 100 trucks, representing 70 different manufacturers. There is a remarkable variety in the painstakingly restored collection, encompassing not only the bodies but transmissions, tires, and ornamentation. They date from a beauty from 1901 (the year A. W. was born) to some of the more recent Peterbilt monsters that now rule the highways.

Chances are your guide will be A. W. himself, a gentleman who spends his days since retirement caring for this unique collection. A. W. can still replace a fender and fabricate a wooden steering wheel with the best of them, and he is filled with stories about each of his prized possessions. (A. W. is also full of homespun humor. He told me his associates call him "Aw," his friends call him "Pop," and his wife calls him to dinner.)

He started in the trucking business by driving for other truck owners, delivering produce from the farms around Woodland to the San Francisco markets. During the Depression he scraped up enough money to buy his own truck. His business was so good that soon he had several trucks and the desire to start a collection.

According to Aw, the most unusual truck in his collection is a made-in-San Francisco model with a hauling platform only 14 inches above the ground. This was made before hydraulic lifts to make it easier to load the truck. I'm sure it worked just fine, but one pothole would surely cause the bottom to scrape the road.

Even if Aw isn't on hand for a tour, you'll do just fine on your own. Each exhibit is set up with a card with all the vital information. As you walk down the line of vehicles, a history of transportation in America unfolds, and you begin to see how the demand for moving goods created our highway system. You'll also see some great-looking machines.

A. W. HAYS ANTIQUE TRUCK MUSEUM, *2000 East Main Street, Woodland. Phone: (916) 666-1044. Usually open 10 A.M. to 4 P.M. Monday through Friday, and sometimes on weekends if A. W. feels like being there. Call first, as this is a* *very informal operation. Admission: Adults, $3; teens and younger, $1. Wheel-chair accessible.*

HOW TO GET TO THE TRUCK MUSEUM: *From San Francisco, take the Bay Bridge and stay on Route 80 heading for Sacramento. About an hour after the bridge, assuming you're in normal traffic, you will come to the Route 113 exit for Woodland. Take Route 113 North to Main Street in the town of Woodland. Turn right (east) and go to the corner of Route 102, where it intersects with Main. The museum is on your right.*

WOODLAND OPERA HOUSE ⑧

While you're in Woodland, you ought to see some of the town itself, and that simply involves a short ride down Main Street from the truck museum. As you move into the town's center, you can see this is a lively community. Thirty thousand people live here, and the modern Yolo County Courthouse is a focal point of activity. But Woodlanders have a keen sense of history, too, and they have preserved some of the town's most precious buildings.

On Main Street at Second you will find one of the finest of these, the Woodland Opera House, a beautifully restored brick building that is now open for shows and for tours. This was a very busy theater back in the late 1800s. All the shows on the circuit from Seattle to San Francisco stopped here. Not much in the way of grand opera was performed, but every traveling melodrama and dog-and-pony show packed 'em in. Young actors like Walter Houston and Sidney Greenstreet honed their craft here before moving on to more illustrious careers. John Phillips Sousa played his marches here. The place was boarded up in 1913, however, after someone fell in the theater and sued the owner. It stood as a decaying relic of the past until the 1960s, when a group of citizens raised enough money to restore it. Now it is a state historic site and is busy once again, with a new professional director and an ambitious program of plays, films, recitals, and concerts.

When the concerned citizens went inside to fix the place up, it was as if they had entered a time capsule. Costumes still hung in the downstairs dressing room; yellowed advertising posters adorned the walls. The gas stage-lighting panel was found in the wings. There were also tons of dust. After years of work, much of it volunteer, the Opera House reopened for tours in phase one. Then, the theater was totally renovated with plush seats, new paint and design, and historic displays in the lobby. It is a must stop for anyone interested in theater or architecture. It's a jewel of a house, with rounded balcony, high ceilings, perfect acoustics, and the proverbial "not a bad seat in the house."

WOODLAND OPERA HOUSE, *340 Second Street (Second and Main Streets), Woodland. Phone: (916) 666-9617. Open for tours 10 A.M. to 3:30 P.M. Tuesdays or by appointment. It's a good idea to call ahead. Admission: Donations accepted.*

HOW TO GET TO THE WOODLAND OPERA HOUSE: *From San Francisco, follow the directions for the truck museum. From there, follow Main Street past Route 113 to Second Street. The theater is on the northwest corner.*

Nearly every county has a historical museum these days, and after a while they start to blend together. This is not the case in Yolo County at the Gibson House Museum.

This county museum stands out from the rest for two reasons. First, the building looks like it belongs in the Old South. That's because William Gibson, the original occupant, was from Virginia, and to feel at home in the Wild West he embellished his 10-room house with impressive white columns, a la Tara in *Gone With the Wind*. The museum's other distinction is its director, Monica Stengert, whose background is unique indeed. Before moving to Northern California in 1975, Monica worked at the largest museum in her native Warsaw, Poland. She brings to her current job not only a world view of history but also a great appreciation for the immigrants who settled and built the town of Woodland. A visit with Monica is worth the trip, but the museum is an added treat.

The Gibson House is arranged to show the various periods during which the Gibson family lived here, from 1850 to 1940. Each room represents a different era and a different generation of Gibsons.

One of my favorite displays is the collection of barber-shop glass. This includes two display cases of beautiful bottles used for lotions and shampoos by the town barber, back in the days when the barber shop was an unofficial gentlemen's club. Some of the bottles were made in Venice and Murano, others were made locally; they are all spectacular.

Outside you'll find three smaller buildings, which housed the dairy, the root cellar, and the washroom. Each of these is operational, so you can have a hands-on experience churning butter or turning a hand-cranked washing machine. There is also a small display of antique farm equipment, an herb garden, and a park for picnicking. It can get very hot in the summer in Woodland, but the shade provided by a 200-year-old oak and other trees makes for a comfortable parklike setting on the property's 5 acres.

The Gibson House has been in operation only since 1982. It's another example of community volunteers getting together to enrich their town. For many years the home had been abandoned; local legend said it was haunted. Then a historical society was formed and the county was convinced to buy the house. Volunteers spent nearly 10 years fixing it up and acquiring donations for the exhibits. Today it's a county treasure.

YOLO COUNTY HISTORICAL MUSEUM AND GIBSON HOUSE, *512 Gibson Road, Woodland. Phone: (916) 666-1045. Museum is open noon to 4 P.M. Saturday and*

Sunday, 10 A.M. to 4 P.M. Monday and Tuesday; office hours are 8 A.M. to 5 P.M. Monday and Tuesday. Admission: Free. You can arrange to see the museum by appointment on Wednesday, Thursday, or Friday, but there is a $1 per person fee.

HOW TO GET TO THE GIBSON HOUSE: *From San Francisco, follow the directions to the truck museum, but when you reach the shopping center at Gibson Road, turn left. From the opera house, go back to Route 113 at Main Street. Turn right, heading south. After several blocks, you will come to a stoplight at Gibson Road, with a shopping center entrance on the left. Turn right and continue for a few blocks. The Gibson House is on the left side of the road.*

CHAPTER **10** The Delta

AREA OVERVIEW   California epitomizes America's love affair with the automobile. But the Sacramento Delta is one place in the state where the car loses out to the boat. The Delta is truly a marvel: 1000 miles of waterways connecting some 55 islands. (More about how to use those waterways later.)

In this boaters' paradise there is still much to see by taking a drive. This is an agricultural area, with levees along the roadside, built to control the flow of the Sacramento and San Joaquin rivers. These levees were the work of Chinese laborers who had come to the United States for the Gold Rush and stayed to work on the continental railroad.

There are few towns. What you see on a drive on the main road, Route 160, is scenery and history. Even though you're only an hour or so away from the Bay Bridge, you're a long way from the "California chic" of the Bay Area. Restaurants are not called "Chez" or "Casa de"; they are called Sid's, Doc's, and Al's. Beer outsells white wine by a wide margin.

The roads are mainly two-lane, and they meander. The best plan for a drive is to pick just one or two destinations and simply wander, taking a turn to see where it will lead you. Sooner or later the maze will always get you back to Route 160. If there is one "must see" town in the Delta, it is Locke (see page 170).

If you have some time, the absolute best way to see the Delta is by water. Boats are available for rent at several locations. You can rent a small boat by the hour and simply putt around. Because of high insurance rates, it is now difficult to rent a houseboat and live on the Delta. Marinas with waterfront services such as grocery stores and restaurants are easy to find. Portions of the Sacramento

Delta are reminiscent of the Mississippi Delta, with channels that take you through narrow aisles of moss-covered willow trees. In fact, movie producer Samuel Goldwyn remarked, when looking for a place to shoot *The Adventures of Huckleberry Finn*, "It looks more like the Mississippi than the real thing." Don't worry; there are no alligators here. A word to the wise: This is a popular place in the heat of the summer, and I do mean heat. A beautiful slough can lose some of its glamour when you are trying to navigate your way past a houseboat full of amateur sailors. The best time for a trip on the Delta is in the late spring or early fall. How to get to the Delta: From San Francisco, the most direct route is to take the Bay Bridge to Route 80 North to Fairfield. Turn right on Route 12 and follow it into the town of Rio Vista (see Yolano map). Once you cross the bridge onto Route 160, you are at the beginning of the Delta. This is the spot where Humphrey the Whale made his world-famous visit in 1985. Another route, which will take you near the scenic town of Benicia, is to take the Bay Bridge to Route 24 toward Walnut Creek. Route 24 eventually joins Route 680. Follow 680 North to Route 4 toward Antioch until it meets Route 160. Take Route 160 all the way through as much of the Delta as you wish to visit.

For information about rentals, write or call the Rio Vista Chamber of Commerce for a list of agencies. The address is 60 Main Street, Rio Vista, CA 94571. Phone: (707) 374-2700.

FOSTER'S BIG HORN

The town of Rio Vista, the gateway to the Sacramento Delta, went relatively unnoticed by the rest of the world until the fall of 1985, when a huge whale named Humphrey magically and inexplicably appeared in the town's canal.

But as impressive a specimen of mammal life as Humphrey was, he was small potatoes compared to the big game to be found in Foster's Big Horn Saloon.

The name "Big Horn" ought to provide a clue to the kind of place this is. The walls of the barroom and back dining room are covered with every kind of animal head you can imagine: lions and tigers and bears, oh my! And elephants, too. In fact, the best seat in the house is right under an enormous elephant's head with huge tusks. Groucho Marx fans love to sit under it and say that in Alabama the tusks are looser.

If Bill Foster were alive today he would be the target of every animal's rights group in the world, and rightly so. But his hunting was done back in Hemingway's time, when shooting game was accepted as sport. And what he left behind is a collection as remarkable as anything you could imagine.

This collection is even more incredible in light of the fact that every specimen was shot by Foster himself. It is heralded as the largest one-man collection of big horns and heads in the world. Foster apparently zipped off to Africa quite regularly; in its heyday, Foster's Rio Vista joint was a gambling parlor successful enough to fund frequent safaris. Foster would return with more prizes to decorate his saloon.

Before Foster retired in 1950, his Big Horn Saloon had everything: gambling, hooch, big spenders from the city on their way to do some pleasure-cruising on the Delta. Today the place is much quieter. It is owned by the son of the woman who bought the place from Foster. It is a hangout for locals who drop by for a drink or a bite to eat and an attraction for tourists who drop by to see if what they've heard about the place could possibly be true; they are seldom disappointed.

FOSTER'S BIG HORN, *Main Street between Front and Second, Rio Vista. Open 10 A.M. to 2 A.M. daily. Phone: (707) 374-2511.*

HOW TO GET TO FOSTER'S BIG HORN: *From San Francisco, take the Bay Bridge to Highway 80 toward Sacramento. At Fairfield, exit onto Route 12 and follow it all the way to Rio Vista. On entering town, bear right at the sign for the business district. Foster's will be on your right on Main Street.*

RIO VISTA MUSEUM

We have the 1976 Bicentennial celebration to thank for the plethora of town historical museums that can be found throughout the United States. In the Bay Area, in the Delta town of Rio Vista, a group of citizens decided they should do something to celebrate the nation's 200th anniversary, so they turned an old blacksmith shop in the middle of town into a museum. Therein lies the beauty and the problem of these new museums.

Since a history had not formally been organized, categorized, and cataloged for the town until 1976, creative methods had to be devised. The call went out for all locals to bring in anything they thought might be of interest. Practically nothing was refused. Then W. H. K. Dunbar, a 50-year resident of Rio Vista and a retired electrical engineer, set about the task of creating a showplace.

When I visited, Mr. Dunbar was well into his eighties but still full of energy and still trying to organize the place. He calls the collection "mostly junk," but I found it a fascinating representation of the town—of the entire nation, as a matter of fact. People brought in newspapers from hometowns across America and Dunbar framed the front page of each one. The result is a wall of nationwide headline history, from the turn of the century through world wars, assassinations, depressions, and space voyages. Below the newspapers an ever-changing display of artifacts is arranged: old typewriters, early radios, personal pictures, even an amusing assortment of beverage containers including jars of sarsaparilla, a can of Billy Beer, and tiny airplane-service-size whisky bottles.

There are several rooms, each filled to the ceiling with what I can only call "stuff." The original part of the building, the blacksmith's shop, is filled with farm equipment from the area's earliest agricultural days. This is a very charming place, and I hope you'll get a chance to meet W. H. K. Dunbar, too.

RIO VISTA MUSEUM, *16 North Front Street, Rio Vista. Phone: (707) 374-5169. Open 1:30 to 4:30 P.M. Saturday and Sunday only. Admission: Free, but a donation of $1 is greatly appreciated.*

HOW TO GET TO THE RIO VISTA MUSEUM: *From San Francisco, take the Bay Bridge to Highway 80 toward Sacramento. At Fairfield, exit onto Route 12 and follow it all the way to Rio Vista. When you enter town, bear right at the sign for the business district.*

MUSEUM OF DREDGING

I have been to the town of Rio Vista several times in the past few years. For reasons that may seem obvious, I always avoided visiting a place called the Museum of Dredging. Really, what could sound more drab and boring? Well, I'm happy to report I was wrong. This place is neither drab nor boring, and it is a stop I can heartily recommend.

The Dutra Museum of Dredging happens to be set up in a beautiful old house in a residential section of this picturesque town. It's the kind of house every boy or girl in the 1940s wished were home: a stone structure with a beautiful garden and a porch that goes from the front all the way around the side to the back of the house. You can imagine sitting on a swing or glider on a hot day, waiting for the ice-cream truck to come by.

This has been the Dutra home for years, and Mrs. Linda Dutra has opened the place to tourists to show the private collection of memorabilia and models and to tell the story of the Dutras' involvement with developing the Delta region. Linda begins the tour at a huge mural that shows how the Dutra family first came to the United States, then headed west by wagon train to California. Several generations ago the Dutras developed what is called the clamshell style of dredging. Using huge cranes that look like giant clams, they cut the intricate series of canals that now make up the Delta. Of course their work never ends because the flow of the rivers brings new silt that must be continually dredged to maintain a navigable depth. Every room in the house is decorated with memorabilia from the exploits of the clan. You wouldn't believe that there could be so many fascinating pieces of machinery to see; there are scale models of early dredges and a working hydraulic model to show you the latest in equipment.

But for me, the personal stories were the most fascinating. In seeing the history of this one Portuguese-American family, complete with personal photographs and mementos, you see a dramatic illustration of the American dream through their eyes. This is a family that made it, accumulated a lot of money, and is still working to keep the Delta open.

There are several bittersweet elements to a visit here, too. Edward Dutra, the patriarch of the family, suffered a crippling stroke a few years ago and sits in a corner watching his wife give the tours. He is unable to speak. There is also a twinge of bewilderment from Mrs. Dutra that some environmentalists oppose the kind of work they do and have made the Dutras a symbol for rallying supporters to their cause.

Linda says that most people expect to stop in for just a few minutes but end up staying a long time. She says the men get fascinated by all the equipment and the women fall in love with the house.

DUTRA MUSEUM OF DREDGING, *345 St. Gertrude's Avenue, Rio Vista. Phone: (707) 374-5015. Open by appointment. Admission: Free.*

HOW TO GET TO THE DREDGING MUSEUM: *From San Francisco, follow the directions to the Rio Vista business section ("Rio Vista Museum"). From Main Street, turn right on Fourth Street and follow it to the corner of St. Gertrude's Avenue. The house is directly across from the high school.*

RIDE THE J-MAC

Do you love boat rides but don't have the time for a long trip? Maybe you like the idea of the high seas but are subject to *mal de mer*? Do I have a ride for you!

Because there are so many inland waterways to cross in the Sacramento Delta, the state provides free ferryboat service from island to island. The quickest, shortest ride is on the J-Mac, which connects Grand Island and Ryer Island, crossing the Steamboat Slough. You drive your car right onto the ferry, which looks like a glorified barge. In less than two minutes you are on land again, on the other side. The smooth sailing comes courtesy of such pilots as Early Whiteley, who makes the trip back and forth every day. This is a guy who spent years on a sailboat in the Pacific, and he says the river is so fascinating that he always sees new things.

The J-Mac ferry crosses 160 times a day, and there are lots of other ferries at crossings all along Route 160. It's the only way to get between the many islands of this unique region.

For more information call Caltrans. Phone: (415) 923-4444.

LOCKE: THE TOWN THAT TIME FORGOT

Of the few towns in the Delta, none is more interesting or unusual than Locke. This was one of California's original Chinatowns, constructed for the Chinese laborers who built the intricate systems of levees that control the flow of water in the Delta. There isn't much left of the town, and every now and then somebody comes up with a grand scheme to buy the place and turn it into a commercial enterprise. One such plan was to build a theme park to compete with Disneyland. But for now this is a one-block village with a past. In 1915 discriminatory laws did not allow the Chinese to own land. A white farmer named George Locke leased a parcel of his land to the Chinese to build a town; by 1920 Locke was an active community with a school, church, and population of around 2000.

During the Depression, since Locke was really out in the sticks, it became a place to which city slickers could come for a night of gambling; the Star Theater, which had once hosted operas every week, became the town brothel.

Today the Chinese population has dwindled to 45. Their fate has been a sad one. The younger generation has moved on to the cities, and most of the old businesses that served the once thriving community have closed. There is some concern about the longevity of the ramshackle wooden buildings that line the town's one street; they tend to lean a bit, and these structures may not last long, so a visit to this little town should not be put off. It represents a slice of history that doesn't exist anywhere else. A stroll through Locke will probably include a visit to the old Star Theater, the Chinese schoolhouse, and the Dai Loy Gambling Museum.

The only real action is at Al's, an old-time bar in the front where regulars pass the time of day and night. But Al's main claim to fame is the culinary offerings in the rear dining room. For years, people have come from all over for the house specialty at Al's: steak and peanut butter. You order a grilled rib steak that comes with a side of toasted, buttered French bread. On each table there is a big jar of peanut butter and a companion jar of jelly. Some put the condiments on the bread, others on the steak. Some make a sandwich of the whole thing. But everyone in the place seems to get a kick out of the fact they are eating such a weird lunch.

I should mention that the new food consciousness has even caught up with Al's. A few years ago they added an alternative for those cutting down on the consumption of red meat: chicken. So now you have your choice of steak or chicken with peanut butter. By the way, they only offer the smooth kind. No chunky.

LOCKE, *right off Route 160, the main road through the Delta. Park your car and then walk in. The street is very narrow, and no parking is available on Main.*

AL'S DINER, *on Main Street in Locke. Phone: (916) 776-1800. Open for lunch and dinner.*

DAI LOY GAMBLING HOUSE MUSEUM, *13951 Main Street. Phone: (916) 776-1246.*

Several destinations four and five hours from San Francisco are still considered to be part of the Bay Area. These places add to the pleasure of visiting or living in this part of the world, offering access to snow and skiing in the winter, crystal clear lakes and water sports in the summer, and forests and wilderness activities all year-round.

Many of the destinations in this section require more planning than the places in the other chapters. Overnight accommodations will be necessary, and during peak seasons reservations are a must.

The closest Gold Country destinations can be reached in 2 hours from San Francisco. Mendocino and Carmel are 2½ to 3 hours away, and Yosemite, Lake Tahoe, and the Redwood Empire are at least 4 hours away. These are average driving times, which are to be used only as a point of reference. I recommend taking your time, stopping now and again to examine the curiosities along the way.

AREA OVERVIEW   Imagine California before the Gold Rush in 1848. Hollywood didn't exist. San Francisco was only a tiny waterfront. Monterey was the capital city of this Spanish-American outpost of farmland and cattle. Then word went out around the world that fortunes were to be found in "them thar foothills" of the Sierra, and people have flocked to the Golden State ever since.

For a few short years the action was in the area known as the Gold Country. Boomtowns housed thousands upon thousands of people; saloons, hotels, and other businesses sprang up overnight to provide services. In fact, many who found fortunes during the Gold Rush were suppliers to the miners—companies like Levi Strauss, Studebaker, Armour, and Ghirardelli.

But the Gold Rush fever cooled rapidly, and most of the people who had arrived from points all over the globe headed to San Francisco or Sacramento to build new lives. Only a few stayed behind. The Gold Country was more or less abandoned.

Today there is still gold in the hills, but it's simply too expensive to be mined by small companies. Major corporations are now running giant mines, and are pulling more gold out of the hills now than during the Gold Rush. For small fry, though, the new gold is the tourist trade. The nine counties in the mother lode area have banded together to try to strike it rich. Every effort is made to make the area a year-round attraction. The most popular time for tourists is between May and October, when the weather is warmest and the counties hold fairs. The most famous of these is the Calaveras County Fair, site of the annual jumping frog contest, an event first made famous years ago by a local newspaper writer named Mark Twain.

The weather for the region is more like the Bay Area than the neighboring mountains of the Sierra. Most of the Gold Country is below the snow line, and roads are passable throughout the year. The days get very hot during the summer, but the nights tend to cool off.

The main road connecting the counties of the mother lode is appropriately named Route 49 (gold miners seeking their fortune were called "forty-niners," just like San Francisco's professional football team). Route 49 leads you 317 miles from the southern tip of the Gold Country at Oakhurst to the northernmost town of Downieville. No one should try to take it all in on one trip. The best plan is to select one section and concentrate on it. No matter where you go you will find beautiful scenery, often corny remnants of the Gold Rush days, and towns with wonderful names like Fiddletown, Grub Gulch, Bootjack, and Humbug.

I recommend that you concentrate on one of the three general areas: the Southern Mines, centered around Columbia; the Central Mother Lode, centered around Jackson; or the Northern Mines, centered around Nevada City. Each area has its own local historical museum and its own particular flavor.

TO GET TO THE SOUTHERN MINES, take Highway 580 out of Oakland to Highway 205 to Route 120 to Oakdale; then take Route 108 to Route 49, which you pick up a bit south of Jamestown. You might recognize Jamestown as the site for numerous movies such as *High Noon* and *The Virginian*. Continue on Route 49 to Sonora, the closest thing to a booming city in the county, then on to Columbia. The entire town is a state historic park, faithfully restored like Williamsburg, Virginia, but on a much smaller scale.

TO GET TO THE CENTRAL MOTHER LODE, follow Interstate 80 from the Bay Bridge to Route 50 in Sacramento; then take Route 16, following the signs to Jackson. Here, visit the towns of Jackson, Sutter Creek, Volcano, and the wine region in the Shenandoah Valley. For history, Coloma is another town that became a state park. Here you can see how the Gold Rush began. If you have time, you might want to take a look at the town of Ione, which used to be called Bedbug. In fact, the town's one hotel was actually called Bedbug Hotel. A very impressive castle overlooks the town; it was formerly used as a boys' reform school, but now it's left empty and the school is in a new building.

TO GET TO THE NORTHERN MINES, take Interstate 80 from the Bay Bridge to Route 49 North at Auburn and continue to the towns of Grass Valley and Nevada City. In Auburn, you'll wonder about the giant statues rising high above various points in the city. They were all created by a local dentist named Ken Fox who started building statues as a hobby. His 42-foot-high concrete and steel creations include gold miners, Amazon warriors, and Chinese laborers. Because of their size, the statues will probably outlast Dr. Fox's fillings. In Nevada County, the Chamber of Commerce is located in the house once occupied by the legendary actress Lola Montez; the flower planter out front is her bathtub ("It was the only clean thing about her," one of the Chamber of Commerce people remarked). It's located at 248 Mill Street, Grass Valley. Phone: (916) 273-4667.

Also of note, just south of town, is the Empire Mine State Historic Park. This was the largest and richest of all the hard-rock gold mines in the state and operated for more than 100 years. A tour of the mine and its many buildings and passages is offered by park personnel. A highlight is a visit to the home of the owner of the mine, William Bourne, whom we met earlier as the owner of Filoli in Woodside.

In terms of distance from San Francisco, most areas of the Gold Country can be reached in 2½ to 3 hours. The roads that take you there are all good and fast. Route 49 is slow and requires that you take your time.

Keep in mind that night life is close to nonexistent in the Gold Country, and great restaurants are few and far between. Columbia in the south has its City Hotel, and Sonora offers a place called Hemingways, but it gets to be slim pickings after that. Nevada City and Grass Valley also have good restaurants, as well as many attractive homes and neighborhoods.

I'm sure you will find your own special places simply by driving around the backroads off Route 49. To get you started, here are some spots of special interest, arranged south to north along Route 49.

For general information about traveling in the Gold Country, contact the Golden Chain Council of the Mother Lode, P.O. Box 1246, Auburn, CA 95603. Phone: (916) 885-5616.

MERCER CAVERNS

About a mile north of the town of Murphys is a tourist attraction that is corny, predictable, and too good to pass up. Mercer Caverns has been a tourist attraction since 1885, after a gold prospector, Walter J. Mercer, discovered the place. The legend is that after a long, fruitless day of searching for gold, Mercer stumbled across these caverns while looking for some water (and considering that he was nearly 40 years behind everybody else, it's not surprising he was tired and thirsty). He noticed some bay bushes growing near a bluff of limestone; upon further investigation he found an entrance leading to the caverns. Since then, thousands have paid admission for the experience of visiting the wonders inside Mother Earth.

Today you will be led through the caverns by tour guides who have preset speeches yet manage to seem fascinated by the material. They will tell you how Mercer probed in the darkness, risking life and limb to see what was there. They will tell you of his discovery of an ancient Indian burial ground. They will explain stalagmites and stalactites, and, as a climax to the tour, they will turn off the flashlights to show you what it is like to really be in the dark.

Before the lights go out, what you will see is truly spectacular. It's a constantly changing show of underground rock formations, illuminated by colored lights and seemingly reaching to endless depth. I liked the weird formations named for items they resemble. For example, the area named "Chinese Meat Market" features shapes hanging from the ceiling that look like the objects to be found hanging in the butcher's shop (sort of). The "Organ Loft" is to be found in a section with a vaulted chamber, and with a little imagination it does remind one of a giant church organ. Other formations with names like "Angel Wings" and "Rapunzel" are self-explanatory. (Look, you paid for the tour. Does it hurt to let your imagination go for a while?)

This is a place to visit in the summer, when the temperature outside hovers around 100 degrees. It's always about 55 degrees inside the caverns, and it feels wonderful. You will want to wear good walking shoes, and the tour is not recommended for anyone who might have trouble climbing back up the steep stone steps.

MERCER CAVERNS, *Murphys. Phone: (209) 728-2101. Open 9 A.M. to 5 P.M. daily, Memorial Day through September; 11 A.M. to 4 P.M. Saturday, Sunday, and school holidays October through May. Admission: Adults, $4.50; children 11 and under, $2.25; under 5, free. The tour takes about 45 minutes.*

HOW TO GET TO MERCER CAVERNS: *From San Francisco, take the Bay Bridge to Highway 580 East, which becomes Route 205. Follow Route 205 to Route 120 to Oakdale; then take Route 108 to Route 49. Continue north on Route 49 until you come to Route 4 at Angels Camp. Take Route 4 into Murphys. Mercer Caverns is 1 mile north of Murphys, off Highway 4, on the Ebbetts Pass Highway.*

THE JEWEL OF THE STATE PARK SYSTEM

Not far from Mercer Caverns is a less commercial but equally spectacular destination. Long before Walter Mercer or any other white man even dreamed of settling in California, this was the home of giant sequoia trees. In fact, not only are these trees thousands of years old, but they are the largest living things in the world. When they named this park Big Trees, they weren't kidding.

How big are the trees? Well, when the grove was discovered in the 1850s a group of businessmen cut down one of the trees to take it on the road as a traveling exhibition. The remaining stump was large enough to be used as a dance floor. For many a Saturday night, an orchestra, dancers, and the crowd of onlookers would gather on this 27-foot-diameter tree stump. Fortunately, after the parks service was established, further abuses of the forest were prohibited. Today visitors may walk on the stump while enjoying the majesty of the trees towering over the site of their fallen relative. This park is practically devoid of gimmicks; other than the stump and a tree with a hole that you can walk through, every effort has been made to preserve the natural beauty of the area.

Guided tours by park rangers are available and recommended. In places such as this, the rangers are thrilled to be where they are and love to share their enthusiasm. My guide was Kurt Craft. He calls his outpost "the jewel of the state park system." And no wonder. His territory includes 6000 acres of mountainous terrain, deep canyons, riverside beaches, two groves of giant sequoias, and mountain meadows. He says people come here for hiking, peace, and a chance to lose themselves in the woods for a while. The park features more than 40 miles of hiking trails, most of them easy to navigate. Highly recommended is the Three Senses Trail, an area that encourages the use of sight, smell, and hearing

—not only fascinating but therapeutic.

CALAVERAS BIG TREES STATE PARK, *Highway 4, near the town of Arnold. Open all year. For information about camping, swimming, and fishing, phone (209) 296-7488.*

HOW TO GET TO BIG TREES STATE PARK: *Follow the directions to Mercer Caverns, but continue on Ebbetts Pass Highway until you come to the park. It's about a half hour from the caverns.*

AMADOR COUNTY MUSEUM

Did you ever see the Will Rogers movie *Boys Will Be Boys*? How about the television series *Petticoat Junction*? Both have a connection to the Amador County Museum, a former residence that sits high on a hill overlooking the town of Jackson. Rogers used the house as the setting for his 1920 epic, and the train from the TV series sits outside, with a paint job designed to remind visitors of the Gold Rush days.

These examples will give you some idea of the flavor of the museum, an eclectic, show-bizzy collection of items that tell the story of the Central Mother Lode.

The main house is a lovely two-story brick building, filled with furniture from the period. The place is arranged as if the family still lived there and had stepped out for the afternoon. The kitchen is ready for a meal to be prepared; the parlor has been tidied up for guests.

Then there are the show-biz touches. In the parlor you'll see a 1920s vintage radio on display, and you'll hear the crooning sounds of Russ Columbo and young Bing Crosby (but if you peek behind the radio you'll find a modern tape recorder). Out back in the old livery stable you'll find a working scale model of one of the largest mines in the area, the Kennedy Gold Mine. You will first be ushered into the stable, probably under the guidance of museum curator Cedric Clute. Then he will turn out the lights, rush over to yet another tape recorder, and begin a 10-minute multimedia presentation about the mine and how it operated. It is great fun, and the miniature mine actually works.

After viewing the model, it is recommended that you drive up to the top of the hill on Route 49 to overlook the remains of the original mine. Much of it is underground, but you can still see the huge wheels and other gizmos used in the process of gold mining.

Back at the museum, you can ask Cedric about the infamous heart-shaped plaque that is no longer on display in town. It was a tribute to the ladies of the Gold Rush who came to work in the brothels. Replicas of the original are available on a key chain in almost every trinket shop in the area.

As for the *Petticoat Junction* train, a resident heard that the Hooterville Cannonball was sitting around on an empty lot in Hollywood, so he bought it and contributed it to the museum. It doesn't go anywhere, but it's interesting to find it here.

AMADOR COUNTY MUSEUM, *225 Church Street, Jackson. Phone: (209) 223-6386. Open Wednesday through Sunday 10 A.M. to 4 P.M.; closed Monday and Tuesday. Admission to the museum is free, but the mine program costs $1.00 for adults, 50 cents for kids.*

HOW TO GET TO THE AMADOR COUNTY MUSEUM: *From San Francisco, take the Bay Bridge to Interstate 80 toward Sacramento. In Sacramento, exit to Route 50 East toward Lake Tahoe. Take Route 16 off Route 50 toward Jackson. Follow Route 16 to Route 49, the main road of the Gold Country. Turn right (south) on Route 49 and follow the signs to the town of Jackson. You will be on Main Street. Turn left onto Church and follow it up the hill to the museum.*

VOLCANO

This is one of the prettiest towns in all the Gold Country. It is a very small place with a very large sense of community pride. A visitor isn't in town long before being reminded that Volcano is the home of many "firsts" in the state, including the first circulating library, theater group, private law school, and solar still.

When you drive into town, the first thing you will see in this one-street town is the quaint though obligatory National Hotel (in the Gold Country, restored National Hotels are like wineries in the rest of the state—they are everywhere). You will also see shops and lovely historic buildings, all surrounding an inviting parklike town center. There's a bench out in front of the general store, facing a large grassy knoll. In front of the knoll there are a few exteriors of old buildings being held up like stage sets, offering a flavor of the old town.

Also on display is the town cannon, set up to deter a possible Confederate uprising during the Civil War. It has never been fired, so apparently it was effective against the rebels.

Then you will see the town's sore thumb, the modern, ranch-style post office. If you want to start a conversation with anybody, just ask about the post office. You'll hear all about the town's battle with the U.S. government. It seems that the post office used to be in a beautiful old building across the street from the hotel. That was fine, but the residents didn't get along with the postmaster. You must understand how important the post office is to a community like this. People come down from the hills and mingle with the townsfolk as they all pick up their mail; it's as important a community center as the neighborhood pub is in England. The good folks around Volcano complained loud and long to the powers that be in Washington, D.C., and eventually they got their way, sort of.

To make a long story short, according to the residents' version of the story, they were able to get rid of the postmaster, but as punishment the government took away their nice post office building, claiming it was no longer suitable.

Stuck with an ugly old trailer, the citizens battled long and hard to get a more suitable building, possibly restoring the old historic one and bringing it up to code. No luck; the government finally got rid of the trailer but put up a modern building that looks like it might be a dry cleaner's.

If you are really lucky, you might run into a fascinating man named George Oxford. He looks a lot like Walter Cronkite. In fact, George did spend his career in broadcasting, but not as a newsman. To Bay Area listeners of the 1950s he was Jumpin' George. He says that as a native Southerner, he had an affinity for black rhythm-and-blues music. He introduced the sounds of the Penguins, the Moonglows, and the Orioles to radio listeners while affecting a jargony delivery that made most people assume he was black, too. Jumpin' George was a smash, and he has wonderful stories to tell about people's reactions when they would discover he was a white man. Now retired, this distinguished-looking gentleman loves to tell stories about the old days of radio. His wife runs the county Chamber of Commerce.

If you visit in the spring, George, or anyone else in town, will surely direct you to a favorite spot around here, Daffodil Hill. Each April the 300,000 bulbs that have been planted on the hillside will be in bloom. It is a dazzling show.

VOLCANO, *about 20 minutes from the larger town of Sutter Creek. The county Chamber of Commerce can tell you if Daffodil Hill is in bloom. Phone: (209) 223-0350.*

HOW TO GET TO VOLCANO: *From Jackson, take Route 88 to the Pine Grove Road until you reach Volcano Road. Turn left and follow for a few miles into Volcano.*

HOW TO GET TO DAFFODIL HILL: *It's 3 miles beyond Volcano, still on the Pine Grove-Volcano Road. There are signs to the hill.*

INDIAN GRINDING ROCK STATE PARK

Several places in Northern California are dedicated to preserving the lifestyle of the original Indian inhabitants of the state. In my opinion, the most impressive of these is outside the town of Volcano at the Indian Grinding Rock State Historical Park.

There is much to see and do here, but it is best to start at the park's namesake rock. Until the turn of the century original Indians of the High Sierra would travel to this meadow to gather food. The rock was used for grinding acorns from the surrounding oak trees into meal, a staple of the Indian diet. This giant slab of limestone, 173 feet by 82 feet, was the social center for women; while the men hunted, the women would gather the acorns and other seeds and pulverize them while swapping stories and tending their children. The rock is the largest of its kind in California and is fenced off with a platform for public viewing.

There's another part to the story. After the Indians left, the property was in the hands of a family that passed the land down from generation to generation.

The family knew the rock had significance but wasn't sure how to protect it for the future. In the 1950s the family enlisted the support of Muriel Thebaut, the county's unofficial historian and a wonderful lady. She took it upon herself to convince the authorities that something should be done to preserve the rock. She went to the county supervisors, suggesting that a park be established, but they weren't interested. She went to some local Indian families, who said they were sure no one cared about their heritage. Finally, she went to the state parks department, who became interested. After years of lobbying, a park was finally established. Muriel remains a park docent and an active board member.

The park features 21 campsites with tables and stoves, a picnic area, many hiking trails, several re-created Indian dwellings and a wonderful cultural center with displays from several tribes and occasional demonstrations of Native American crafts. The center is built in the style of an Indian roundhouse and is quite beautiful.

INDIAN GRINDING ROCK STATE HISTORICAL PARK, *14881 Pine Grove-Volcano Road, about 15 minutes outside the town of Jackson. Open 8:30 A.M. to 4:30 P.M. Wednesday through Friday, 9:30 A.M. to 5:30 P.M. Saturday, Sunday, and holidays. A nominal fee is charged for parking. Phone: (209) 296-4440.*

HOW TO GET TO THE STATE PARK: *From Jackson, take Route 88 to Pine Grove, then bear left and follow the Volcano Road to the park.*

NEVADA CITY

Many people are surprised to learn that Nevada City is in California. That's nothing, Virginia City is in Nevada. The Gold Country is full of surprises.

There is something special about Nevada City. Perhaps it's the setting, framed against the foothills of the Sierra. Maybe it's the crisp air, or the energy of the residents, or the attractive architecture. Whatever it is, the town itself is a gem and a worthy destination. Its historical buildings, including a number of Victorian homes, are beautifully restored. And considering its location, Nevada City is quite cosmopolitan; several shops downtown sell everything from chic clothing to Gold Rush memorabilia, and there are good places to eat and stay. Nevada City is also one of the few places in California where you can find fall foliage as lovely as that in the East, thanks to the many trees brought in by transplanted Easterners.

Like so many Gold Country towns, Nevada City has an obligatory National Hotel, this one famous for the fact that the papers that led to the creation of the Pacific Gas and Electric Company were signed in one of its suites. Herbert Hoover was a regular guest here when he was a young mining engineer.

One place in town worth checking out is the Miner's Foundry Cultural Center. Until recently, this complex was called the American Victorian Museum, which was an ambitious community center, combined with a museum and retail outlet for Victoriana. Now, the Victorian antiques have been moved to a small room, and the building's main display areas are devoted to local history. This old stone building really was a miner's foundry. It still houses the community-owned radio station (KVMR 89.5 FM, the call letters still standing for Victorian Museum Radio), a large stage for community theater productions, and the Great Stone Hall, which is a dining room decked out in Victorian-era treasures. Here Sunday brunch is served, and annual events, including Thanksgiving, Christmas, and Robert Burns's birthday, are celebrated. Call or write ahead for a schedule of events.

The best way to enjoy Nevada City is to drive into the center of town and park. The Chamber of Commerce office is at the foot of Main Street and can offer brochures and maps for a walking tour. If you walk up Broad Street and then branch off onto any of the side streets, you can't go wrong.

MINER'S FOUNDRY COMMUNITY CULTURAL CENTER, *325 Spring Street, Nevada City, CA 95959. Phone: (916) 265-5040. Reservations for Sunday brunch are advised.*

HOW TO GET TO NEVADA CITY: *From San Francisco, take the Bay Bridge to Route 80 toward Sacramento. Exit onto Route 49 at Auburn and follow Route 49 into Nevada City.*

MALAKOFF DIGGINS Almost everything in the Gold Country is what I would call "cute." Everywhere you see icons of grizzled old prospectors, Wild West saloons, and mementos of the good old days of the forty-niners. It's all done in a fun, corny way. But the Malakoff Diggins illustrates the dark side of gold fever. Malakoff Diggins is a huge pit cut out of what was once a beautiful ravine. During the Gold Rush, this was the largest hydraulic mining operation in the world. In a literal rush to get at the gold in the hills, huge hoses attached to powerful pumps were brought in to blast away indiscriminately at the landscape. As the hillside gave way, the gold would be extracted and the rest allowed to wash away down the Yuba River. The gold fever was so intense that in the mining town of Relief, residents stood on the banks of the river with nozzles and washed away the foundations of their own homes.

The environmental impact was felt well beyond the Gold Country. Silt-filled rivers caused flooding 40 miles away in the towns of Yuba City and Marysville and even clogged San Francisco Bay, inhibiting the shipping industry. A lawsuit was brought to stop hydraulic mining. The result was the first major court decision in favor of the environment. The abusive practice was stopped, and much gold still remains in the area. But before packing your prospecting gear, you should know that the gold is protected by law and too scattered to be worth the effort to extract.

Now operated as a state historic park, Malakoff Diggins has several good vantage points where you can walk out to the edge and view the valley cut by greed. In the past century some vegetation has had the opportunity to grow, but you can imagine what a desolate wasteland the area must have been in 1884.

A visitor's center has been set up within the park in the town of North Bloomfield. During the Gold Rush the town had 1500 residents; today there are 16. They oper¬te the town's restored general store, livery stable, and the museum that tells the story of the area.

MALAKOFF DIGGINS STATE HISTORIC PARK, *16 miles northeast of Nevada City on North Bloomfield Road. Phone: (916) 265-2740. The 3000-acre park is open year-round and has primitive campsites and accommodations for motor homes (but no hookups). The restored historic town of North Bloomfield is open 10 A.M. to 4:30 P.M. daily from April to October, 10 A.M. to 5 P.M. weekends November to March. Demonstrations of the hydraulic mining monitor are given on weekends. The North Bloomfield town museum is open November through March; call ahead for open times.*

HOW TO GET TO MALAKOFF DIGGINS: *Take Route 49 out of Nevada City and turn right onto the North Bloomfield Road. Follow the North Bloomfield Road into the park. It's about a half hour from Nevada City.*

ROUGH AND READY WEDDING CHAPEL

Colorful names abound in the Gold Country. There's Fiddletown, Grub Gulch, and Humbug, for example. The origin of most has been lost, but no matter; they add to the unsophisticated, fun-loving atmosphere of this part of the world.

One of the most interesting of these towns is Rough and Ready. In 1850, when the U.S. government imposed a tax on mining claims, this northern Gold Country burg seceded from the Union. The citizens of this new republic elected their own president and signed a constitution similar to that of the United States. However, this nation didn't last for more than a few months; by the time the Fourth of July rolled around, Old Glory was hoisted up the flagpole, and the short-lived Republic of Rough and Ready became a very minor footnote in history.

Today the place looks neither rough nor ready for anything in particular. Visitors come to town to see the historic buildings that show what town life must have been like in the Gold Rush days—the remains of a one-room school built in 1868, a blacksmith shop the Chamber of Commerce opens for public viewing once in a while, and the Old Post Office, now operated as a little store.

The main tourist attraction in town is rather new, built in 1959. It is the Little Wedding Chapel, and it looks like the sort of place you'd find in a fairy tale. This incredibly cute, one-room chapel is run by Jackie Kelley, whose mother founded the place. Kelley says the wedding chapel is the result of a shipwreck. Her parents were on a voyage from Portland, Oregon, to San Francisco when the ship sank. Her mother promised God she would dedicate her life to providing a service to humanity in return for her survival. She lived and followed up on her promise.

Today brides and grooms come from all over the world to be married in this chapel. The unusual thing is that most people who travel a great distance to get married continue a bit farther across the state line into Nevada, where they can get a quickie ceremony with no prerequisite tests or licensing hassles. Because this chapel is in California, a valid marriage requires advance planning.

Yet this chapel thrives. Weddings take place every weekend, booked well in advance. In fact, some children who are the product of weddings performed here have made reservations for their own nuptials.

The chapel can provide just about anything you might need: a minister or justice of the peace, an organist, caterers, flowers, candles, even witnesses who can't help crying at weddings. And no matter where you are in town, you'll know the bride has been kissed when you hear the ringing of the carillon bells.

LITTLE WEDDING CHAPEL, *on Highway 20, a few miles west of Grass Valley in the town of Rough and Ready. The chapel is also available for baptisms. To make arrangements, phone (916) 273-6678. For more information about the town, call the Chamber of Commerce at (916) 273-8897.*

HOW TO GET TO ROUGH AND READY: *From Nevada City, take Route 20 West. Rough and Ready is about 20 minutes away.*

CHAPTER **12** Yosemite National Park

AREA OVERVIEW   It's a four- to five-hour drive from San Francisco to one of the most beautiful spots in the world. As early as 1864 its value was recognized by President Abraham Lincoln, who declared the Yosemite Valley and Mariposa Grove to be public parks. In 1890, thanks to the efforts of the Scottish-born naturalist John Muir, the nearly 800,000 acres of wilderness area became our first national park. Since entire guidebooks have been published about this area, I need not go on forever in this section; plus, once you arrive in the park you will be bombarded with maps, printed schedules of events, and lists of services. But I can offer a few tips.

First the bad news. Today there is one aspect of Yosemite that can make the trip unpleasant: crowds. This is one of the most popular of all national parks, and sometimes it's hard to see the trees for the tourists.

The good news is that there are ways to find solitude in this grand wilderness paradise. The way to avoid the crowds is to stay away from the valley in the summer. If you visit on weekdays during any other time of year, chances are there will be no lines of traffic, no wait at the food concessions, and easy access to the cross-country and downhill skiing areas. Winter, though cold up on the mountains, is moderate in the valley. Enticing mid-week offers you can't refuse are presented; these include lodging, ski lessons (cross country and downhill), lift tickets, and babysitting. Also, guest chefs from around the state come to prepare extravagant dinners—a lovely and memorable way to end a day in the snow.

Fall offers a changing of the leaves and quite often warm, clear weather. Spring offers pleasant temperatures, spectacular waterfalls, and probably a lot of mud.

If you are a camper, just about any time of year you can find hundreds of places to hike and set up camp without seeing another soul. But if you are less physical or more accustomed, as I am, to such things as beds, toilets, and restaurants, the Yosemite Valley is probably the best place for you.

In the valley there is a wide choice of accommodations, from the luxurious Ahwanee Hotel to the middle-range motel-like Yosemite Lodge. Another alternative is to stay in the tiny village of Wawona, near the southern entrance to the park, via Route 41. Here you'll find the gracious Wawona Hotel, founded in 1856, complete with pool, tennis courts, golf course, and riding stables. It's much quieter here than in the valley.

Even more isolated options for spending the night indoors are the Tuolumne Meadows Lodge, which offers tent cabins and a dining hall about 60 miles from the valley near the park's eastern entrance, or the White Wolf Lodge, offering both cabins and tents, about 30 miles from the valley; however, these are open only during the summer months.

All are owned and operated by the Yosemite Village and Curry Company, a division of MCA, the show-biz giant. The Curry Company has the concession on just about every service in the park except the post office. It even runs the free shuttle buses that will take you on any road in the valley and up to the ski areas at Badger Pass.

Once you get here, there's no shortage of things to do. In the valley, you can walk, rest, look around, and breathe the fresh air. In Yosemite Village you'll find an art gallery dedicated to the work of the great photographer Ansel Adams, who masterfully captured the unique qualities of the national park. Next door, at the art center, free watercolor classes are offered at various times of the year; the classes are taught by artists who spend a week at the park and take their students to a favorite place to paint.

The Pioneer Yosemite History Center, located near the Wawona Hotel, which you reach by covered bridge, is a small historical museum. And you can catch a free tram that will take you through the Mariposa Grove of giant sequoias while park rangers tell the stories of these trees, some of the largest in the world.

For an overview of the park, check into the visitor's center in Yosemite Village, where there are displays of the history of the park and all of the activities available at the time of your visit.

If you're lucky, you'll be there to catch Lee Stetson, an actor who portrays John Muir on stage at the Yosemite Theater. This one-man show, called "Conversation with a Tramp," is based on Muir's ideas about the environment and mankind's duty to preserve it. On weekends Stetson, still in character, leads tours to some of Muir's favorite spots in the valley. Either way, it is an unforgettable theatrical experience that offers new appreciation for the wilderness.

YOSEMITE NATIONAL PARK. *For general park information, phone (209) 372-0264. All accommodations can be reserved through the Yosemite Park and Curry Company. Phone: (209) 373-4171. For camping reservations, sites can be reserved through Ticketron or by writing the National Park Service, Western Regional Office, 450 Golden Gate Avenue, San Francisco, CA 94102.*

HOW TO GET TO YOSEMITE: *From San Francisco, the most direct route is to take the Bay Bridge to Route 580 East to Route 205 to Route 120 all the way to the park.*

HOW TO GET TO WAWONA: *Follow the same route but leave Route 120 onto Route 99 South to Route 140 East at Madera. Follow Route 140 until it connects with Route 41, and take Route 41 into the park.*

If you want a real backroads experience and you are not in a hurry, you can follow Route 580 to Route 205 to Route 120 to Route 99 South. Exit onto Route 132 at Modesto and follow Route 132 into the park. This is the old Yosemite Road, which follows the Tuolumne River past the Old West town of Coulterville; it eventually connects with Route 120 for the entrance to the park.

HERSHEY CHOCOLATE FACTORY

Here is a worthwhile stop along the way to or from Yosemite. It's the Hershey's chocolate plant in the town of Oakdale. This is the only Hershey plant that offers public tours. If you go to the Pennsylvania town named after the company, you get a simulated factory and an amusement park.

This place is paradise for chocoholics. As soon as you step inside the door of the huge plant, the aroma of roasting cocoa beans gets you. Then there's the sight of hundreds of huge vats of melted chocolate being mixed by giant granite mixers. As you walk through, your guide will point out the drums of peanut butter on their way to the Reese's Peanut Butter Cup line, the molds for the various bars, the Kiss inspector, and just about everything else you fantasize a

Hershey factory to be. And after the tour, everyone gets a complimentary chocolate bar. I should also warn you that you end the tour in the gift shop, so you will probably walk out with a few more items, too. The tour itself takes about a half hour.

This is a huge operation, making all the Hershey's products for 11 Western states and the Far East. I even learned something that came as a major jolt to a man who is prone to Mr. Goodbars: the biggest seller for Hershey is . . . Reese's Peanut Butter Cups. Hmmm . . .

HERSHEY CHOCOLATE FACTORY, *Albers Road, Oakdale. Phone: (209) 847-0381. No appointment necessary for tours, unless your group has 15 or more people. Tours Monday through Friday from 8:15 A.M. until 3:00 P.M., except major holidays; closed weekends. Admission: Free.*

HOW TO GET TO THE HERSHEY FACTORY: *From San Francisco, take the Bay Bridge to Route 580 and stay on it when it becomes Route 205. Follow Route 205 to Route 120 past Manteca all the way into the town of Oakdale. In Oakdale, turn right onto County Road J-14 (also called Albers Road) and continue a mile south of town until you see the large Hershey plant on the right.*

CHAPTER **13** Lake Tahoe

AREA OVERVIEW

Lake Tahoe is a spectacular natural attraction, one of the most beautiful mountain lakes in all the world. That alone would be enough to make it an irresistible destination. But there's more. For skiers, the Lake Tahoe area is a winter wonderland a mere four hours from downtown San Francisco. For sun worshipers, the area offers a marvelous blend of hot summers, clean mountain air, and crystal-clear water for swimming and water-skiing. Last but not least, for gamblers, the Nevada side of the lake is Las Vegas North, with fortunes to be won and lost in the 24-hour casinos.

Some quick facts: The lake itself is 22.5 miles long and 12 miles wide. It covers some 70 miles of shoreline in California and Nevada. It's the second deepest lake in the country, after Crater Lake in Oregon—Tahoe's maximum depth is 1645 feet. In the summer the lake's temperature averages 68 degrees. In the winter, despite the huge snows above, the lake never freezes, cooling only to about 50 degrees. Finally, if you want an idea of how much water is in the lake, Tahoe could supply everyone in the United States with 50 gallons of water a day for five years.

Archaeologists tell us that ancient civilizations lived here. The Washoe Indians gave the lake its name; Tahoe means "big water in a high place." The lake was first mapped by John C. Fremont's expedition in 1844, not long before the great Gold Rush nearby; water from the lake was used to flush out the gold. In the 1870s lumber barons decided to turn the lake into a fashionable resort. One still finds very fashionable digs, as well as many reasonably priced accommodations.

Make no mistake about it: Lake Tahoe is a major tourist attraction, and a lively tourist-oriented industry has been set up to cater to just about every whim. You don't have to worry about investing a lot of money when trying out a new sport; every kind of equipment imaginable is for rent. In addition to hedonistic temptations, there are 9 museums, 10 state parks, 30 campgrounds, and thousands of acres of national forest in the area.

Most of the action is on the south shore of the lake. If you do not wish to be alone, this is the spot for you. This is where you'll find plenty of franchised restaurants and souvenir shops. The town of Stateline is the home of most of the casinos, and the main road on the south side can get very crowded. You can get away and head into beautiful country from the south shore if you head out Route 88 toward the Kirkwood ski area, and the town of Markleeville.

The north shore and the Nevada side of the lake above Stateline offer more seclusion and a less hectic scene. If this interests you, look for accommodations in the communities of Tahoe City or Carnelian Bay. Compared to the south side they are low-key, and it's an easy drive in any direction to a wilderness trail or state park.

To the north, off I-80 are the Donner summit with its state park facilities, lake, and monument to the famous Donner party. There's also an interesting ski museum at Boreal Ridge. Nearby is the town of Truckee, which used to be a funky little old west town and is fast becoming filled with shops and restaurants. Note the huge rock that hangs above town on a hillside. Legend has it that this large rock used to rest in perfect balance on a smaller stone, and that it would move at the slightest touch. Nervous town fathers cemented it down many years ago, and enclosed it in a fenced-in gazebo. Still, the rocking stone adds a bit of local color to Truckee.

There are many motels and hotels, and even some nice bed-and-breakfast inns in the Tahoe area. It's also relatively easy to get a cabin or a condo that comes complete with a modern kitchen and comfortable furnishings. Some of the condo complexes even offer maid service, pools, and hot tubs.

If you visit in the summer, you might want to take a drive out to Emerald Bay State Park to visit Vikingsholm, a 38-room mansion open for tours July through Labor Day. Built in 1929 and patterned after a ninth-century Norse fortress, it's the kind of place that simply couldn't be built today. It is said to be the finest example of Scandinavian architecture in this country and is filled with Norwegian furnishings and weavings. Emerald Bay and Vikingsholm are located on the southwestern side of the lake, 17 miles south of Tahoe City. The road, Route 89, is often closed because of snow during the winter. For those interested in gambling, all the casinos are on the Nevada side of the lake, and they range from opulent (like Harrah's and Caesar's Tahoe) to funky (the parlors you'll find along the road on the North Shore).

There are several ways to get here. You can fly into Reno or South Lake Tahoe. At the airports you can rent a car or take a bus or a train (some hotels offer transportation).

For toll-free information on accommodations available, phone the Tahoe North Visitors and Convention Bureau, (800) 822-5959 from California or (800) 824-8557 from out of state; or the Tahoe South Visitors Bureau, (800) 822-5922 from California or (800) 824-5150 from out of state. For information on Emerald Bay, phone (916) 525-7277.

SKI MUSEUM, *Boreal Ridge. Phone: (916) 426-3313. Open every day. Winter hours: 11 A.M. to 5 P.M. Tuesday through Sunday; summer hours: 11 A.M. to 5 P.M. Wednesday through Sunday. Admission: Free.*

HOW TO GET TO THE NORTH SHORE OF LAKE TAHOE: *From San Francisco, take the Bay Bridge to Route 80 North and take it all the way to the Truckee exit. You can stop at Truckee or you can take Route 89 South to Tahoe City.*

TO GET TO THE SOUTH SHORE OF LAKE TAHOE: *Take the Bay Bridge to Route 80 but exit near Sacramento onto Route 50. Then take Route 50 all the way into South Lake Tahoe.*

CHAPTER **14** Mendocino County

AREA OVERVIEW

As you drive north from Sonoma County into Mendocino County, the change is immediate. If you're inland on Route 101, the four-lane highway becomes a country road that takes you through—not around—the town of Hopland. If you're on the coastal route, Route 1, the road takes even more twists and turns, and the sandy beaches give way to a rocky shoreline.

For the most part, Mendocino County is an unspoiled beauty. It's where San Franciscans go to feel like they're far from home. In this sprawling county of inland farms and rugged beaches, the largest town, Ukiah, would be considered a small town in just about any other part of the world. The major destination in the area is Mendocino. Thousands of tourists flock here each year, yet this village is so small that it isn't even incorporated.

There are three ways to get to the village of Mendocino.

One is to drive straight up the coast. This is not only the longest route but also the most trying for those who tend to get carsick when driving on constantly curvy narrow roads while hugging the ocean's edge. However, this shoreline road does take you to some lovely areas, including Sea Ranch and the old coastal town of Gualala. Sea Ranch is the famous private community of modern homes designed to blend in with the landscape. The homes are architecturally significant, and many of them are available for weekend rentals. There are also a lodge that offers overnight accommodations and a restaurant. Around Gualala the main features are the Old Milano Hotel which still looks like it did when it was new in 1905, and, a bit north of town, St. Orre's, an inn and restaurant that looks like a small Russian palace.

A quicker, and less winding way to get to Mendocino is by going north on Route 101 to the intersection of Route 128 in Cloverdale, then taking Route 128 through the Anderson Valley to the coastline. This joins Route 1 near the town of Albion for the short ride up to Mendocino. The third way is to continue on Route 101 to Ukiah and then come over on the Ukiah/Comptche Road.

HOPLAND As the name might suggest, the town of Hopland is a place where hops were grown. In fact, this town was once a major supplier of hops to the American brewery industry. This claim to fame ended in the late 1940s when giant breweries stopped using hops in mass-produced beer. Hopland became a quiet farming community that travelers zipped past on the road to the Redwood Empire.

But today Hopland is experiencing a new lease on life, and if you stop to look around, there's a good chance you'll want to stay awhile.

One must stop is the Mendocino Brewing Company, aka the Hopland Brewery, Tavern, Beer Garden, and Restaurant, a thriving business that has brought beer back to Hopland. This is the place that started the latest California craze of brewery pubs, places that make beer in the back and sell it in front. Housed in what was 100 years ago the Hop Vine Saloon, this family-style pub is a very inviting brick building, with inside walls covered with original ornamental stamped tin. In one room there is a handsome, hand-crafted oak bar, reminiscent of pioneer California. The pub also includes a stage for performers on weekends and a dart area, where employees will buy you a beer if you can beat them. On a warm day you can rest a spell in the beer garden, shaded by a grape arbor, while the kids play in a sandbox.

Good pub food is available, too, including giant hamburgers, sausages, vegetarian dishes, and various daily specials, all inexpensive. As for the main attraction—the homemade beer—the pub offers four different beverages, ranging from pale ale to dark, thick stout. For the person who prefers not to drink alcohol, the pub also offers their own Hopland Seltzer, made from the same local H_2O that makes the beer so delicious.

But what if your taste runs to sweet things? Well, next door to the pub is a place called the Cheesecake Lady. This is a giant bakery and wholesale operation serving the Bay Area and Sacramento, with many types of luscious desserts available for consumption on the premises. This huge operation at first seems out of place in this neck of the woods, but the owners were able to get a lot of space for low rent in Hopland, so low that it is worth the effort to truck their goodies long distances. To accommodate visitors, there are tables and an espresso machine. After consuming a cappuccino and a slice of their chocolate mousse cake, I could have driven straight to Canada, no problem.

There are more places to visit in Hopland, right on the main road, including Country Christmas, a store featuring holiday decorations and a 9-foot teddy bear, and the California Yurt Company. In case you don't have the faintest idea what a yurt is (I didn't), it is a type of housing developed in Afghanistan, most often used as a one-room home or a giant sauna. There's a small complex of yurts sitting off the highway just south of town.

And lest we forget, the town of Hopland has a busy wine industry. The Milano Winery was first, opening in 1975 in an old hop kiln just a mile south of town. A few years later Fetzer bought the old high school and turned it into a visitor's complex called Hopland Station, complete with a wine-tasting room, a crafts gallery, a gift shop, a good restaurant called the Sun Dial, and a larger conference and garden center called Valley Oaks. And just a few miles east of town on Route 175, McDowell Valley Vineyards is proud of being the nation's first solar-integrated winery.

HOPLAND BREWERY, TAVERN, BEER GARDEN, AND RESTAURANT, *13351 South Highway 101, Hopland. Hours vary each day. Tours of the brewery are possible by prior arrangement. Phone: (707) 744-1015 or (707) 744-1361.*

HOW TO GET TO HOPLAND: *From San Francisco, cross the Golden Gate Bridge and take Highway 101 about 90 miles north to the place where Route 101 changes from a four-lane highway into a busy country road. A note of caution: Logging trucks seem to appear from nowhere on this curvy stretch of road; be careful whenever entering the highway.*

LITTLE LAMBS

If this section were on television instead of in a book, it would be easy to convince you to visit this place. I would start by showing you a shot of a baby lamb staring into the camera, then racing off to its mother. Then the camera would pull back and show you hundreds of little baby lambs, all adorable and fuzzy, wobbling around on unsure legs.

We all have the image of California as the place where movies are made, high-tech industries are born, and going to the beach is a way of life. But the fact is that agriculture is the main business of the state. It's no wonder, then, that the University of California runs nine different research facilities around the state to study land use, animal behavior, and ecology.

The Hopland Field Station is one of these university-run experimental farms. Here the specialty is sheep, thousands of them. And while researchers are studying breeding, nutrition, grazing management, and wool production, visitors get a rare opportunity to mingle with some of the most entertaining and lovable creatures on earth.

Hopland is the largest of the university's field stations. More than 5300 acres encompass low valleys and brush-covered hills. You can wander around at your leisure or schedule a tour at the range office. A small community of full-time workers lives down by the barns, and they love to have visitors. You can drive down to the visitor's center and not worry about great distances, if you are not a hiker.

What you will see depends on what time of year you visit. From mid-January through March is ramming time, when the ewes give birth. If you miss the actual event, you will certainly see lambs just a day or two old. In spring the hills are awash with wildflowers, and it's shearing time. At all times of the year the daily routines are interesting to watch. It's not every day we get to see a sheepdog and shepherd in a pasture rounding up 50 sheep, the dog moving them exactly where the master wants them to go.

When I was there, I simply sat alone on a hillside, away from all the barns and experimental activity, just watching and listening. There were no cars, no airplanes, just a symphony of baa-a-a-s.

HOPLAND FIELD STATION, *4070 University Road, Hopland. Phone: (707) 744-1424.*

HOW TO GET TO THE FIELD STATION; *From Hopland, take Route 175 East toward Lakeport. When you come to Valley Oaks Ranch, turn left at the fork and follow the signs to the Hopland Field Station.*

MENDOCINO: CALIFORNIA'S NEW ENGLAND VILLAGE

If you are feeling adventurous, and it's broad daylight, you can cut over to the coast and the village of Mendocino by taking Orr Springs Road out of Ukiah and then hooking up with the Comptche-Ukiah Road. This trip will take about an hour from Route 101, and will put you deep into the woods (therefore you want to do this during the daylight hours) before you arrive at the ocean and Route 1. Then, to the north as you get your first glimpse of Mendocino in the distance, you will understand immediately why this is a popular destination. The entire village sits high on a bluff overlooking the ocean. In the foreground, the blue Pacific rushes up to a cove. In the background, red, yellow, and blue Victorian homes dot the landscape, as do seasonal wildflowers. It is a spectacular entrance.

Everything in town is designed to bear the look and charm of a nineteenth-century New England town. In fact, Mendocino looks so much like New England that it has been used as the set in such movies as *The Russians Are Coming! The Russians Are Coming!* which was supposed to be taking place in Gloucester, Massachusetts.

Critics say the town is too precious and that too many of the shops and inns cater to the tourist trade instead of the locals. But I think there is also a genuine quality to the place, especially when you get away from the main shopping area. Mendocino first gained fame as an artist's colony, and that tradition is still alive. There's a lively art center in town, with a display gallery and gift shop where you can purchase ceramics and paintings by local artists. One of the more outrageous creative people around town is Larry Fuentes, whose "trash art" sculptures have been featured on the cover of *National Geographic*. He told me he likes living in Mendocino because it's just like high school. Everybody knows everybody, and there is a protected, predictable quality to the place.

Equally colorful is another local fixture of the art world, Byrd Baker, whose enormous sculptures of whales are to be found all over town (there's one downtown in front of MacCallum House, a bed-and-breakfast inn at 45020 Albion Street, for example). He is a large, Hemingway-like figure who wears an eye patch and has helped lead the fight for the protection of the gray whale, which can be seen swimming offshore at various times of the year. Byrd sees the whale as a symbol of life in Mendocino; he says that by saving the whale, the citizens are saving the traditions of small village life.

While in the area, you may notice bumper stickers and window decals that depict an offshore oil well with a red slash through it. That's because there is a very active stop-offshore-drilling movement here, spearheaded by Rachel Binah, owner of Rachel's Inn, a bed-and-breakfast place in the adjacent town of Little River. As Rachel points out, this area is not just the Mendocino coast, it is the Kansas coast; in other words, it belongs to all Americans and if it is spoiled it affects us all. Most restaurants bear the "stop drilling" symbol on their front doors and in their advertisements; at Rachel's you may leave your business card in a large pot which will be added to the collection of giant mayonnaise jars filled with business cards that Rachel plans to take to Washington, D.C. someday. So, if you are a heavy supporter of offshore oil drilling, Mendocino may not be an ideal vacation spot for you.

THE MENDOCINO ART CENTER *is located at 45200 Little Lake Street. Phone:*

(707) 937-0228. Call for current gallery hours and exhibition information.

For more information about the stop-offshore-drilling movement, contact Rachel Binah at Rachel's Inn, Post Office Box 134, Mendocino, CA 95460; phone (707) 937-0088.

FORT BRAGG AND ITS SKUNK TRAIN

About 20 minutes north of Mendocino on Route 1 is the larger town of Fort Bragg, which is the center of the lumber industry in these parts. Fort Bragg doesn't have the architectural charm of Mendocino, but there are other attractions. South of town is the lovely Mendocino Coast Botanical Gardens. Noyo Harbor is a lively fishing port with working fishing fleets on one side and restaurants and cafes on the other. This is also the site of the world's largest salmon barbecue, held at the harbor on July 4th each year. If this spot looks familiar, it was also used for the East-West standoff in the movie, *The Russians Are Coming*.

The main attraction in Fort Bragg is a working railroad called the Skunk Train. The train got its name from the days when steam locomotives ran on these tracks; you could smell one coming from miles away. Today the aroma is gone (they have switched to diesel engines), but the atmosphere and scenic ride through redwood forests are the same as in the old days. The trip is 40 miles each way, with a running commentary over a public address system pointing out significant sights along the way. You can sit inside railroad cars or stand outside in open-air cars. During the summer months it's not unusual to find a guitar-playing troubadour hired by the train company to roam the trains singing old American traveling songs.

You can spend the day on the train, taking the 80-mile round trip through the redwoods to the town of Willits. A shorter alternative is to ride the train for 20 miles to the redwood grove, where there are rest rooms, refreshment stands, and souvenir shops, and catch the next train back to Fort Bragg. This is a half-day excursion.

SKUNK TRAIN DEPOT, *located at the foot of Laurel Street. Phone: (707) 964-6371. Call for current schedule information. Reservations are advised, especially during the summer.*

TO GET TO THE SKUNK TRAIN, *just take Main Street, which is Route 1, through downtown and watch for the signs. Laurel is one block to the west, or left, of Main.*

PYGMY FOREST

Before we leave the Mendocino area, I should mention that there are several wonderful parks up and down the coast. One of my favorites is Van Damme State Park, which is the home of the Pygmy Forest. This is a grove of trees that have been dwarfed by a twist of fate, not to mention geological and climatic conditions (the ranger on duty can give you a more thorough explanation). These are full-grown evergreens that are about knee-high. The kick for me is to be able to walk through a forest and look down on the trees.

VAN DAMME STATE PARK, *3 miles south of Mendocino on Route 1; it's well marked. Phone: (707) 937-0851.*

BOONVILLE AND THE BEAUTIFUL ANDERSON VALLEY

If you return from Mendocino by taking Route 128, it will bring you through the very interesting little town of Boonville. If you read the gourmet magazine writers, you've probably heard of the New Boonville Hotel, an extraordinary restaurant that transformed this little town into a tourist attraction. It started out as an ambitious project, a restaurant that would raise its own animals and grow its own food. Though the restaurant was excellent, the dream was never fully realized. Then in a turn of events from a B movie, the owners got into deep financial difficulties and left town one night under the cover of darkness.

The new owners, who call the place simply The Boonville Hotel, have more realistic ambitions, a smaller menu, and as a result don't have the draw of the former incarnation. Still, it's the best restaurant for miles, and, anyway, Boonville is definitely worth knowing about. It is the only town in California, maybe even the United States, that has its own language. The citizens speak English, but some of them also speak Boontling—a funny locally created lingo that the locals started years ago. The town coffeeshop is called the Horn of Zeese, which is Boontling for "cup of coffee." Outside you can use the Buckey Walter, which is the telephone. Almost anywhere in town you can pick up a booklet with the most important phrases.

Boonville also happens to be in the center of the beautiful Anderson Valley, a worthy destination on its own or a pleasant stop on the road from San Francisco to Mendocino. There are several places to stay, including a place that is a combination inn-and-craft gallery fashioned out of a stagecoach stop built in 1888.

The Anderson Valley also has several fine wineries; in fact the buzzword is that this threatens to become "the next Napa Valley." However, due to its distance from San Francisco and the lack of major highways, my guess is that Anderson Valley is unlikely to ever become as commercial or crowded. (Remember you read it here first.) However, the grape-growing conditions here are so ideal that Roederer, the very fancy French champagne producer, has built a huge production facility here. Though no public tours of this plant are offered, you can visit another special vineyard across the yard. Husch Vineyards not only has the claim to fame of being the oldest winery in the Anderson Valley, it is one of the few wineries anywhere that welcomes visitors into the vineyards. Here you can wander around 21 acres of pinot noir, gewürztraminer, and chardonnay grapes, get a lovely hilltop view of the surrounding valley (including the Roederer facility across the way), and walk down to a pond with a gazebo, followed by wine tasting in the tasting room. Other fine wineries in the area include Navarro Vineyards and Edemeads.

If you'd like to get your historic bearings, the Anderson Valley Museum is the place to go. It's a little red schoolhouse—the real thing—filled with a thoughtful and well-organized collection of household gadgets, tools, family photos, quilts, clothing, and other artifacts donated by locals. Most of it is on display in the schoolhouse, built in 1891. A more modern building next door serves as an annex where you can see blacksmithing and viticulture exhibits. Also on display is antique farm equipment, including the nation's only four-sheep-at-a-time shearing contraption. It's a valuable resource for "the way things used to be" in this agricultural valley.

The most valuable resource for "the way things are" is the *Anderson Valley Register*, a wonderful weekly newspaper run by a big, bearish fellow named Bruce Anderson. Bruce is a throwback to the old small-town newspaper editor who takes it upon himself to tell it like he sees it. His paper is opinionated, funny, and enterprising. He challenges the establishment, provokes the pompous, and raises hell on every issue. All this has made Bruce a controversial figure in the community, but he's also responsible for keeping people on their toes. Pick up his paper and see what you are missing in your hometown daily.

THE ANDERSON VALLEY, *Route 128 between Routes 101 and 1.*

THE BOONVILLE HOTEL, *Highway 128, Boonville. Lunch and dinner Wednesday through Sunday. Phone: (707) 895-2210.*

ANDERSON VALLEY HISTORICAL MUSEUM, *Highway 128, Boonville. Phone: (707) 895-3207. Open Friday through Sunday, 11 A.M. to 4 P.M. in summer, 1 P.M. to 4 P.M. the rest of the year; closed Christmas and New Year's Day. Admission: Free.*

PHILO POTTERY INN, *8550 Route 128, Philo. Phone: (707) 895-3069.*

HUSCH VINEYARDS, *4400 Highway 128, Philo. (707) 895-3216. For more information about local wines, you can contact the Anderson Valley Winegrowers Association, Box 63, Philo, CA 95466.*

CHAPTER **15** Redwood Empire

AREA OVERVIEW The giant redwoods of Northern California are legendary. The largest, most impressive concentration of these awesome trees is called the Redwood Empire, a stretch of forest that begins inland around the town of Leggett and continues north to the coastal city of Eureka. This is an area with many worthwhile destinations. The trip on Route 101 from San Francisco will take four to five hours, but it is an easy drive, and there are many diversions along the way.

The coastal redwoods alone are worth the trip. Nowhere in the world are there more majestic trees or more beautiful forests. I also doubt if anywhere in the world you can find so many roadside attractions, ranging from truly tacky to just plain funny.

You will see the signs as you near the town of Leggett. There's the Drive-Thru Tree Park, a 240-acre operation with a picnic area, a store, many trails, and, yes, a tree with a road going through it. It costs $2 to enter the park, and you can stay as long as you like, driving through the tree as many times as you like. A quick tree fact: the drive-thru tree is alive, which is proof that the nutrients for the giant redwoods are located on the outside, not the inside, of the trunk.

AVENUE OF THE GIANTS

Route 101 becomes a four-lane highway north of Garberville, and that's where you should look for the turnoff for the Avenue of the Giants. This is a 33-mile stretch of road that parallels the freeway. Actually it's the old Route 101, a two-lane, tree-lined drive through a majestic redwood forest.

From the avenue you can take a backroad that leads to the best of the redwood groves, called the Rockefeller Forest. Many of the trees to be found here are virgin growth, meaning they have never been cut. These trees are believed to be at least 3000 years old. You can stay in your car and drive around, or you can park and then walk into areas where you will be virtually alone with nature.

This grove contains what is said to be the tallest tree in the West. In case you're wondering how anybody figures out this sort of thing, park rangers used to measure by floating balloons connected to a kind of measuring tape to the top; but since it's difficult to see the tops of the trees from underneath, it was a less than accurate technique. Today they use elaborate laser beam technology, but even so it's still a matter of estimates.

The Rockefeller Forest is part of Humboldt Redwoods State Park. If you have the time, stop in at park headquarters, which is located right on the Avenue of the Giants, just 2 miles south of Weott. This is the largest of California's state parks. A sawmill for public viewing is in operation in the Rockefeller Forest. They only saw trees that have fallen down naturally, and the wood is then used to build facilities for other park centers. If you are on a tight schedule, the rangers recommend that you at least visit Founder's Grove. This is right off the Avenue of the Giants north of Weott and features a scenic, easy-to-walk, self-guided nature trail. The grove is dedicated to the founders of the Save the Redwoods League, the group responsible for stopping the wholesale logging of the area in the 1920s.

HUMBOLDT REDWOODS STATE PARK, *2 miles south of Weott. Phone: (707) 946-2311. Open sunrise to sunset daily. No fee just to drive around. Camping: $10 per car per night; day-use fee, $3.*

HISTORIC FERNDALE

The town of Ferndale, or "Historic Ferndale," as the road signs on Route 101 call it, is almost too cute to be real. It is an almost perfect Victorian village, filled with color and colorful characters. This small town of 1100 residents features such things as a repertory theater, a rare-book store, a blacksmith shop, two bed-and-breakfast inns, and clean public rest rooms with a Victorian exterior. There's a pool hall called Becker's where the locals gather for lunch, cards, reading, and conversation—everything except pool because Becker's has no pool table.

The characters, who are only too willing to put on a show for you, include Carlos the bookstore owner, who won his place in a poker game, he says with a wink. Maybe he did, maybe he didn't, but it doesn't really matter; it's the story that counts. Carlos is one of the town spokesmen, a world traveler who settled in Ferndale about 20 years ago. He points to the fact that Ferndale looks the way it does because it never suffered a major fire or other catastrophe, so it never needed to be rebuilt.

Joe the Blacksmith has another way of looking at the authenticity of the town. He calls Ferndale "the old town that other cities are trying to create." As you walk down Main Street, the point becomes clear. The stores and services are not just for tourists. You'll find a full range of community services: pharmacy, hardware store, butcher shop, jeweler, bank, bakery, dry cleaner's, and so on, with a few boutiques and candy shops tossed in for the visitors.

What's there to do? The Chamber of Commerce schedules several events throughout the year that draw attention from all over the world. One is the Foggy Bottoms Milk Run, a race through three of the area's dairy farms, held each March. Another is the Arcata-to-Ferndale Cross-Country Kinetic Sculpture Race, a three-day affair held each Memorial Day weekend. This race is the brainchild of Hobart Brown, who runs the local art gallery. He's also a sculptor, and he collects crazy-looking vehicles that look like soapbox racers on drugs. Participants in the race build these exotic machines, powered by the individual's own energy, usually by pedaling. The contraptions are truly amazing, and the race eventually turns into one big party.

If there has ever been a town where you can simply take off your watch and forget about the rest of the world, Ferndale is it. It is a place for doing nothing but hanging out and talking to people. It will stay that way, too; the state has declared it a historic landmark, giving it protection from wholesale development or other major changes.

FERNDALE. A walking tour map is available from the Ferndale Chamber of Commerce, 428 Francis Street. Phone: (707) 786-4477. You can also write for a brochure of events scheduled throughout the year: Ferndale Chamber of Commerce, P.O. Box 525, Ferndale, CA 95536.

HOW TO GET TO FERNDALE: From Route 101, there are ample signs directing you. Ferndale is approximately 30 minutes south of Eureka.

SCOTIA: A COMPANY TOWN

Scotia is a must stop on a trip to the redwoods. It is one of the few official company towns left in the United States. By "official company town" I mean that the entire town is owned by one business, in this case the Pacific Lumber Company. The only other one I know of is in the coal-mining region of West Virginia, which is hardly as attractive a setting for visitors as Scotia.

Located about 30 miles south of Eureka off Route 101 and south of Ferndale, Scotia is smack in the middle of the Redwood Empire, surrounded by forests, rolling hills, and the Eel River. You know you're in a lumber town right away when you see two of the more imposing buildings in the center of town. They are made entirely of redwood, including the doric columns, which would be made of marble or cement anywhere else.

One of these buildings is City Hall, which is really the main office of Pacific Lumber. Here you'll be greeted and given a glossy visitor's guide that tells you the history of the firm and all about forest management. I should point out that Pacific Lumber was always regarded by environmentalists as one of the most enlightened lumber companies. In fact, even as far back as the 1920s they held off logging what is now Humboldt State Park until the Save the Redwoods League could buy the land for the state park system. However, in 1986 the company changed owners in a hostile takeover, and the jury is still out on how the company will operate in the future.

The visitor's guide includes a small piece of redwood on which is printed the directions for a self-guided tour through the mill. Do it, by all means. You can see the entire process, from the unloading of newly cut trees to the final cutting of boards. Most people spend an hour or two, mesmerized by the sight of huge logs being tossed around by even bigger machines. Two of the highlights are the hydraulic barker (which strips bark off the tree with giant bursts of water) and the edgerman (an area where giant saws are maneuvered by remote control to shape the logs into specific sizes). Everything on the tour is bigger than life, just like the redwood trees. It is also very loud.

As for the town itself, take the time to drive around and visit with the residents. Many are second- and third-generation Scotians. They live in company-owned houses, go to company-run schools, and begin and end life in the company-owned hospital. Scotia has some 300 homes of varying sizes. A typical three-bedroom unit rents for about $200 a month, deducted from the worker's paycheck.

Another thing about life in a company town: You never have to set an alarm. The whistle blows at 6:30 A.M. to wake everyone up and again at 7:25 A.M. to let people know they have five minutes to get to work.

Scotia has a downtown of sorts, with a grocery, a hardware store, a clothing store, and even a diner—all owned by the company but leased to private operators. The diner, by the way, is remarkably good, especially considering it's the only eatery in town that's open for lunch. At the counter you'll see the names of Pacific workers at each setting. They are apparently born into their own counter seat. Visitors should ask where they may sit. The booths are fair game.

The Scotia Inn is a nice place to stay, with fairly luxurious rooms and a formal dining room. In the olden days this grand hotel was for guests only and workers were discouraged from entering. Nowadays locals are encouraged to use the hotel facilities. Many community events take place here, so this is another good place to get to know the town. Overnight guests will also get the 6:30 A.M. wake-up call; there's no way to avoid it.

Much to the chagrin of many of the ladies in town, the company also runs a men's club, meaning for gentlemen only. Inside there's a color TV and pool table —the sort of things one would expect to find in a den of males. One of the wives described it to me as "just a place where men can go to get away from their wives" (it makes me wonder where the women go to get away from their husbands). Visitors must be accompanied by a member.

SCOTIA. *Tours of the town are offered without appointment (unless you have a group of 10 or more) weekdays from 7:30 to 10:30 A.M. and 12:30 to 2:30 P.M. A logging museum is open to visitors in the summer. For visitor's information, call (707) 764-2222.*

SCOTIA INN. *For reservations and information, call (707) 764-5683.*

HOW TO GET TO SCOTIA: *From San Francisco, cross the Golden Gate Bridge and take Route 101 North about four hours. Follow the signs to Scotia.*

EUREKA "Eureka" is the motto of California, the exclamation shouted by the Greek scientist Archimedes when he discovered a way to determine the purity of gold. In the town of Eureka, some real treasures are to be found.

Treasure Number One: Here you'll find the most elaborate, unbelievable, astonishing Victorian home in the world. The Carson House overlooks the old town from the foot of Second Street. From a distance it looks unreal and becomes no less fantastic as you stand outside the gate. Unfortunately, that's as close as you'll get since it is now used as a private club and no tours are offered.

But that hardly diminishes the spectacle. Built in 1884 by a lumber baron named William Carson, the home features a 68-foot tower, eight gables, balconies, porches, pillars, intricate moldings, stained-glass windows, and gingerbread trim. It sits alone surrounded by lush lawns and colorful gardens. Legend has it that more than 100 craftsmen worked on the mansion. It apparently inspired other homeowners and builders, as the city features many Victorian gems. The Chamber of Commerce offers a pamphlet with the location of more than 30 homes worth seeing.

Treasure Number Two: Down the street from the Carson House, in the center of the restored Old Town, is the Romano Gabriel Sculpture Garden. The story of this rare work of folk art tells you a lot about this city and its priorities.

Romano was a reclusive old gent who lived alone in a quiet section of town. Over the course of several years he built an elaborate sculpture garden in front of his little house, fashioning brightly colored figures and flowers and trees out of old orange crates; eventually the entire house was blocked from view. Locals believe that this "art" was his way of communicating with the town.

When Romano died in the late 1970s no one knew what to do with the sculpture garden. The new owners of the house didn't want it, so finally some art-loving citizens intervened, the historical society bought the sculptures, and the city provided a permanent display area.

This is primitive art. Like much of modern art, it is what you think it is, and you could spend hours admiring the intricate details.

Also of interest: Fort Humboldt State Historic Park, a small redwood park just outside of town. This is where Ulysses S. Grant was stationed in the 1850s and early 1860s. There was little to do, and apparently he was drunk most of the time. He got wind that he was to be court-martialed, so, to avoid the inevitable, Grant turned in his resignation only to be informed he would be needed for the Civil War. The rest, as they say, is history. He went on to become a general in the Union Army, then president of the United States, but apparently never did stop drinking. Today the pre-Civil War outpost has been partially restored, and there are displays of pioneer logging methods. The view of Humboldt Bay makes this a nice spot for a picnic.

I should note that Eureka is a town in transition. It has been hit hard by a bad fishing economy and a changing lumber industry. There is a move to establish tourism as a major industry, but there are not a lot of attractions or services yet. Still, the city offers great hospitality and can be used as your headquarters for a visit to the Redwood Empire. There is one grand old inn in the Old Town section, the Eureka Inn, which offers comfortable rooms for much less than you would pay for the same room in a larger city. I should also point out that the weather is often cloudy or rainy. Count on summers to be foggy, with only occasional periods of sunshine. As in San Francisco, your best bet for sunny and warm weather is either spring or fall.

EUREKA CHAMBER OF COMMERCE *is located at 2112 Broadway. Phone: (707) 442-3738.*

THE CARSON HOUSE *is located at Second and M Streets. It is a private club, so you can't go in, but the sight from the outside is spectacular.*

THE ROMANO GABRIEL SCULPTURE GARDEN *is on display at 315 Second Street between D and E Streets.*

FORT HUMBOLDT STATE HISTORIC PARK, *3431 Fort Avenue, above Route 101 at the south end of town. Phone: (707) 443-7952.*

THE EUREKA INN *is located on the corner of Seventh and F Streets. Phone: (707) 442-6441.*

HOW TO GET TO EUREKA: *From San Francisco, cross the Golden Gate Bridge and take Route 101 North 235 miles.*

CHAPTER **16** Monterey Peninsula

AREA OVERVIEW   The area surrounding Monterey Bay is one of the prime attractions for visitors to the San Francisco area, as well as for locals. Carmel was a major destination, long before Clint Eastwood had his short stint as mayor. Bing Crosby's golf tournament brought fame to the Pebble Beach golf course. And there are lesser known spots where you can avoid the crowds.

The beach resort of Santa Cruz sits on the northern tip of Monterey Bay. On the other side is the Monterey Peninsula, which you can reach by continuing south on Route 1. Here you will find Monterey and Carmel, as well as the more manageable town of Pacific Grove.

An Italian friend once prepared me for a visit to Venice by saying that it was Italy's version of Disneyland. I think the same holds true for Monterey and Carmel. They are Northern California's Disneyland. Not only does everything appear to have been arranged for tourists, but there is also a fantasy quality to these places; the countryside and coastline are almost too beautiful to be real, and the shops and restaurants (especially in Carmel) look like stage sets. Still, these are wonderful places to visit. Since the idea of this book is to offer alternatives to the crowded tourist scenes, I will concentrate here on places you may overlook. Some of the locations are not really on the Peninsula, but are in the general area or on the way to Monterey.

Most of the towns along the Bay Area's backroads have attractions. In the case of San Juan Bautista, the town *is* the attraction, preserving California as it was in pre-statehood days. In this tiny village you will encounter almost every phenomenon that made California famous: sunny weather, movies, and earthquakes.

There are two main sections of town to visit. One is the downtown, a collection of Mexican restaurants, antique stores, and such businesses as the San Juan Bakery, the oldest continuously operating bakery in the West. In fact, the family that now owns the business never lets their huge oven cool; it keeps burning all night, and they keep churning out wonderful breads and pastries, many from Portuguese recipes (many Portuguese came to California to fish, though some moved inland to farm).

Downtown also features the John Cravea clothing store, which has more goods crammed into a tiny space than you would think possible. Outside the store is the Liar's Bench, where locals sit to pass the time and tell stories (don't ask them for directions; you might end up in San Diego).

Not far from the bench is a garden tended by a charming little old man named Chepito. Sometimes he can be seen wandering around town selling his specialty, garlic braids. But most of the time he can be found in his little garden along the main drag behind a homemade sign bearing his name. If you play your cards right, he'll take you to his home, around the corner, where he braids his "stinking roses" and keeps a menagerie of parakeets and a collection of lanterns, pots, and items I can classify only as folk art. According to Chepito, people come from all over the country to buy his garlic braids. He also says ladies find it difficult to resist his charms.

The other destination in town is the old plaza, a state historical park that features several Old West re-creations including a replica of the town's original hotel, jail, and blacksmith shop. The buildings face a large parklike square where you can sit on benches and watch the world go by. The park surrounds the beautiful mission, founded in 1797, and a church built in 1812. Movie buffs will recognize this as the setting for several scenes in the classic Alfred Hitchcock film *Vertigo*. There is a belfry tower atop the chapel, though the tower in which Jimmy Stewart and Kim Novak played their final scene was grafted onto the mission by Hollywood special-effects magic. Visitors may tour the building, which is the largest of all the 21 California missions.

Unfortunately, when the well-meaning Franciscans chose the San Juan Bautista site, they didn't know that the San Andreas Fault ran through its back yard. On the grounds near the mission the fault line is marked, and you can see the damage done to the terrain and the bleachers of the nearby rodeo stadium. There is also a seismograph and an exhibit about earthquakes.

Earthquakes or no earthquakes, Catholic services are held in the church regularly, and at Christmas there is a lavish pageant worth making the trip to see. It is presented by the internationally famous theater group El Teatro Campesino, the troupe that grew out of the Farmworkers Union struggle during the heyday of Cesar Chavez. Founder, director, and playwright Luis Valdez has since won acclaim for the film *La Bamba* and for such theatrical productions as *Zoot Suit* (also made into a film directed by Valdez) and *Corridos*. El Teatro still operates out of a former spinach-packing factory in San Juan Bautista. No matter what time of the year you may visit, if the Teatro is performing, take advantage of the opportunity.

SAN JUAN BAUTISTA STATE HISTORIC PARK, *open 10 A.M. to 4:30 P.M. daily. Phone: (408) 623-4881. To inquire about El Teatro Campesino, located at 705 Fourth Street, call (408) 623-2444.*

HOW TO GET TO SAN JUAN BAUTISTA: *From San Francisco, take Highway 101 South, past San Jose and Morgan Hill, and watch for the exit to San Juan Bautista, near Gilroy. The entire town is quite small, so I recommend parking as you enter the main town section. You can walk past the shops and walk to the mission and plaza, which are just a block or two away.*

FREMONT PEAK TELESCOPE

The Bay Area is a popular site for astronomy buffs. Why? Perhaps there is a feeling that after you go West and can't go any farther on land, the next place to go is up. Whatever the reason, a subculture of people with telescopes has developed. They spend their spare time roaming the hills away from the city lights in hopes of getting a glimpse of the heavens above.

And thanks to the efforts of two such buffs, Kevin and Deborah Medlock, this state park is developing into an astronomer's paradise. Fremont Peak State Park is a remote jewel, only about 200 acres and well removed from the nearest city. It is named for the earth explorer John C. Fremont, who was the first to stab an American flag into California soil. For years amateur astronomers have been lugging their telescopes to this peak because it sits above the Bay Area fog, giving them a clear shot at the stars.

Kevin had the idea to build one giant telescope for everyone to use on the peak. From his Oakland home, he and wife Deborah spent five years scrounging around for junk metal parts and buying the necessary items to build an imposing, 13-foot-long telescope with a 30-inch mirror—to their knowledge the largest telescope ever made available to the public absolutely free, with no institutional connections. Kevin says he invested a total cash outlay of $2600; purchased new, such an instrument would cost about $60,000.

With the help of volunteers and of park ranger Enrique Morales, the astronomers have also built a house with a retractable roof for the telescope and have plans for a visitor's center. Again, all of this has been accomplished with no help from the taxpayers, only volunteer time and money plus some help from corporations that Kevin was able to interest.

It is wonderful to visit here, far removed from the often institutionalized feeling of observatories. Kevin and Deborah remind me of modern-day Mickey Rooney–Judy Garland types: "Hey, we've got the brains and the talent—let's build our own telescope!" They are so involved with astronomy that they were married at an observatory; their big thrill is watching your reaction when you take your first look through their telescope. What can you see? I saw an extreme close-up of the surface of the moon, which to the naked eye is a small and distant crescent. Kevin says he has been able to see rings around Saturn quite clearly.

There are a few things to know when planning a visit. Though nights at sea level can be pretty warm, it can get cold on the peak, especially in winter, so bring something warm just in case. Die-hard astronomers like to do their viewing around midnight, so they bring sleeping bags and camp on the peak. But you can see through the telescope pretty well as soon as the sun sets, particularly if the fog rolls in and covers the nearby lights.

FREMONT PEAK STATE PARK, *on San Juan Canyon Road, south of San Juan Bautista. The state park offers overnight camping facilities, so the peak is accessible almost all the time; however, the telescope schedule varies, so be sure to call ahead. Admission: $3 per vehicle (use-fee for the entire park). Phone: (408) 623-4255 or (408) 623-4526.*

HOW TO GET TO FREMONT PEAK: *From San Francisco, take Route 101 South to Route 156. Head east on Route 156 and turn right at the entrance of Fremont Peak State Park. The observatory is right behind the ranger's residence, the first building you see when you arrive in the park.*

PINK POODLE FARM

For some 30 years, motorists on Echo Pass Road in Prunedale have done a double take when they pass a bright pink apparition along the road. That's the idea: The huge pink poodle and shocking pink buildings are supposed to attract our attention.

This is part of the plan of a shrewd entrepreneur named Una Buckmaster. She is a successful breeder of toy poodles. I should mention that there is not a pink poodle on the premises; the pink refers to the color of the farm buildings, not the animals.

Una says people come here from all over the world to buy her puppies, and dog lovers are invited to drop in just to see her broods. The puppies are kept inside the farmhouse, nurtured by Una until they are seven to eight weeks old and ready for a new home. They range in price from $200 to $1000. Customers range from San Francisco society ladies to big burly truck drivers looking for a small but affectionate traveling companion. I asked if a toy poodle wasn't a tad wimpy for your average teamster, and Una laughed and said I would be surprised by her macho clientele.

The older members of Una's "family" live outside. These 40 or so poodles who roam the yard are not for sale. Some are breeders; others are the dogs Una loves best and wants to keep around. She knows each one by name and can identify them not only by their looks but by the sound of their barks.

When the Buckmasters first moved to California from Oklahoma, Una had troubles with neighbors because she liked to have a few dogs around. Finally she asked her now late husband to get her a house in the country with no rugs, no expensive furniture, and no neighbors so she could keep as many dogs as she liked. (By the way, for Una, dog is synonymous with poodle.) She started breeding them as a hobby and later turned it into a career.

When they first moved to this farm, Route 101 was just a quiet, two-lane road through farmland. Today the highway is four lanes and loaded with traffic. But once you enter Una's yard and hear those poodles barking, you wouldn't know there's a truck for miles.

PINK POODLE FARM, *19000 Morrow Road, Prunedale. Phone: (408) 663-3709. This is a drop-in business, and visitors are always welcome.*

HOW TO GET TO THE PINK POODLE FARM: *From San Francisco, take Route 101 South past Gilroy and look for a huge flea market on the left side of the highway. Then start looking for Echo Valley Road. Exit onto Echo Valley and turn right immediately onto Morrow Road. Then turn left into the poodle farm entrance. It's right off the highway.*

PINNACLES NATIONAL MONUMENT

Though there are several national parks and forests in the Bay Area, there are only two national monuments. What's the difference, you might ask? A national park is created by an act of Congress; a national monument is created by a presidential order. The Bay Area's monuments are Muir Woods (see Chapter 1) and the Pinnacles. Both were declared national treasures by Theodore Roosevelt in 1908.

The Pinnacles is about a three-hour drive south from San Francisco. It is a truly unique spot, with remarkable spirelike formations that have names like Machete Ridge and the Balconies. This place feels as far removed from the rest of civilization as you can get in the heart of California, and I should let you know right off the bat that this is not for a casual drop-in visit. This is a hiker's and rock climber's paradise; very little can be seen without parking the car and traversing some of the 26 miles of trails.

The monument is run by the National Park Service and is separated into east and west sides. Most visitors go to the east entrance, where you'll find park headquarters and the Bear Valley Visitor's Center, complete with a minimuseum, picnic areas, and rest rooms. The west entrance offers a more spectacular view. This is the backside of the monument, and you can see the actual pinnacles—huge, ragged peaks rising dramatically from the hills. They stand where the American plate of the earth's crust meets the Pacific plate, along the San Andreas Fault. In other words, this is a spot with a whole lot of shakin' goin' on.

One of the easiest and most interesting hikes takes about an hour and a half. It begins at park headquarters on the east side, takes you through caves at Bear Gulch (be sure to bring a flashlight), and brings you out on Moses Spring Trail back to park headquarters. A more spectacular view on the east side is offered from Condor Gulch Trail, a four-hour journey through the high peaks and along the monument's reservoir. On the west side (where there is a ranger station, campgrounds, picnic tables, and rest rooms) you'll find a variety of trails overlooking the awe-inspiring view of Machete Ridge and a multihued rock formation known as the Balconies.

Spring and fall are the recommended times to visit; the wildflowers are in bloom, and the often desertlike climate is neither broiling hot nor deathly cold. No matter where you go, you'll be surrounded by the quiet wonders of nature. If you're lucky, you'll meet up with Cecilia Bjornerus, a retired schoolteacher known as the Flower Lady. Cecilia lives in a trailer in the park and is making a list of all the plants that grow there, including the digger pines, blue oaks, and other flora. She leads groups on nature walks. If Cecilia isn't available, the park rangers occasionally offer guided tours.

Campers can settle down in a privately run campground just outside the east entrance, and 24 walk-in sites within the Pinnacles National Monument on the west side are available on a first-come, first-served basis. If camping is not your style, the park offers a list of nearby motels and hotels and places for recreational vehicles.

Again, let me emphasize that this is not a place to visit casually. Plan your trip, bring lots of water, and prepare to walk.

PINNACLES NATIONAL MONUMENT, *Paicines. Admission: Free for walk-ins, $1 fee per car. East-side entrance: Phone (408) 389-4578; West-side entrance: Phone (408) 389-4425; Pinnacles Campground, phone (408) 385-4462.*

HOW TO GET TO THE EAST-SIDE ENTRANCE: *From San Francisco, take Route 101 South past Gilroy to Route 25 toward Hollister. Follow Route 25 all the way south to the Route 146 turnoff, which is marked as the entrance to the monument.*

HOW TO GET TO THE WEST-SIDE ENTRANCE: *From San Francisco, take Route 101 South to Soledad and turn east on Route 146 through town. Follow Route 146 all the way to the Pinnacles entrance.*

MOSS LANDING

As mentioned before, the Monterey Peninsula is one of the most popular tourist attractions in the Bay Area. The city of Monterey has a wonderful aquarium, and the town of Carmel-by-the-Sea has lots of cute shops and restaurants. Unfortunately, most visitors whiz past Moss Landing, which is also picturesque and worth a stop.

This is a real fishing village. Only two types of businesses flourish here, those that cater to the fishing industry and, for some unknown reason, those that deal in antiques.

First, fishing. The town started back in the day when farms covered the surrounding area; Moss Landing was the port for shipping wheat out of the area. Then it became a whaling station and is now an active fishing port. If you ate Monterey Bay squid or prawns in a Bay Area restaurant last night, there's a good chance it came from the water off Moss Landing. It looks like Monterey's waterfront looked 50 years ago, when John Steinbeck wrote about Cannery Row. Fortunately, it doesn't smell that way.

A land bridge takes you to the waterfront. Just park your car on the side of the road and wander around. You will see an active fisherman's wharf with absolutely no tourist attractions like wax museums or souvenir shops. This is the real thing. If you stay out of their way, and if they have the time, some of the old salts will tell you about their unique town. You also can't miss the giant Pacific Gas and Electric plant, which towers in the foreground, across Route 1. There appears to be a peaceful coexistence between the industrial giant and the small town. The power company employs nearly all residents who aren't in the fishing business.

Aside from the colorful fishing area, the major attraction in Moss Landing is antique stores, 23 of them, all clustered around the main drag in town—truly a browser's paradise.

MOSS LANDING, *just off Route 1 on the road to Monterey.*

HOW TO GET TO MOSS LANDING: *From San Francisco, take Highway 101 South to Route 280 to Route 17 South to Santa Cruz. Take Route 1 South from Santa Cruz and look for the huge PG&E towers on the left. Then watch for the sign on* *the right to Moss Landing. It's about a 30-minute drive from Santa Cruz, in light traffic.*

Just down the road from Moss Landing is one of the hidden treasures of the South Bay. Elkhorn Slough is a 7-mile waterway flanked by the largest salt marsh in the state. It all empties into an estuary where salt water mixes with fresh water. This marshland attracts an incredible mix of birds. It is said that more species of birds can be seen here than in any other spot in California—truly a birdwatcher's nirvana.

In addition to our fine-feathered friends, there are easy-to-hike nature trails that lead to places that feel far removed from the hectic world (in spite of the constant hum from the nearby PG&E plant).

Before venturing out to the slough, it's a good idea to stop at the visitor's center to find out the best place to visit for the time of year you're there. If it's spring or summer it's likely they'll suggest you head for the shallows, where you'll see a school of leopard sharks and bat rays giving birth. At other times of the year they may suggest a visit to the old barns left over from the days when the area was a dairy farm, where you're likely to spot some birds of prey.

Elkhorn Slough is also an active research facility, so even though you may feel like you're in the middle of nowhere, there is always something going on, and there are enthusiastic people interested in showing you around.

ELKHORN SLOUGH NATIONAL ESTUARINE SANCTUARY, *1700 Elkhorn Road, 2 miles from Moss Landing. Phone: (408) 728-2822. Open 9 A.M. to 5 P.M. Thursday through Sunday. Admission: Free.*

HOW TO GET TO ELKHORN SLOUGH: *From San Francisco, take Route 101 South to Route 152 West to Route 156 to Castroville Boulevard, which you will come to just before entering the town of Castroville. Turn right on Castroville Boulevard. When you come to a yield sign, veer to the right and then take the next left onto Elkhorn Road. Follow it a short distance to the visitor's center. From Moss Landing, cross Route 1 and follow the road inland, adjacent to the power plant. That is Dolan Road, and it will take you to Castroville Road. Turn left on Castroville and then follow the signs to Elkhorn Slough.*

The great writer John Steinbeck is usually associated with the Monterey Coast and the Cannery Row that he made famous. His home, however, was in Salinas, about an hour inland. Today Steinbeck is honored by the town public library, which is named for him. His statue stands on the lawn outside the library, as if beckoning visitors to come see the rare collection of Steinbeck memorabilia inside.

On the main floor is a room entirely devoted to the American author. Here you will find most of his books, plus photos, magazine stories about him, awards, newspaper clippings, and correspondence. All this reminds you of the major role he played in our literary history. The real treasures, however, are downstairs, locked away behind a steel gate in the Steinbeck Archives, a destination for Steinbeck scholars from all over the world. This basement room, about the size of a junior executive's office, is accessible to the general public with advance notice.

Here you will see his family photos, personal mementos, and first editions and autographed copies of his books. Perhaps the real treasures are the original hand-written manuscripts. Steinbeck didn't use a typewriter; what he wrote every morning on lined notepads would be typed by a secretary in the afternoon. In this day of word processors, it is remarkable to pore over the meticulous pages and imagine the author at work.

The archives also has oral histories of the man, told by folks who knew him during various stages in his life. One tape features Steinbeck himself, reflecting on his life and the endless battles he fought because he was committed to writing what he had to say about the human condition.

Try to meet library director John Gross. He is a charming scholar who can offer additional insights into Steinbeck and his community. He told me that Steinbeck was hated in the area during his lifetime. After he published Cannery Row, the Monterey town council threatened to tar and feather him if he ever showed his face in town. In Salinas, where he exposed the dark and sad side of life in this quiet farming area, he was considered an enemy of his class. But as Gross pointed out, "All prophets are unpopular in their own town because they write the truth and don't care who they might hurt to tell it."

Today Steinbeck is not only forgiven but is a figure of pride in the area. Even his former home, a lovely Victorian just off Main Street, has been carefully restored and is operated by a women's guild as a popular luncheon spot.

STEINBECK LIBRARY, *110 West San Luis Street, Salinas. Phone: (408) 758-7311. Open 10 A.M. to 9 P.M. Monday through Thursday, 10 A.M. to 6 P.M. Friday and Saturday. An appointment is required to see the archives.*

JOHN STEINBECK HOUSE *is just a few blocks from the library at 132 Central. Open for lunch with seatings at 11:45 A.M. and 1:15 P.M. Monday through Friday. Reservations requested. Phone: (408) 424-2735.*

HOW TO GET TO THE STEINBECK LIBRARY AND ARCHIVES: *From San Francisco, take Highway 101 South to Salinas. Take the north Main Street exit and continue to San Luis Street. Turn right and go one block to Lincoln; the library is on the corner of San Luis and Lincoln.*

If the crowds in Monterey get to you, head south to Pacific Grove. This is a more relaxed and quaint waterfront community, filled with Victorian homes, inviting parks, and nice restaurants and inns. Pacific Grove's claim to fame is that it is the monarch butterfly capital. Like the swallows that return to Capistrano each year, millions of monarch butterflies arrive in Pacific Grove every October to lay their eggs. You're likely to find them in the trees adjacent to the Butterfly Grove Inn, 1073 Lighthouse Avenue; another winter home is Washington Park, which is bordered by Sinex, Short, Alder, and Melrose Streets. If you time it right, you'll also see the annual October festival to welcome the monarch, a celebration that includes a parade of marching bands and children dressed as butterflies.

Another attraction in Pacific Grove is the less costly alternative to the 17-Mile Drive, which most guide books list as a must-see. This is a beautiful, privately owned stretch of oceanfront property that takes you through the Del Monte Forest (owned by the giant canning company) and past luxurious homes, pristine beaches, and the famous Pebble Beach Golf Course.

The only problem is it costs $5 per car to take the drive. Since it irks me even to pay bridge tolls, I can't get myself to plunk down five bucks to drive on the Del Monte company's road. Instead, I take the free 4-mile drive along Ocean View Beach in Pacific Grove and spend the extra five bucks on lunch. Along the way are beautiful Victorian homes, a terrific view of the ocean, tidepools, and the Point Pinos Lighthouse. Built in 1855, it is the oldest continuously operating lighthouse on the Pacific Coast. It stands at the entrance to Monterey Harbor, at the end of Ocean View Boulevard. The lighthouse is open to the public Saturday and Sunday 1 to 4 P.M., with tours given by the Coast Guard. Phone: (408) 373-3304.

Near the lighthouse along the ocean you will come to the often empty beach at Asilomar, a name that means "refuge by the sea." This is a state-run park and conference center, which includes 103 acres of pine forest. Business groups and others may rent the facilities, which include a lodge, several housing units, meeting rooms, and a dining area. Individuals and couples may rent inexpensive accommodations, when available. Phone: (408) 372-8016.

Until the Gold Rush turned San Francisco into a boomtown, Monterey was the center of activity in Northern California. Today, Monterey is still the county's Big City, though most of the action is around the Fisherman's Wharf area and Cannery Row. Both places are collections of touristy shops and attractions, the kind you'll find at San Francisco's Fisherman's Wharf. However, the wonderful Monterey Aquarium is there and should not be missed. Get a reservation and go.

You can visit a real working wharf at the foot of Figueroa Street, where commercial fishing boats unload the catch of the day into huge processing plants. No organized tours are offered, but you can stroll around and watch the operation on your own.

Monterey State Historic Park, near the downtown area, features a Path of History, a walking tour of 37 important buildings, some you can go inside, others you simply admire and read about from the sidewalk. These include the Custom House, where the stars and stripes first flew over California; California's first theater, where performances still take place; and Stevenson House, where the writer Robert Louis Stevenson lived when he first came to California, chasing after the love of his life. You can pick up a map of the historic buildings at the Custom House, located at 1 Custom Plaza.

MONTEREY BAY AQUARIUM, *886 Cannery Row, Monterey. Phone: (408) 375-3333. Open daily 10 A.M. to 6 P.M.; closed Christmas. Admission: Adults, $7; students and seniors, $5; children 12 and under, $3. Advance tickets are available through Ticketron.*

MONTEREY STATE HISTORIC PARK, *Monterey. Phone: (408) 649-2836. The museums are open from 10 A.M. to 5 P.M.; several are closed during the lunch hour.*

CARMEL If you want crowds, you'll find them in Carmel or, as the Chamber of Commerce likes to call it, Carmel-by-the-Sea. This is a picture-postcard little village, and it ought to be seen at least once. Carmel's success seems to be due to its original intended charm, a simple coastal town and colony for artists and writers. The buildings have no address numbers, billboards and large commercial signs are prohibited, and there is very little in the way of street lighting.

Yet this very quaintness, not to mention the spectacular beach at the end of town, draws more and more visitors each year. And ever since the town's most famous resident, Clint Eastwood, was elected mayor in 1986, even more tourists are flocking in. (In all fairness to the ex-mayor, I should point out that Eastwood has also been active in preserving the historic part of Carmel. A couple of years ago the Mission Ranch, an old dairy farm that has been used as a family resort for years and years, was in danger of folding, and Eastwood bankrolled the place to keep it in business.) My advice is to see Carmel's downtown briefly, then head to two of the area's historical attractions, Tor House and the Carmel Mission.

ROBINSON JEFFERS'S CARMEL Tor House was the home of the late poet Robinson Jeffers. Though it is only a few miles from the center of town, it feels like another world entirely. The home is a symbol of the original Carmel, before it became a tourist mecca.

Jeffers was a man of nature. He was also an outspoken man of letters, and he was a constant thorn in the sides of those who wanted to turn Carmel into a tourist paradise. He hated them, and they hated him. At his home you will see Jeffers's vision of how the coast should be treated. He personally built the house of rough rock so that it is in harmony with the natural landscape. He also built a stone tower that affords a magnificent view of the ocean if you're willing to climb to the top.

Inside, the home is just as it was when the poet was living and writing here. Many of his manuscripts remain, as do the personal artifacts of his life. His widow still occupies the home in front of Tor House. The house is maintained by a group of local residents who want to perpetuate Jeffers's memory and to keep the original artist colony spirit alive in Carmel. They charge a small admission for touring the home and also hold readings and other fund-raising events throughout the year to pay for the upkeep.

TOURS OF TOR HOUSE *are given on Friday and Saturday. Admission is $5. For reservations and more information, you can contact the Tor House Foundation at P.O. Box 1887, Carmel, CA 93921, or by phone at (408) 624-1813. They will give you directions to the house.*

CARMEL MISSION

The Carmel Mission is located at the south of Rio Road. This is where Father Junipero Serra established headquarters for the Northern California mission system. It was his residence and headquarters until his death in 1784. Father Serra's remains are buried here, in front of the altar in the faithfully restored basilica. The mission will probably be crowded with tourists (even Pope John Paul II visited in 1987), but there are quiet places on the grounds to rest and reflect, particularly in the courtyards that link the various parish buildings. The mission also includes a museum with some of the original artifacts from Father Serra's day.

CARMEL MISSION, *3080 Rio Road, Carmel. Phone: (408) 624-3600.*

HOW TO GET TO THE MISSION: *From downtown Carmel, get back on Route 1 and head south until you come to Rio Road, which is a major intersection. Turn right on Rio Road, and the mission is just a few blocks away on the left.*

BIG SUR

It's about an hour's drive from Carmel down the coast to Big Sur, and I heartily recommend it. In fact, this is one of the most scenic drives in the world.

Many visitors come to the area looking for a town called Big Sur. Well to paraphrase Gertrude Stein, there is no Big Sur in Big Sur. It is 70 miles, more or less, of craggy peaks, beautiful forest, and breathtaking coastline that does not have any official boundaries. The residents, many of them artists and writers, like it that way.

Route 1 is the main road through Big Sur, and almost any attraction you would like to see is right along it. One way to explore the area is to pull into one of the several state parks and start walking. Pfeiffer State Park, for example, features a self-guided nature hike. Along the way you're likely to see coastal redwoods, sycamores, and cottonwoods, raccoons, wild boar, and unusual birds like water ousels and belted kingfishers. This park is located about 37 miles south of Carmel. For more information about state parks in the area, call (408) 667-2315.

Big Sur is also the home of the famous Esalen Institute, where many of the innovative psychotherapists of the 1960s first explored the human potential movement. It is still a center for healing and experimentation, closed to the public except during the middle of the night, when they open their hot springs for a fee. Phone ahead first for the current schedule and directions: (408) 667-2335.

The major literary figure in Big Sur was Henry Miller, who lived here from the late 1940s to the mid-1960s. His former home is now a memorial library, containing many original manuscripts and mementos from Miller's life. The library is run by the late author's old friend, painter Emile White, and is open by appointment only from 9 A.M. to noon daily. Phone: (408) 667-2574.

If there is one must stop in Big Sur, it is Nepenthe, located on the right side of the road (going south) a few miles past a series of small resorts on the Big Sur River. It is well marked. Even though you are likely to run into a lot of other tourists, you'll also be able to rub elbows with the locals. It's the unofficial community center of the area. The name comes from a mythical Egyptian drug meaning "no sorrow."

Nepenthe is definitely a place to see. Sitting 800 feet above the ocean, with a remarkable view of the coast, Nepenthe is a restaurant, a gift shop, or just a place to sit in the sun with a drink in your hand. A protege of Frank Lloyd Wright designed the main restaurant; following the teachings of the master, the buildings look as though they have always been a part of the landscape. The design is spectacular in its simplicity, and whether you are outside on the huge deck or inside the dining pavilion, you always have the sense you are nowhere else but Big Sur.

The place has a romantic history. The original main house was spotted in the 1940s by Orson Welles and Rita Hayworth as they were driving from Carmel to Los Angeles. They decided it would be a perfect honeymoon cottage and bought the place. According to the present owners, Orson and Rita spent about eight hours on the site, arguing about the drapes and this and that, and never came back.

The food is decent, ranging from standard hamburgers to vegetarian specials. If you are hungry and the wait is too long in the restaurant, down below there's a smaller cafe, the Cafe Amphora, adjacent to the combination art gallery and gift shop (which is called the Phoenix). At the Amphora you'll find light fare like sandwiches, good coffee, and wonderful desserts you can enjoy outdoors on the lower terrace. Nepenthe opens at noon daily. Phone: (408) 667-2345.

HOW TO GET TO BIG SUR: *Simply continue south on Route 1 from Carmel for about an hour.*

Index

217